Delivering Business Analytics

WILEY AND SAS BUSINESS SERIES

The Wiley and SAS Business Series presents books that help senior-level managers with their critical management decisions.

Titles in the Wiley and SAS Business Series include:

Activity-Based Management for Financial Institutions: Driving Bottom-Line Results by Brent Bahnub

Big Data Analytics: Turning Big Data into Big Money by Frank Ohlhorst

Branded! How Retailers Engage Consumers with Social Media and Mobility by Bernie Brennan and Lori Schafer

Business Analytics for Customer Intelligence by Gert Laursen

Business Analytics for Managers: Taking Business Intelligence beyond Reporting by Gert Laursen and Jesper Thorlund

The Business Forecasting Deal: Exposing Bad Practices and Providing Practical Solutions by Michael Gilliland

Business Intelligence Success Factors: Tools for Aligning Your Business in the Global Economy by Olivia Parr Rud

CIO Best Practices: Enabling Strategic Value with Information Technology, Second Edition by Joe Stenzel

Connecting Organizational Silos: Taking Knowledge Flow Management to the Next Level with Social Media by Frank Leistner

Credit Risk Assessment: The New Lending System for Borrowers, Lenders, and Investors by Clark Abrahams and Mingyuan Zhang

Credit Risk Scorecards: Developing and Implementing Intelligent Credit Scoring by Naeem Siddiqi

The Data Asset: How Smart Companies Govern Their Data for Business Success by Tony Fisher

Demand-Driven Forecasting: A Structured Approach to Forecasting by Charles Chase

The Executive's Guide to Enterprise Social Media Strategy: How Social Networks Are Radically Transforming Your Business by David Thomas and Mike Barlow

Executive's Guide to Solvency II by David Buckham, Jason Wahl, and Stuart Rose

Fair Lending Compliance: Intelligence and Implications for Credit Risk Management by Clark R. Abrahams and Mingyuan Zhang

Foreign Currency Financial Reporting from Euros to Yen to Yuan: A Guide to Fundamental Concepts and Practical Applications by Robert Rowan

Human Capital Analytics: How to Harness the Potential of Your Organization's Greatest Asset by Gene Pease, Boyce Byerly, and Jac Fitz-enz

Information Revolution: Using the Information Evolution Model to Grow Your Business by Jim Davis, Gloria J. Miller, and Allan Russell

Manufacturing Best Practices: Optimizing Productivity and Product Quality by Bobby Hull

Marketing Automation: Practical Steps to More Effective Direct Marketing by Jeff LeSueur

Mastering Organizational Knowledge Flow: How to Make Knowledge Sharing Work by Frank Leistner

The New Know: Innovation Powered by Analytics by Thornton May

Performance Management: Integrating Strategy Execution, Methodologies, Risk, and Analytics by Gary Cokins

Retail Analytics: The Secret Weapon by Emmett Cox

Social Network Analysis in Telecommunications by Carlos Andre Reis Pinheiro

Statistical Thinking: Improving Business Performance, Second Edition by Roger W. Hoerl and Ronald D. Snee

Taming the Big Data Tidal Wave: Finding Opportunities in Huge Data Streams with Advanced Analytics by Bill Franks

The Value of Business Analytics: Identifying the Path to Profitability by Evan Stubbs

Visual Six Sigma: Making Data Analysis Lean by Ian Cox, Marie A. Gaudard, Philip J. Ramsey, Mia L. Stephens, and Leo Wright

Win with Advanced Business Analytics: Creating Business Value from Your Data by Jean Paul Isson and Jesse Harriott

For more information on any of the above titles, please visit www.wiley.com.

Delivering Business Analytics

Practical Guidelines for Best Practice

Evan Stubbs

WILEY

John Wiley & Sons, Inc.

Library of Congress Cataloging-in-Publication Data:

Stubbs, Evan.
    Delivering business analytics : practical guidelines for best practice /
Evan Stubbs.
        p.   cm. — (Wiley & SAS business series)
    Includes bibliographical references and index.
    ISBN 978-1-118-37056-8 (cloth); ISBN 978-1-118-55954-3 (ebk);
    ISBN 978-1-118-55945-1 (ebk); ISBN 978-1-118-55944-4 (ebk)
        1. Business planning.   2. Strategic planning.   3. Decision
making.   I. Title.
    HD30.28.S785 2013
    658.4'013—dc23
                                                                2012041500

Printed in the United States of America

10   9   8   7   6   5   4   3   2   1

*To the dreamers, the innovators, the visionaries,
and those who know things could be
better—this book's for you.*

Contents

Preface

I had an interesting conversation during a book signing for my previous book, *The Value of Business Analytics*. I'd just come off a fairly intense trip that included talking to hundreds of executives about how they could drive better value through the use of business analytics. Over drinks after one event, I ended up talking to a friendly fellow who, rather apologetically it must be said, seemed like he had something to share.

It took a while, but after enough prompting he eventually built the courage to tell me what was on his mind. Paraphrasing, it was that "I liked your book but it didn't seem like you'd explained anything I didn't already know. . . . "

Of all the possible reactions he was expecting, I think laughter had to be pretty far down the list! Much to his surprise, I wholeheartedly agreed with him; objectively, I don't think anyone would disagree with anything I've written. Pragmatically, I think much of it is self-obvious. What fascinates me more than anything else is that so few teams *actually do* what's apparently self-obvious. If everyone did, business analytics wouldn't be seen as an arcane, confusing, and arguably mystical discipline.

Arthur C. Clarke once said that any piece of sufficiently advanced technology is indistinguishable from magic. Like it or not, that's where we sit with business analytics; those who haven't been skilled in the secret ways by past masters are left at a significant disadvantage.

The Value of Business Analytics was written for a general audience. It tried to help the doers make their lives easier by explaining how and why organizations fail to get behind business analytics. Drawing from a wide variety of case studies and research, it highlighted the four major characteristics of successful business analytics teams. The more I dealt with effective teams, the more I saw that they were unique.

They were exceedingly good at defining the value they were going to create. They paid specific attention to communicating that value to the broader organization. They understood the importance of delivering to a strategic road map, and possibly most importantly, they measured the value they created. I wrote the book because I felt that, although there's an increasing library of books talking about business analytics, there are relatively few that provide practical, pragmatic advice on how to succeed on a day-to-day basis.

This book is more technical than my last; it drives into the detail. This is deliberate—where my last book was written for the doers, this book is written for the designers. I have made every effort to validate the approaches described in this book with a variety of knowledgeable practitioners across different industries, different sized organizations, and different geographies. All their input has been invaluable and any oversights in this book are solely mine. Some may disagree with what I've written. However, debate is good; if we are to develop as a discipline, the best place to start is with best practice.

This book aims to give data scientists and architects the ammunition they need to succeed. The biggest disservice the profession does for itself is hoarding information; many apparently challenging problems have already been solved, repeatedly in many cases. Unfortunately, finding these solutions is nearly impossible; although there are a multitude of books that deal with the specifics of strategy, data mining, business intelligence, or other highly focused areas of interest, there are few if any that try to establish a core toolkit from which common problems can be solved.

That, in a nutshell, is the focus of this book. It describes a variety of solutions to common problems, focusing specifically on those involving assets, information, technology, skills, and processes. Although it avoids referring to specific technologies, it drives into enough detail to help an architect establish a core requirements list. Although it doesn't provide a series of role definitions, it outlines sufficient detail to help a newly appointed chief data scientist or chief analytics officer drive the greatest value out of the organization's investment in business analytics. Finally, although there isn't a single piece of code through this whole book, it will still help analysts understand how they can better design their applications to support enterprise-level execution.

WHY YOU NEED TO READ THIS BOOK

Why do you need to read this book? For a few simple reasons: Hopefully, it'll give you the edge you need. It'll almost definitely make your job easier. It should start you thinking about what does and doesn't work in your specific context.

At its core, business analytics is about transformation and change. It's about making more with less, creating insight from seemingly impenetrable information, and outperforming everyone else. Succeeding in business analytics will help you drive competitive differentiation as well as your own career. We live in a digital age, and those that know how best to take advantage of it will have the greatest success.

The thing is, we often don't know what we don't know. Knowing what's possible is usually half the battle—theory helps provide some insight but a few hours' worth of guided discovery can eliminate years of experience fueled by first principles. Practice makes it real. To make the examples as real as possible, this book emphasizes case studies wherever possible.

Every book needs at least one reason to exist. This book's reasons are to explain why:

1. *Business analytics is different from analytics.* Where analytics is about generating insight from data-driven processes, business analytics is about leveraging analytics to create measurable, tangible value.

2. *Business analytics drives sustainable competitive advantage.* It exhibits economic characteristics, which, when harnessed, lead to cost and quality advantages. Where applicable, it does so by creating production efficiencies as well as driving better results. These benefits are created through economies of scale, economies of scope, and higher-quality outcomes.

3. *Operational analytics is the key to sustained value creation.* Converting the intangible value associated with insight into tangible value is usually a case of operationalizing this insight through decisioning systems.

4. *Best practice involves aligning with these philosophies and driving a culture of continuous improvement and assessment backed by measurement theory.*

You can't demonstrate success or improve things if you don't measure them. Driving the right culture is essential. So is having the metrics by which you can optimize your investment.

By reading this book, you'll understand the logic behind each of these statements and discover ways to help simplify execution in a variety of situations. It distills decades of practical experience with business analytics into a small set of best practices, management principles, and general solutions.

These haven't been defined arbitrarily—they were identified after repeatedly seeing some teams succeed and many fail. By reading this book, you'll build an understanding of how business analytics drives competitive advantage. You'll understand why some projects are more successful than others. And you'll learn how to go about managing the analytically focused technology and data that will underpin your organization's use of business analytics.

These guidelines and principles help establish the right philosophies and management patterns. What they can't do, however, is tell you how to do it. To bridge the gap between theory and practice, this book provides practical solutions to common problems across:

- *People and process*, or how to go about solving problems related to developing competencies and creating reusable processes.
- *Systems and assets*, or how to go about managing assets and designing and managing technology architectures.
- *Data and decision making*, or how to go about capturing and managing data as well as how to improve operational decision making.

These principles haven't appeared overnight—they are the result of extensive work with a variety of organizations ranging in size from thousands of employees to businesses with less than a hundred. This book draws from the successes and failures of these organizations and synthesizes them into a basic framework from which managers, designers, and architects can draw.

Some of these organizations have been using business analytics to do everything from advanced risk simulation to viral marketing. Others have been more interested in simply establishing a common platform from which they can start eliminating inefficient spreadmarts.[1] Although their use and execution has varied, the logic behind their successes (and failures) hasn't.

If you already know everything there is to know about leveraging business analytics, this book will serve as a way of communicating and validating your hard-earned experience. It will solidify most of what you already know into a series of principles you can communicate and foster. If you are studying the field as part of an undergraduate or postgraduate course, this book will help give you some practical insights into how business analytics is applied. If you are entering the field for the first time or are interested in moving beyond creating insight into driving change, this book will help provide a series of field-tested patterns to build on.

HOW TO USE THIS BOOK

The book is divided into five parts:

1. Business Analytics Best Practices
2. The Data Scientist's Code
3. Practical Solutions: People and Process
4. Practical Solutions: Systems and Assets
5. Practical Solutions: Data and Decision Making

In the main, this book lacks narrative. Each section has been written such that it can be picked up and read independently from the rest of the book. This is very deliberate; rather than being written to be read cover to cover, this book was written to provide specific answers to specific questions.

The main benefit of this approach is that readers are free to consult this book as a reference, dipping in and out as items of interest catch their eye. Although the book structure offers a consistent internal flow and it *can* be read from beginning to end, there's nothing that forces a reader to do so. Instead of a book that's read once and left on the bookshelf, this book is intended to assist as a constant help, kept close by managers and analysts for reference and guidance. The breadth of content is such that everyone from newly created to highly mature teams should find something of interest between these covers.

Because of this, different sections contain an inevitable degree of repetition. When reviewing management guidelines, it would be impossible to emphasize the importance of retaining one's intellectual property without referencing the risks and benefits of engaging an external consultant. It would be equally impossible to talk about the specifics of how to best engage external parties without at least referencing the reasons behind the recommendations.

Although it would have been possible to condense material into fewer topics with longer chapters, this would have had the undesirable effect of making the topics less "chunkable." We don't always have enough time for a full meal; sometimes all we need to keep going is a snack. To help readers understand these interdependencies, each section includes a list of related sections.

Part One, Business Analytics Best Practices, provides the major premise of this book: that best practice in business analytics stems from favoring approaches that emphasize the microeconomic advantages of business analytics. It provides the core vocabulary used throughout and outlines the link between business analytics and competitive advantage.

Part Two, The Data Scientist's Code, provides a variety of principles to keep in mind that, if followed, help data scientists move toward best practice. These are general philosophies rather than specific answers—they represent some ideas and concepts that, if kept in mind, help make it easier to find a better path.

The last three parts provide a number of solutions to specific problems. All of these map into the general guidelines in some way. However, they don't cover every possible solution—if the guidelines define the boundaries of the sets, the solutions fall within those sets. These solutions explain why some projects are not as successful as they could be, and they provide specific recommendations on how to go about improving day-to-day planning, design, and management.

As much as possible, the reasons behind these solutions are explained using case studies. These are based on real examples, albeit modified to protect the identity of the organizations in question. Although they sometimes provide positive examples, many of them aim to highlight how poor design decisions can limit effectiveness.

While it's possible that some readers may feel like they refer to their organization specifically, I sincerely hope they don't!

These solutions focus on how organizations can avoid commonly faced problems in the practical application of business analytics. They provide a starting point for managers, architects, and practitioners to design their business analytics systems and solutions. Equally though, they should not be treated as a limited set of options; innovation comes from attempting the impossible and succeeding. Although the approaches described in this book represent a good snapshot of the most successful approaches used by organizations today and range from being simple to highly complex, they're not an exhaustive list and should not be read as such.

To make it easier to interpret and apply these solutions, each one follows the same broad structure:

- An overview of why it's worth reading the section.
- The background that leads to the issue.
- A description of the pains and symptoms stemming from the issue.
- A list of common solutions that, while logical, tend to lead to more problems.
- A general solution that aligns with the best-practice principles described in this book along with associated benefits and limitations.

Each solution starts with an overview of the problem it solves and when it can be applied. Specific exclusions or warning are noted. The specific context and forces that define the situation are then explained, along with a practical example of how this context can emerge.

This context creates a problem with corresponding challenges and symptoms. The solution is then outlined, along with the benefits that stem from applying the solution as well as important limitations to the solution.

Readers are recommended to use the solutions described in this book to expand their awareness of what their peers are doing, to consider alternative approaches, and to develop a fuller understanding of the very practical advantages and disadvantages of different designs. Readers are also recommended to design their solutions based on the best-practice principles identified within this book unless, of course, it would mean sacrificing value or renewable return for the sake of complying with a series of bullet points. They help, but there's always more than one way to solve a problem.

Part Three, People and Process, deals with the challenges associated with finding the right people, developing the right competencies, and driving effective use of technology at a resource level. Rather than focus on cultural considerations, this part focuses on structural considerations including techniques to assist with team retention, how best to augment existing enterprise resource planning (ERP) processes with analytical insight, how to treat intellectual assets as the value-creation property they are, and how to structure technology and teams to drive efficiency and avoid bottlenecks. Readers interested in the people management and process aspects of business analytics will find a great deal of valuable information in this part.

Part Four, Systems and Assets, deals with technology and asset related aspects of business analytics. It focuses on solutions associated with information processing, computation, and systems management. It covers the importance of establishing the right architectural principles in platform design, the value chains needed to support effective execution, considerations in technology selection, and the various technology management options available. Readers interested in understanding the implications of leveraging desktop computing, server-based processing, or cloud computing will be especially interested in this part.

Part Five, Data and Decision Making, deals with information management aspects of business analytics, covering both data storage and generating actionable insight. Key considerations covered within this part include the benefits and limitations of tightly coupling with the enterprise data warehouse, how the time available to make a decision influences design, and how to manage the often conflicting dynamic of analytical measures against business rules. It examines both how information storage can be managed as well as how to execute analytically based decisions in an operational context. Readers interested in designing operational systems will find this part highly informative.

NOTE

1. The painful situation in which spreadsheets are used not to visualize data but to store permanent data.

Acknowledgments

This book would have been impossible without the deep support that so many people provided. Thanks are due to Bill Franks, David Hardoon, and Felix Liao for providing their tremendously valuable insight and experience. As is his wont, Peter Kokinakos managed to clarify what was a rather clumsy structure into something that was tighter, punchier, and more persuasive. Thanks must go to Brendon Smyth whose advice fundamentally changed the book's structure for the better at the eleventh hour.

There are a few people who went far above the call of duty to help me during my editing process. Despite being given a very rough early draft, Marnie MacDonald battled through what was in reality a very fragmented structure to give valuable feedback. Thanks to a shared taxi after a rather serendipitous conference, Warwick Graco somehow managed to tear through one of my late drafts, sparking tremendously valuable thoughts in the process. Neil Fraser was a constant support, providing very detailed feedback and suggestions for further research, without which this book would have greatly suffered.

On a more personal level, I'd also like to thank my sister Cassie who somehow managed to review copy while also getting married, making her own wedding rings, renovating her house, and looking after a rolling progression of friendly dogs. Your feedback helped with this book and the next.

More than anyone else, I'd like to thank my wife Vanessa for her absolutely tireless reading and rereading of multiple drafts, even when they were largely incomprehensible messes of unstructured discourse. Without her help and support, this book would have literally been impossible. I'd also like to thank two of my most important advisors: my daughter Amélie, who kept me company and kept me going in my study when the deadline was fast approaching, and my son Calvin, whose laughter lit my life, even when I was exhausted. I love you all.

PART ONE

Business Analytics Best Practices

W e don't know what we don't know. This creates an interesting dynamic. We can accept the way things are as a given, and by doing so doom ourselves to mediocrity. Or we can experiment, hopefully innovate, and grasp new opportunities. Unfortunately, innovation requires taking chances. For many organizations, taking that first leap into business analytics is already seen as being risky enough.

Every day, we push the boundaries of what's possible. Facebook has over a billion customers. A billion! Every day, the limits of what we don't know decrease. Every problem we solve frees us to focus on the next, harder problem. In aggregate, we're making faster progress than we've ever made since the first caveman decided to try and predict where his next hunt should take place.

The paradox is, of course, that these advancements aren't shared. For most of us, our individual awareness of how to drive innovation through business analytics has lagged tremendously compared to the industry leaders. This shouldn't be surprising—that same knowledge is justifiably seen as a competitive advantage to the organizations that generate it. So despite the general benefit that would come from sharing information, important insights and understandings remain hidden.

The basics aren't hard. Successfully leveraging business analytics for competitive advantage requires understanding how to generate insight, how to manage information, and how to action that insight. The real secret is that business analytics isn't about insight; it's about change. And that makes all the difference.

Business analytics is about doing things differently; it's about using information to test new approaches and drive better results. The challenging thing is that this *does* actually mean things need to change. Insight is great, but when we use the same management approaches we always have, we usually end up with the same result.

Ignoring the need to develop new competencies in our people generally leads to unchanged outcomes. Trying to shoehorn traditional data warehousing models into a business analytics context limits the insight that's possible, not because the fundamentals of warehousing are wrong but because the discipline and objectives are different. They are related, but different, and running the same process will inevitably lead to the same outcome.

As a professional discipline, this holds us back. There remains a lack of clarity around how to solve what are, more often than not, common problems. We repeatedly reinvent the wheel, wasting valuable time, resources, and money, and there's no good reason for it. Although it's true that organizations that cannot overcome the simplest hurdles are held at a disadvantage compared to their peers, we do ourselves a disservice by not developing a broader industry maturity.

We learn from knowing what's possible. We innovate by trying to overcome the impossible. Without knowing what other people are doing, we usually fail to do either.

This book attempts to fill that gap by sharing what others have already learned. To the first-time reader, some of it may seem obvious, some of it novel. Critically though, what's seen as obvious varies from person to person; to someone who's an experienced retailer but has never managed a business analytics project, even the simplest things can be surprising. On the other hand, to someone who's completely wedded to retaining control over all aspects of information management, the way others are using cloud computing and leveraging external resources may be surprising.

Drawing from extensive experience and numerous real-world applications, this book distills a wide variety of successful behaviors into a small number of highly practical approaches and general guidelines. I hope that everyone, regardless of how experienced they are, will discover some novel and useful ideas within the covers of this book. By knowing what's possible, we increase the odds of success.

CHAPTER **1**

Business Analytics: A Definition

Before we define the guidelines that establish best practice, it's important to spend a bit of time defining *business analytics* and why it's different from pure analytics or *advanced analytics*.[1]

WHAT IS BUSINESS ANALYTICS?

The cornerstone of business analytics is pure analytics. Although it is a very broad definition, analytics can be considered any data-driven process that provides insight. It may report on historical information or it may provide predictions about future events; the end goal of analytics is to add value through insight and turn data into information.

Common examples of analytics include:

- Reporting: The summarization of historical data
- Trending: The identification of underlying patterns in time-series data
- Segmentation: The identification of similarities within data
- Predictive modeling: The prediction of future events using historical data

Each of these use cases has a number of common characteristics:

- They are based on data (as opposed to opinion).
- They apply various mathematical techniques to transform and summarize raw data.
- They add value to the original data and transform it into knowledge.

Activities such as business intelligence, reporting, and performance management tend to focus on what happened—that is, they analyze and present historical information.

Advanced analytics, on the other hand, aims to understand *why* things are happening and predict *what* will happen. The distinguishing characteristic between advanced analytics and reporting is the use of higher-order statistical and mathematical techniques such as:

- Operations research
- Parametric or nonparametric statistics
- Multivariate analysis
- Algorithmically based predictive models (such as decision trees, gradient boosting, regressions, or transfer functions)

Business analytics leverages all forms of analytics to achieve business outcomes. It seems a small difference but it's an important one—business analytics adds to analytics by requiring:

- Business relevancy
- Actionable insight
- Performance measurement and value measurement

There's a great deal of knowledge that can be created by applying various forms of analytics. Business analytics, however, makes a distinction between relevant knowledge and irrelevant knowledge. A significant part of business analytics is identifying the insights that would be valuable (in a real and measurable way), given the business' strategic and tactical objectives. If analytics is often about finding interesting things in large amounts of data, business analytics is about making sure that this information has contextual relevancy and delivers real value.

Once created, this knowledge must be acted on if value is to be created. Whereas analytics focuses primarily on the creation of the insight and not necessarily on what should be done with the insight once created, business analytics recognizes that creating the insight is only one small step in a larger value chain. Equally important (if not more important) is that the insight be used to realize the value.

This operational and actionable point of view can create substantially different outcomes when compared to applying pure analytics. If only the insight is considered in isolation, it's quite easy to develop a series of outcomes that cannot be executed within the broader organizational context. For example, a series of models may be developed that, although extremely accurate, may be impossible to integrate into the organization's operational systems. If the tools that created the models aren't compatible with the organization's inventory management systems, customer-relationships management systems, or other operational systems, the value of the insight may be high but the realized value negligible.

By approaching the same problem from a business analytics perspective, the same organization may be willing to sacrifice model accuracy for ease of execution, ensuring that economic value is delivered, even though the models may not have as high a standard as they otherwise could have. A model that is 80 percent accurate but can be acted on creates far more value than an extremely accurate model that can't be deployed.

This operational aspect forms another key distinction between analytics and business analytics. More often than not, analytics is about answering a question at a point in time. Business analytics, on the other hand, is about sustained value delivery. Tracking value and measuring performance, therefore, become critical elements of ensuring long-term value from business analytics.

CORE CONCEPTS AND DEFINITIONS

This section presents a brief primer and is unfortunately necessarily dry; it provides the core conceptual framework for everything discussed in this book. This book will refer repeatedly to a variety of concepts. Although the terms and concepts defined in this chapter serve as a useful taxonomy, they should not be read as a comprehensive list of strict definitions; depending on context and industry, they may go by other names. One of the challenges of a relatively young discipline such as business analytics is that, although there is tremendous potential for innovation, it has yet to develop a standard vocabulary.

The intent of the terms used throughout this book is simply to provide consistency, not to provide a definitive taxonomy or vocabulary. They're worth reading closely even for those experienced in the application of business analytics—terms vary from person to person, and although readers may not always agree with the semantics presented here, given their own backgrounds and context, it's essential that they understand what is meant by a particular word. Key terms are emphasized to aid readability.

Business analytics is the use of data-driven insight to generate value. It does so by requiring business relevancy, the use of actionable insight, and performance measurement and value measurement.

This can be contrasted against *analytics*, the process of generating insight from data. Analytics without business analytics creates no return—it simply answers questions. Within this book, analytics represents a wide spectrum that covers all forms of data-driven insight including:

- Data manipulation
- Reporting and business intelligence
- Advanced analytics (including data mining and optimization)

Broadly speaking, analytics divides relatively neatly into techniques that help understand *what happened* and techniques that help understand:

- What *will* happen.
- Why it happened.
- What is the best course of action.

Forms of analytics that help provide this greater level of insight are often referred to as *advanced analytics*.

The final output of business analytics is *value* of some form, either *internal* or *external*. Internal value is value as seen from the perspective of a team within the organization. Among other things, returns are usually associated with cost reductions, resource efficiencies, or other internally related financial aspects. External value is value as seen from outside the organization. Returns are usually associated with revenue growth, positive outcomes, or other market- and client-related measures.

This value is created through leveraging *people, process, data,* and *technology*. *People* are the individuals and their skills involved in applying business analytics. *Processes* are a series of *activities* linked to achieve an outcome and can be either *strongly defined* or *weakly defined.* A strongly defined process has a series of specific steps that is repeatable and can be automated. A weakly defined process, by contrast, is undefined and relies on the ingenuity and skill of the person executing the process to complete it successfully.

Data are quantifiable measures stored and available for analysis. They often include transactional records, customer records, and free-text information such as case notes or reports. *Assets* are produced as an intermediary step to achieving value. Assets are a general class of items that can be defined, are measurable, and have implicit tangible or intangible value. Among other things, they include new processes, reports, models, reports, and datamarts. Critically, they are only an asset within this book if they can be automated and can be repeatedly used by individuals other than those who created it.

Assets are developed by having a team apply various *competencies*. A competency is a particular set of skills that can be applied to solve a wide variety of business problems. Examples include the ability to develop predictive models, the ability to create insightful reports, and the ability to operationalize insight through effective use of technology.

Competencies are applied using various *tools* (often referred to as *technology*) to generate new assets. These assets often include new processes, datamarts, models, or documentation. Often, tools are consolidated into a common *analytical platform*, a technology environment that ranges from being spread across multiple desktop personal computers (PCs) right through to a truly enterprise platform.

Analytical platforms, when properly implemented, make a distinction between a *discovery environment* and an *operational environment.* The role of the discovery environment is to generate insight. The role of the operational environment is to allow this insight to be applied automatically with strict requirements around reliability, performance, and availability.

The core concepts of people, process, data, and technology feature heavily in this book, and, although they are a heavily used and abused framework, they represent the core of systems design. Business analytics is primarily about facilitating change; business analytics is nothing without driving toward better outcomes. When it comes to driving change, establishing a roadmap inevitably involves driving change across these four dimensions. Although this book isn't explicitly written to fit with this framework, it relies heavily on it.

NOTE

1. Astute readers will notice that this section draws from my prior book, E. Stubbs, *The Value of Business Analytics* (Hoboken, NJ: Wiley, 2011).

CHAPTER 2

The Competitive Advantage of Business Analytics

B usiness analytics enables competitive advantage.[1] Regardless of whether one uses classic SWOT (strengths, weaknesses, opportunities, threats) analysis, Porter's five forces, the resource-based view of the firm, or Wilde and Hax's delta model to identify and drive toward competitive differentiation, business analytics helps develop sustainable competitive advantage.

Intuitively, this makes sense: Smarter organizations that act on their insights tend to be more successful. Organizations that better understand their customers' preferences and design their products to suit will easily differentiate themselves in the market. Insurers that have better awareness of the cost of risk will carry lower exposure than those that don't.

It's pithy, but it's true: Making better decisions leads to better results, and business analytics helps organizations make better decisions. Counterintuitively, however, the specifics behind why this is so are harder to explain. Even those with extensive experience in the field often struggle to explain how business analytics supports competitive advantage beyond saying that "it creates better outcomes."

Although true, it lacks clarity, and the link between being smarter and achieving success remains vague.

Some organizations are willing to take this leap of faith. Through experience or experimentation, they succeed. Through a combination of time, trial, and error, they develop an awareness of what works and what doesn't. These organizations are in the minority; most organizations are relatively risk averse and may not want to be the first to experiment with a new idea or initiative. Rather than start from first principles, they would rather make their investments with some degree of confidence that the approaches they'll be following are grounded in both good theory as well as practical application.

Taking advantage of others' experiences is reasonable and pragmatic. Despite this, it is a general rule is that the majority of projects involving either change[2] or information technology (IT) delivery fail. Beyond just knowing that success is possible, success is easier when one knows the *reasons behind* success and encourages the behaviors and approaches that increase the odds of successful delivery. Unfortunately, the relative immaturity of business analytics as a discipline means that these best-practices and execution patterns are either not yet developed or largely ill-defined. Those who already know what works succeed, whereas those who don't are forced to work off trial and error supported by guesswork and assumptions.

Compounding the challenge is that there is no one best policy or practice that fits all organizations. The best business-analytics applications support an organization's unique business model and its strengths. They are a relative endeavor, one that capitalizes on an organization's specific context and environment to achieve organization-specific tactical and strategic goals.

This uniqueness means that there's no one-size-fits-all process that guarantees success. In this respect, business analytics has many parallels with strategic planning: Although there are high-level things that need to happen, the details are inevitably highly organization specific. Much as there isn't one business model that fits all organizations, there isn't one approach to business analytics.

This creates an apparent paradox. On one hand, it's painfully obvious that some organizations are more successful than others when it comes to business analytics. Clearly, not every approach is equally effective.

On the other hand, though, it's also painfully clear that every organization needs a different approach to drive maximum value. So it's not simply a case of copying one's competitors!

The obvious answer is to hire a guru. The teams that do succeed usually have the benefit of a grizzled, battle-scarred individual with hard-won experience. However, success shouldn't rely on the one capable individual. Like anything else, there are patterns and behaviors that increase the odds of success. This goes beyond making sure initiatives are aligned to strategy or having an understanding of how initiatives will create economic returns. The best guidelines are those that enable the process.

Ask a random sample of practitioners what they think drives success and they'll inevitably say one or more of the following:

- Having strong data management capabilities
- Engaging with the right areas of the business
- Being able to innovate
- Giving the business what it needs rather than what it wants
- Making sure information is accurate and trustworthy
- Responding to business requests in an acceptable time frame
- Delivering measurable value to the business
- Having the trust of the business

These are all true. Unfortunately, they're also imprecise. Although they enable success, they also fail to give any guidance on how to do it. Without knowing the general reasons that these are so significant in driving success, practitioners stick with what they know and are hesitant to try anything new.

This book aims to clarify this uncertainty. The rest of this chapter investigates the structural and economic reasons behind business analytics that lead to competitive differentiation. By doing so, it establishes a framework for establishing best practice. Although it's unrealistic to expect that one process will fit all organizations, it's eminently reasonable to have a series of guidelines that, if followed, will lead to best practice.

These will form the foundation for the rest of this book. Every best-practice guideline and solution described in this book aligns to the drivers described later; more than anything else, they establish an objective litmus test to check whether any given change could be seen as moving toward best practice. If a change runs counter to the recommendations described later, more likely than not it is a movement away from best practice and will create inefficiencies rather than efficiencies.

ADVANTAGES OF BUSINESS ANALYTICS

Strategically, business analytics enables differentiation. Knowing this doesn't actually help explain *why* it's true. And, without knowing why, it's impossible to plan for the "how." Without knowing how business analytics creates and augments competitive differentiation, it's hard to know how best to go about improving things.

Business analytics, as a discipline, is primarily about driving change. This in turn means that those driving change must define what that change will look like. Some things are easier to define than others. For example:

- Technology architectures are generally designed based on vendor-specific best practices. For these, the best approach is largely defined by reference-technology architecture.

- Outcomes and predictions can be benchmarked on their accuracy and robustness. For these, the best approach is largely defined by the method that produces the best prediction when taking into account the need for stability and other statistical measures.

- Information-management activities can be benchmarked on storage efficiency, query performance, and ease of interrogation. For these, the best approach is largely defined by quantifiable measures.

It's great that some things are clear. Unfortunately, these represent a small proportion of the change needed! Getting the most from business analytics also requires people and process change, both of which generally lack easily quantifiable measures. Driving this change requires working out how things should look.

It's tempting to try and approach best practices in business analytics as a series of standardized, expert-defined processes. This works well in other fields; enterprise resource planning systems and other operational systems are often based on a series of strongly defined process templates that help drive maximum efficiency across different organizations.

Unfortunately, this doesn't really work. Common and specific best practices don't exist in any useful sense in business analytics; because business analytics is aligned to organizational strategy, there can only ever be general advice. What works for one organization may not work for others.

The biggest reason that a strongly defined approach tends not to work is because there are too many activities that require weakly defined processes. Exploratory data analysis, for example, is by definition exploratory; one doesn't know what's going to work until one's found it! Even worse, business analytics is also heavily linked to innovation. When you're the first person to try a new approach, it's impossible to base that process on an already-defined best-practice approach!

At this point, it may appear that best practice in business analytics is an oxymoron. This is obviously patently false; if it were true, there'd be no performance differences among organizations. There *are* certain principles that help drive efficiency, success, and competitive differentiation.

Consider the classic situation in which someone generates significant insights on their desktop PC using niche, nonenterprise tools. Once they understand what needs to be done, they call the execution team and send across a variety of reports that identify who should be contacted. To make sure it happens, they follow up repeatedly with the team and, over time, they deliver real economic value.

Now, consider another situation in which someone generates those same insights on an enterprise platform, thereby giving their peers the ability to capitalize on their insights. At the end of their analysis, they transform their insights into an asset that is then deployed into the contact-center management system, immediately updating the execution team with a refined contact list.

Both situations go through the same activities and both arrive at the same outcome. In this sense, each is as good as the other. However, the second offers a number of clear advantages. Minimally, it:

- Cross-pollinates knowledge processes across the organization
- Increases the odds of the execution team acting on the insights
- Minimizes the time it takes to move from insight to action

These provide tangential benefits that go beyond the direct economic value they create. Through these extra benefits, they help drive competitive advantage. It is these extra benefits that help define whether a given change is directionally correct in moving toward best practice.

Competitive Advantage

From a microeconomic perspective, business analytics drives competitive advantage by generating:

- Economies of scale
- Economies of scope
- Quality improvement

However, there are two key factors that hinder best practice and, when ineffectively managed, they can actively undermine competitive advantage.

These are:

1. Transaction costs
2. Bounded rationality

Given this framework, best practice in business analytics can then be defined as any movement toward these positive outcomes that simultaneously avoids the associated negative constraints. With this, we have a tightly defined litmus test against which every process can be compared against best practice.

Maximizing Economies of Scale

Economies of scale occur when the average cost per output falls as production increases. This frequently occurs when fixed costs are proportionally higher than variable costs. When sunk costs are higher than the variable costs associated with production or service delivery, organizations have a strong incentive to increase production to maximum capacity to minimize average cost. The reason is simple—the first good produced carries all the cost!

The classic example for this lies in manufacturing. Plant and materials are usually many orders of magnitude more expensive than the variable costs associated with assembly. Setting up the factory might cost a few billion dollars, but the variable costs associated with assembling the product from raw materials might only cost in the tens of thousands of dollars. Given a well-defined cost curve with high sunk costs, the manufacturer needs to manufacture as much as they possibly can to achieve maximum price competitiveness.

Other sources of economies of scale can be achieved by reducing transaction costs or minimizing risk and volatility through volume. Many areas of modern business experience economies of scale to some degree:

- Marketing can reuse their copy across multiple markets, driving down average campaign costs.
- Finance can obtain lower interest rates by borrowing greater amounts of money.
- Vendor management can achieve greater discounts through bulk purchasing.

When they exist and can be harnessed, economies of scale drive cost advantages. Markets that offer economies of scale allow first-mover organizations to achieve either a cost advantage or a margin benefit as they move across their production curve. Over time, this cost advantage may disappear as competitors also achieve economies of scale, assuming they can capitalize on them.

This is not always a guaranteed outcome—achieving true economies of scale may require know-how, unique intellectual property (IP), or unique technology that only the original organization has access to.

When this occurs, those cost advantages become a form of sustainable competitive advantage rather than a transitory competitive advantage.

Business analytics exhibits a number of characteristics that lead to economies of scale. First, there are weak cost advantages to scaling the use of business analytics within an organization. Licensing models vary, but most current technology (hardware and software) tends to be licensed on a structural/capital cost basis. Volume purchasing allows organizations to insist on discounts, decreasing their average cost per processing unit or user.

Organizations reduce total capital investment by taking advantage of oversubscription. They may start by investing in hardware, software, and support for 50 PCs with 4 cores and 8 gigabytes of RAM each. Although the organization is paying for a total processing pool of 200 cores and 400 gigabytes of RAM, none of the users can actually capitalize on this pool; they're all limited to their personal PC.

If these users all follow the typical burst processing pattern (in which their PCs all sit largely underutilized most of the time), the same organization could take advantage of these patterns and achieve the same outcome with a single blade environment that has 64 cores and 64 gigabytes of pooled RAM. Not only does every user get access to a higher-performing environment, but the organization also reduces its capital and support costs, driving economies of scale.

Of greater influence are the sunk costs that go along with driving sophistication. Although analytical solutions don't *need* to leverage advanced techniques, sophistication *can* act as a source of competitive differentiation. More advanced techniques require significant amounts of experience and training, each of which carries heavy time and monetary costs. Becoming proficient in a specialized area can take years of postgraduate education and practical experience. Once developed, however, these same advanced techniques can be applied across multiple problems, driving sophistication across multiple problems. When these advanced techniques drive greater productivity or accuracy, organizations that successfully capitalize on them experience moderate to strong economies of scale.

Business analytics helps drive weak *and* strong economies of scale, partly for generic IT reasons and partly for discipline-specific characteristics. Probably more important, the broader industry has yet to effectively capitalize on these economies of scale, giving those organizations that do capitalize on them a current and possibly sustained competitive advantage.

Taking advantage of these economies of scale is the first way organizations achieve comparative cost efficiencies and drive competitive advantage against their peers.

Maximizing Economies of Scope

Economies of scope drive slightly different cost economies—rather than being related to volume, efficiencies come from breadth. Economies of scope occur when the average cost of production falls as the scope of activities increase. This is independent to an organization's scale of operations, Rather than being related to volume of activity, efficiencies come purely from reusing inputs or competencies across multiple production lines.

Renewable energy is an often-cited source of economies of scope. A major byproduct of most manufacturing processes is heat. If left untapped, this heat acts as both a waste product as well as a source of market failure. The public cost of this negative externality is rarely factored into the market cost of the good. In isolation, manufacturers might see these byproducts as an inherent cost of production.

Approached from a different perspective though, these byproducts can actually create cost advantages through economies of scope. Progressive manufacturers have realized that these byproducts can be used for competitive advantage. Heat can be used to drive alternative sources of energy—by capturing heat-based waste products and blending them with other inputs such as water, manufacturers can reduce their costs in other areas. They can displace central heating in colder climates by recirculating heat. They can use this energy to drive secondary turbines, reducing externally sourced energy requirements. Or they can offset risk in volatile environments by using this energy to maintain backup power supplies. This general solution has applicability beyond pure manufacturing; another common context is managing data centers, the major byproduct of which is heat.

In each of these cases, consuming the byproducts of one value chain helps drive cost efficiencies across the business. At an aggregate level, economies of scope exist when diversifying activities across value chains that have correlated inputs and outputs helps drive down the average cost of production.

Compared to economies of scale, economies of scope occur less frequently. Typically, they manifest when the non-value-adding output of one value chain is a valuable input into an independent value chain. One of the reasons that economies of scope are rarer is that fewer markets or production processes have the necessary commonality of input or outputs within independent value chains.

Business analytics offers moderate to strong economies of scope, largely due to the incremental cost of developing assets using generalized competencies. To understand why, it's important to revisit the value chain of a business analytics team. They will normally take a large set of data and use a variety of tools in conjunction with experience and technical skills to generate one or more intellectual property-based assets. These assets help drive a positive economic outcome for the business within a particular context (such as customer retention or inventory management) by providing automated recommendations and/or actions. These recommendations are of a higher quality than existing activities and, when executed, drive better outcomes.

The major drivers behind business analytics' economies of scope lie in its reusable skills and direct linkage to higher-quality outcomes. Capitalizing on business analytics requires technical skills to varying degrees. At their simplest, these skills can be developed with a minimum of investment; given the right data, learning how to build a simple report in a well-designed toolkit should only take a matter of hours. At their most advanced, these skills can take years of theoretical training along with decades of practical experience. The most advanced forms of analytics can require highly advanced skills in mathematics, computer science, or information-systems design.

Business analytics generates economies of scope because its supporting skills can be reused to solve multiple business problems. Developing new skills carries significant costs; people are rarely productive while they come to terms with their new competencies. Becoming effective in a new area, therefore, carries substantial sunk costs. However, once developed, these competencies can be leveraged within multiple value chains and different contexts with relatively minimal incremental cost. Although this leads to moderate yet constrained economies of scale, it offers significant economies of scope.

For example, the competencies required to drive cross-sell and propensity-based marketing are the same as those needed to identify intentional noncompliance and active fraud. This reuse drives economies of scope, generating cost advantages in organizations that are successful in encouraging cross-functional applications of business-analytics resources.

Significantly, though, this cost advantage is only available to organizations that successfully overcome their internal resistance to reusing competencies across the business. Although this may seem like an obvious approach to take, very few organizations have developed a sufficient level of maturity in business analytics to realize that these economies exist and that they can capitalize on them.

Taking advantage of these economies of scope is the second way organizations achieve comparative cost efficiencies and drive competitive advantage against their peers.

Quality Improvement

Business analytics helps organizations do things better. It's this aspect that provides the final key to competitive advantage: the ability of business analytics to drive higher quality. This in itself can be both profound and confusing.

Quality is a complex concept, one that seemingly defies definition. We know it when we see it, but explaining how it comes about is difficult. No one would argue that there's a big difference between a performance sports car and budget hatchback, but trying to explain why can be frustrating. Usually, it devolves to a case of comparing features or simply saying that one is better, neither of which is entirely satisfactory.

A tremendous amount has been written on the metaphysics of quality, spanning right from the philosophical musings of Pirsig's (1974) Zen Buddhist bent right though to Juran's (1951), Sittig's (1963), and Turner's (1969) attempts to economically link cost to quality. A common theme within the research is that quality correlates highly with return, regardless of how difficult it is to define. Crosby

(1979) went so far as to insist that quality played such a strong role in driving efficiency and savings that, in effect, quality is free.

This text takes the soft road. Rather than try and create a comprehensive definition for quality, it merely acknowledges the role that quality plays in driving better outcomes. For those looking for a more concrete definition, this book adopts the perspectives of both Deming (1988) and Drucker (1985): Quality helps drive both internal efficiencies (through reducing costs and driving productivity) as well as improving the customer's end experience, increasing the amount they're willing to pay or spend.

Although it's a subjective concept, it's useful to think of it as a comparative measure. Given a target outcome with multiple production options and a selection of common inputs, the production process that produces the best outcome can be seen as the higher-quality process. The best outcome is usually dictated by context; production efficiency, market demand, defect management, or a host of other measures may dictate which is the better outcome.

Practical examples abound. One approach may lead to better offer redemptions. One approach may lead to lower product variability. One approach may lead to a lower frequency of fraudulent claims. Given a series of quantifiable outcomes, an organization can benchmark every possible approach and identify which offers the highest quality.

Business analytics is not the only way to drive higher-quality outcomes. However, it's a major one. Information and data, when effectively used, reduce a tremendous amount of uncertainty and, in almost all cases, they lead to a better outcome as long the insights are accurate and acted upon. There are two specific reasons for this. Business analytics:

1. Allows us to consider a broader set of information than would be humanly possible.

2. Scales to allow for highly differentiated treatment patterns

The first is quite simple: In the absence of technological support, we are fundamentally limited in the amount of information we can reasonably consider. Almost everyone feels comfortable thinking about customers or citizens in terms of how much they spend or consume in a given period. We also feel comfortable thinking about them in terms of their average spend or consumption over a longer time period. Depending on our comfort levels, we may even consider 10 or more different dimensions, including age, product holdings, service usage, and so on. Eventually though, we hit a limit; we simply can't consider any more without getting confused or abstracting the information we're considering.

Business analytics has none of these restrictions. Because of its mathematical and algorithmic nature, it matters little whether one is trying to identify common patterns behind 10 or 10 million measures. As long as the data is available, analysis is possible. This helps cast the net wider than would otherwise be possible. In simplifying the information we consider, we run the risk of missing the important things. Business analytics helps reduce the odds of this happening.

Scalability is also critical in driving better outcomes. Better outcomes stem from treating things differently in different contexts. Not every customer or system is the same—people have different preferences, and processes exhibit different dynamics as contexts change. Business analytics helps identify these differences and drive differentiated treatment patterns. For example, rather than have one offer structure for all customers, business analytics allows organizations to make thousands of offers, linking the right offer to the right customer through analyzing behavioral characteristics. This differentiation helps drive both the customer's perception of quality as well as internal efficiencies and productivity gains.

Measuring the impact of insights and activities on quality and using them to drive continuous improvements is the final way organizations leverage business analytics to drive competitive advantage.

CHALLENGES OF BUSINESS ANALYTICS

Just as business analytics offers significant microeconomic advantages, it carries with it various challenges that, when left unmanaged, eliminate major sources of competitive advantage. In the immortal words of Heinlein and Friedman, "there ain't no such thing as a free lunch." Business analytics is a complex discipline and success requires focus. There are many moving parts and when left unattended, chaos and uncertainty tend to be the major outcome.

Minimizing Transaction Costs

It can sometimes seem that practicing business analytics is like trying to assemble a puzzle in which all the pieces are constantly moving. There are at least three groups of individuals who need to be involved to achieve an outcome: the analytics/insights team, the business, and the IT team. Someone needs to provide the answer, someone needs to make it real, and someone needs to act on it.

There is usually a complex technology landscape incorporating multiple-source data systems, at least one (or more) analytical environments, and one or more operational systems that will act as the execution engines. On top of all that, there is a large extended team who will be responsible for acting on the insight, all of whom need to be kept up to speed with how and why the changes will be happening.

Coordinating these activities carries a certain management overhead. Assets and insights need to be migrated between environments and contexts. People need to be briefed and change needs to be managed. Objectives need to be agreed upon, politics managed, responsibilities assigned, and progress tracked. This even goes beyond any single initiative; managers and decision makers also need to coordinate the activities of different teams lest they start creating overly specific processes that have minimal potential for reuse.

Broadly speaking, these start to create diseconomies of scale. As groups get larger, their efficiency starts to drop. Specifically though, these diseconomies are driven by the transaction costs associated with coordination and ensuring consistent quality. Every interaction carries a time and opportunity cost. In a perfectly efficient process, every single one of these transactions is necessary: Assets are deployed once and only once, models pass quality control reviews on their first time, and the outcomes from meetings are both well understood and achieved.

Few processes, however, are perfectly efficient. Controlling transaction costs involves doing two things:

1. Aggressively eliminating all unnecessary points of interaction

2. Identifying and leveraging lower-cost transactional structures

Rather than manually scoring data, teams can use automated scoring processes. Rather than manually supporting decisions by being on call, teams can leverage operational analytics and move toward a system-based approach to decision support. A significant part of this book focuses on a variety of ways organizations can reduce transaction costs.

By understanding the importance of transaction costs and actively managing them, teams greatly extend the degree to which they can achieve competitive advantage through cost efficiencies. When ignored, an artificial cap is placed on the extent to which an organization can realize the economies of scope and scale offered by business analytics.

Bounded Rationality

Despite being rational, based on the information we have access to, the decisions we make are rarely optimal. Decisions need to be made without having access to all the information we would like, the information we work with is frequently imperfect, and we are rarely certain about what's truly important in the first place. To cope with this, we satisfy rather than maximize, blending satisfaction with sufficiency over trying to find the best possible answer—when under pressure, we resort to what we know will work.

To speed decision making, we develop heuristics and rules of thumb that help guide us toward the right outcome in imperfect situations. This is essential given our procedural limits—there is only so much information we can feasibly consider given our limited time and short-term memory capacity. Experience colors our perceptions on what's possible, which in turn constrains our point of view to what our heuristics reinforce.

In the absence of a better solution, satisfying and relying on heuristics makes a great deal of sense. Our cognitive limitations lead to bounded rationality, the situation in which we make the most rational decisions we can, taking into account the time we have available as well as the information we have access to and can process.

Bounded rationality tends to drive locally optimal outcomes over globally optimal outcomes. There is only so much information we can consider and we suffer a variety of psychological biases that lead us to emphasize "closer" information (by time or perceived priority) over "further" information. This encourages functionally applied insights over enterprise applications, undermining economies of scope.

Examples abound of how bounded rationality prevents organizations from developing cost advantages through business analytics. A common one involves how many sales and marketing groups fail to achieve their maximum potential despite making apparently rational decisions. Many groups align their management structures on a product basis where each product group has responsibility over sales revenue. To achieve these targets, these groups will each develop a variety of below-the-line campaigns targeted at specific customer segments. These campaigns culminate in an offer of some form, the outcome of which is hopefully a sale.

Individually, each of these groups targets the customers most likely to be interested in the offer. Inevitably though, these groups end up targeting some of the same customers. The organization only has a finite customer base, and most customers will be interested in more than one product.

Ideally, the organization's final list of offers takes into account the likelihood of acceptance and the expected revenue associated with take-up at a customer level. However, this requires understanding and analyzing a large amount of information. For an organization with tens of millions of customers, this could involve hundreds of millions of product/customer combinations. Therefore, although it's feasible to identify a global solution, most groups devolve back to a variety of local solutions from which they lobby for their preferred outcome. Although rational, it is also substantially suboptimal.

This preference for heuristics and local optima undermines the competitive advantage of business analytics. In the absence of better information, we gravitate toward what experience tells us is most effective. Unfortunately, our experiences are often based on making decisions with imperfect information. Given that one of the biggest advantages of business analytics is its ability to incorporate far more information than would be humanly feasible, our natural tendencies actively prevent us from achieving better outcomes unless we actively manage them.

Improving decision making requires two things. First, it requires trust. Doing things differently requires not only an acknowledged need for change but also a belief that change is possible. Second, it requires evidence to support change. Many of the best practices described in this book are focused on surfacing the evidence required for better decision making. Without knowing what's being sacrificed, it might be entirely rational to make a locally optimal decision. However, if the decision maker can clearly understand the benefits of a globally optimal solution, they'll usually make better decisions.

By understanding the importance of bounded rationality in the decision-making process, teams help overcome many of the barriers that prevent organizations from achieving higher quality as well as economies of scope. When ignored, decision makers tend to gravitate back toward their preferred heuristics and, by doing so, create barriers to change. These actively undermine the benefits offered by business analytics and often block insights from being operationally executed.

ESTABLISHING BEST PRACTICES

At this point, we have everything we need to start reviewing how to move toward best practice. Because of the nature of best practice, it would be impossible to provide an exhaustive list of all possible solutions; there are, quite simply, too many problems that can be solved using business analytics to make this feasible. And it's a developing field; what is cutting-edge today from a technological perspective will likely become a commodity over the next decade.

Still, there are principles that can help guide designers and managers toward better solutions. Armed with the knowledge of the drivers behind competitive advantage, practitioners have an objective framework through which they can constantly move toward best practice. More than just a series of philosophies, we can focus on a series of specific actions by which teams can develop true competitive advantage.

NOTES

1. E. Stubbs. *The Value of Business Analytics* (Hoboken, NJ: Wiley, 2011).
2. *An Inside Job 2000*, viewed September 22, 2012, www.economist.com/node/5958.

PART
TWO

The Data
Scientist's Code

A good data scientist is great at generating insight and driving innovation. The best data scientists understand that business analytics is about more than insight; it's about directly driving real economic value.

To drive competitive differentiation, they manage by the following code:

- Think about competencies, not functions
- Drive outcomes, not insight
- Automate everything non-value-added
- Start flexible, become structured
- Eliminate bottlenecks
- Design your platform for use, not purity
- Always have a plan B
- Know what you are worth
- Own your intellectual property

- Minimize custom development
- Understand your data
- It's better to have too much data than too little
- Keep things simple
- Function should dictate form
- Watch the dynamic, not just the static

CHAPTER 3

Designing the Approach

Moving from insight to value is more than just a glib statement. It represents a major shift in management philosophy. It's also the difference between differentiation and mediocrity. This chapter focuses on five rules that, if followed, help keep organizations focused on value creation rather than just being smart.

THINK ABOUT COMPETENCIES, NOT FUNCTIONS

Business analytics is a competitive differentiator. Treat it as one.

Being better than the competition is the essence of competitive advantage. There are, however, limits to this. Trying to be everything to everyone is a recipe for disaster; there's a reason Amazon and Wal-Mart have different business models.

Competitive differentiation comes from specialization. Specialization comes at a cost: It requires deep skills, time, and investments that carry heavy sunk costs. However, it's hard if not impossible to differentiate by being a generalist. A big part of strategy is simply trying to work out where focus will drive the best return.

Although investment always carries risk, one of the biggest risks is that investing in specialization leads to skills that are rarely transferable. Having the infrastructure to support the world's best supply chain is meaningless when it comes to driving one-to-one customer engagement. For most organizations, it's a case of picking one, maybe two areas to specialize in and being okay everywhere else.

Business analytics turns this constraint on its head. Unlike other specializations, it's entirely reusable across the enterprise. Every business unit faces different challenges. Marketing, for example, needs to retain customers while growing revenue. Finance needs to control costs while enabling growth. The fraud group needs to prevent losses and maximize collections.

Normally, there's little overlap of skills between these domains. Being an experienced marketer rarely helps when it comes to understanding fraud. Being a pricing guru rarely helps when it comes to engaging effectively with customers.

The beauty of statistical skills is that they can be reused across these and many more domains. They can help reduce churn by driving better retention targeting. They can also drive better recovery rates by identifying those who have the highest probability of recovery.

Although these problems are worlds apart, predictive modeling can help improve outcomes for each. By using statistical analysis to create probability-based predictions of future behavior, the organization can improve its ability to reduce churn and increase collections. By investing in these skills once, the organization can use them to solve many problems.

The power of business analytics is that, as long as data is available, it can help solve so many different problems. The skills and infrastructure needed to support business analytics aren't free. However, unlike other specializations, these costs can be amortized across multiple problems. Being skilled in business analytics enables significant economies of scope and creates cost and quality advantages over one's competitors.

Cost efficiencies are one side of the coin. The other is business analytics' capacity to drive higher-quality outcomes. Knowing that certain customers prefer to be contacted via SMS can help drive better response rates. The best way to get this insight is through analytics.

One of the many advantages of business analytics is that it's a renewable source of return. When faced with a problem, there's usually more than one way to solve it. Some approaches may drive higher-quality outcomes at the expense of greater sophistication and time investment. Other approaches may be relatively simple but they may only improve things slightly. On one hand, the greatest thing about business analytics is that it can solve so many problems. On the other, the biggest challenge is that it *can solve so many problems*. There's an almost infinite number of ways any given problem can solved.

What at first may seem like a disadvantage is, in reality, one of the most powerful features of business analytics. Even though there's an abundance of choice, the answer is actually pretty simple. Doing things better doesn't necessarily require heavy sophistication up front. Driving a better outcome is usually simply a case of doing things better than current processes.

Incremental Value Comes from Continuous Improvement

Relatively unsophisticated techniques can still deliver quick wins. However, there's nothing to stop the organization from applying ever-increasing levels of sophistication to help drive further returns. By increasing sophistication over time, organizations can progressively move toward sustainable competitive differentiation while constantly delivering tactical returns.

In an environment plagued by guesswork and gut feel, a team that sets up simple reports that present high-quality information can make some major wins. In the absence of information, even the most elementary analysis can be tremendously valuable. This is a great start. However, they can do more. To further improve outcomes, they can move from reports to alerts. Rather than spend time reviewing information, decision makers would be automatically alerted to potential issues. This increases productivity and gives decision makers more time to run the business.

This is even better, but there's still more! To drive higher-quality outcomes, they can use statistics to isolate the factors that lead to financial success. These help drive focus: Rather than guessing about what drives the business, decision makers can target the right levers to improve performance.

Later on, they might go even further and start predicting what will happen in the future. They might also use optimization to identify how best to allocate resources to achieve a targeted outcome. They may establish automated operational processes that take over certain microdecisions within the organization, giving operational staff more time to focus on high-value activities.

Organizations don't have to start with highly complex solutions. Instead, they can increase the sophistication of their solutions over time. Assuming each is successful, they all help create incremental value. By balancing tactical and strategic returns, business analytics enables continuous improvement and competitive differentiation.

Achieving this level of success requires focus. It requires planning. Possibly most important, the organization needs to treat these skills as a legitimate competency in their own right. Marketing, finance, engineering, and a wide variety of other specialized disciplines require specific management structures if they're to be developed and leveraged.

Business analytics is no different. When these skills are left to develop organically, they're usually only applied functionally. The marketing group may become excellent in predictive modeling, whereas the pricing group may become expert in hedonic pricing theory. Neither benefits from the others' skills. This prevents organizations from capitalizing on potential economies of scope.

Management Principles

Driving ongoing improvement in managing competencies involves emphasizing the following guidelines:

- Identify competencies and nurture them
- Actively look for opportunities to reuse existing competencies

Focus on Value-Creating Skills

The first thing to remember is that skills develop with practice. Sophistication requires experience. When teams spread their focus too thin, they struggle to achieve better-than-average performance. Rather than be mediocre at everything, organizations should identify competencies that are actively creating value and nurture them. As the team's ability to apply these competencies grows, they should slowly extend into new areas.

Reuse Your Skills Wherever Possible

The second thing is to constantly look for opportunities to reuse existing skills. Business analytics offers economies of scope, so that a single competency can solve multiple business problems. For example, predictive models can assist in improving both compliance as well as customer retention. The first initiative usually carries high sunk costs in the forms of skills and technology. However, because the second initiative leverages existing investment, it carries relatively minimal incremental cost.

Competitive differentiation stems from identifying these opportunities to reuse existing competencies. By doing so, organizations can magnify return on investment. This is impossible when organizations don't treat business analytics skills as a domain in their own right and, instead, leave them buried in functional lines of business.

▶ Related Solutions

- Encouraging innovation
- Allocating responsibilities
- Scaling past the PC
- Capturing the right data
- Blending rules with models

DRIVE OUTCOMES, NOT INSIGHT

Insight creates answers, outcomes create value.

Business analytics teams often see their primary responsibility as being the go-to team for answers. It's true, but it's also only half the picture. Insight is important; so are outcomes.

Insight without execution is worthless. Value only comes when someone acts on that insight. This is true regardless of the business, industry, or application. Whether one's in the public or private sector, having the answer isn't as important as using that answer to do something.

A common problem in social services involves influencing behaviors to try and encourage reemployment. The reasons behind unemployment can be complex. A person may be unemployed because they live in a geographically depressed area. They may be structurally unemployed as their skills are no longer in demand. Or they may simply be frictionally unemployed and about to find a new role.

Insight helps identify why someone is chronically unemployed. It may help uncover the drivers behind employment. However, by itself this insight is worthless. It's interesting, but it's still worthless. It's not until the agency uses that insight to change the way they engage that they will create value.

By understanding *why* someone cannot get a job, the agency can better target services and programs to improve the individual's odds of becoming employed. They don't just answer the question, they aim to solve the problem. By acting on their insight, they deliver better social outcomes.

Management Principles

Encouraging best practice in driving value involves emphasizing the following guidelines:

- Focus on the outcome, not just the insight
- Prioritize based on value potential, not just interest

Drive Outcomes Instead of Insight

Insight can be seductive; uncovering relationships and drivers easily becomes an end in its own right. In some contexts, that's a good thing. If your goal is research, insights are invaluable!

However, the goal of business analytics is to drive value creation. Insight is essential, but it's also only an intermediary step. What's equally if not more important is translating that insight into action and achieving an outcome. Always consider what the outcome could be for any given insight and make sure that the outcome is an integral part of the team's objectives.

Emphasize Value over Interest

The other thing to remember is that what's interesting isn't necessarily valuable. We're naturally attracted to the things that interest us the most. Unfortunately, not all things have commercial or practical applications; sometimes, discovery is just for discovery's sake. Although it's true that innovation often comes from experimentation, it's also critical to prioritize activities based on their potential for value creation, not just on what's the most interesting.

When it comes to developing a roadmap or a program of work, interest is essential. A bored team is an unproductive team. However, this needs to be balanced against the probability of being able to drive a tangible outcome. If that outcome can't be defined, odds are good that it shouldn't be a high-priority project. Do it, but don't prioritize it at the expense of higher-value initiatives.

▶ Related Solutions

- Encouraging innovation
- Coping with information overload
- Moving beyond the spreadsheet
- Moving to operational analytics
- Measuring value
- Linking analytics to value

AUTOMATE EVERYTHING NON-VALUE-ADDED

Automation is your friend. Ignore it at your own peril.

We spend far too much time doing things we shouldn't. That doesn't necessarily mean we're focusing in the wrong areas. Usually, we're just inefficient. It's often said that 80 percent of an analyst's time is spent managing data. This is true. What *isn't* as frequently said is that there's a big difference between an efficient 80 percent and an inefficient 80 percent.

Software engineering has struggled with productivity and quality for decades. Brooks,[1] a well-known researcher, highlighted one of the best examples of how big the difference can be between efficient and average resources. One study[2] found that the most efficient programmers could be up to 10 times more productive that an average programmer. This wasn't a one-off finding, either—Glass[3] found that the most efficient programmers could be *28 times* more productive than the worst.

This is also true in business analytics. Consider two analysts, one struggling, the other highly productive. The first spends time copying and pasting data within spreadsheets. The analyst manually edits their data for further analysis. Once the analyst creates insight, he spends a significant amount of time trying to create the table structure he needs to export it to where it needs to go in the right format. He then repeatedly tries to e-mail the data to the person who owns execution, spending even more time trying to explain what every field in the table means. When the next project rolls around, he starts from scratch.

The second analyst uses purpose-built tools to build repeatable processes that automatically extract, cleanse, and transform the data she has into the information she needs. These tools package her processes into assets that can be operationally deployed. Once she has finalized her workflow, she automates it so that it automatically populates (and extends) her analytical datamart.

Rather than find answers through manual effort, she uses her automated assets. And, once she has created these assets, she can migrate these assets into her warehouse. Her final step is to schedule these assets to run as needed, eliminating all need for manual interaction. And when the next project rolls around, she reuses the automated extensions she has already built into her datamart.

When it comes to productivity, experience counts for a lot. Arguably though, automation counts for even more. Every second spent doing things that *could* have been automated is time taken away from generating value.

Management Principles

Encouraging best practice in automation involves emphasizing the following guidelines:

- Minimize the use of approaches that cannot be automated
- Favor approaches that transparently support automation.

Avoid Manual Activities

The reality is that not everything can be automated. Creativity and innovation, in particular, require flexibility. However, whenever one *can* make a choice between an approach that supports automation and one that doesn't, automation should always be a significant consideration. This is true even if it leads to a marginally worse result. After all, although it may marginally reduce return on investment, the team may be able to use their newly found time to deliver more initiatives.

Have Your Tools Do the Work

The other thing to remember is that, although automation is essential, it's not an end goal. As such, it's important to try and minimize the overhead needed to support automation as much as possible.

Generating the right insights already takes long enough. Given all the challenges that come with business analytics, why make the job harder? Tools and technologies have advanced to a point where many natively support automation. Once built, all processes should be capable of being automated regardless of context.

If technology is the constraint, it's probably because the wrong technology is being used. Models should be deployable in a variety of architectures including inside the enterprise data warehouse, in automated scoring processes, or on-demand based on requests from external systems.

If the technology is right, none of these approaches should require substantive reengineering. A great example lies in spreadsheets. Although even spreadsheets support scripting, every second spent writing the code necessary to automate the logic built into the spreadsheet is time that could have been used to drive actual innovation or value creation elsewhere. Just because it *can* be done doesn't mean it *should be done*. Pick the tools for the job; don't constrain the job based on the tools.

► Related Solutions

- Breaking bottlenecks
- Optimizing monitoring processes
- Coping with information overload
- Moving beyond the spreadsheet
- Measuring value
- Measuring performance
- Measuring effort
- Creating data-management processes
- Linking analytics to value
- Enabling real-time scoring

START FLEXIBLE, BECOME STRUCTURED

Businesses don't operate in a static environment. Neither do you.

Analysts operate in a challenging environment. On one hand, their efficiency comes from having disciplined, well-defined processes.

On the other though, innovation comes from experimentation and doing things differently. These work at cross-purposes and in direct contradiction. This presents a dilemma: Focusing on either of these in isolation inevitably destroys value.

One option is to make efficiency the primary priority. When this happens, teams create extremely efficient, well-defined processes. This comes at a cost: They also tend to struggle to adapt to change. Every time things change, their processes usually fail to keep up. To handle these changes, they need large amounts of time and investment to adjust.

The way most organizations manage business intelligence is a prime example. To control risk and manage expectations, they exhaustively scope requirements before they'll even consider developing a report. This has advantages: It emphasizes repeatability, formalizes roles, and substantially reduces uncertainty.

Unfortunately, it's also very inflexible. The business might not know what it needs until it sees it. Or it might require information in a way that's unsupported by the business intelligence team's existing technology. When facing nonstandard and/or unknown requirements, trying to build reports based on predefined requirements is challenging if not impossible.

Conversely, having too much flexibility also introduces issues. The team might make innovation the primary priority. By leaving processes undefined and allowing total freedom, the team may drive real innovation and enable groundbreaking competitive advantage. Unfortunately, this also comes at a cost. When things are undefined, it becomes hard for the team to migrate their resulting assets and processes into production. If the organization's operational framework cannot support the assets developed by the team, much of their work may have to be redesigned.

Management Principles

In the vast majority of situations, the answer isn't to emphasize one or the other. Instead, it's about achieving a balance between the two. It's helpful to keep the following guidelines in mind:

- Maintain flexibility, but not at the expense of execution
- Focus on milestones rather than activities

Flexibility First, Structure After

Where flexibility allows innovation, standardization enables efficiency. To balance these, it can be useful to start by allowing high levels of flexibility during experimentation and discovery. However, as the team hones in on a solution, they need to temper activities if their solution might lead to a situation in which this flexibility would prevent execution. Rather than have one or the other, manage by enforcing a spectrum of control in which things need to be more and more structured as they get closer to operational execution.

Manage by Milestones, Not Activities

The other thing to remember is that creative solutions are hard to define ahead of time. Trying to define and micromanage activities can prevent a team from innovating. Forcing everyone to follow the same specific steps can actually hurt an organization's ability to drive disruptive innovation.

However, the need for flexibility doesn't mitigate the need for *some* standardization. Managers still need visibility over what their teams are doing and whether they're progressing toward a real solution. To balance flexibility with the need for management visibility, teams should manage by milestones rather than by activities.

Each milestone or checkpoint might involve specific outcomes, assets, and review points. Agile development methodologies are a great case study on how rapid iteration can preserve flexibility without sacrificing control.[4] This helps benchmark a team's ability to move from one milestone to the next without limiting their ability to innovate by experimenting with different tools, processes, or techniques.

▶ Related Solutions
- Keeping everyone aligned
- Allocating responsibilities
- Scaling past the PC
- Staying mobile and connected
- Moving to operational analytics
- Enabling real-time scoring

ELIMINATE BOTTLENECKS

You're only ever as strong as your weakest link. Know it, fix it, and move on to the next one.

Business analytics is like a finely tuned watch; when it's working, there are hundreds of moving parts. However, all it takes to break it is one misconfigured spring. Generating insight requires having the right skills, the right tools, and the right data. Acting on that insight requires getting that insight to the people with the authority to do things differently. And making sure it all works seamlessly requires having the right systems and support staff in place.

It's rare that all these people are part of the same team. Most of the time, these people are scattered across the organization—a typical marketing application might require skills from finance, IT, the marketing analytics team, as well as the direct marketing team!

Together, these activities create a value chain, and every activity adds *potential* value. It's only when these activities are linked, however, that this value is *realized*. Because of this, the individual activities aren't anywhere near as important as the overall value chain.

Knowing which customers to contact isn't worth much without the ability to contact them. Being able to deliver more campaigns is of questionable value without knowing who should be targeted to drive the greatest revenue. And, putting in place big-data infrastructure is of dubious value if the organization isn't ready with the skills to understand *how* to leverage big-data analytics.

When linked into a value chain than spans from insight to execution, activities generate tremendous value. They help organizations drive continuous improvement and enable revolutionary transformation. There's a catch, though: Every value chain is only as strong as its weakest link. One of the goals of an effective manager is to find it, fix it, and move on to the next weakest link.

One of the best things about business analytics is that it enables continuous return on investment with relatively minor incremental

investment. Once an organization has developed the right competencies, platform, processes, and information sources, it's relatively
easy for that organization to reuse those assets to solve other problems.
If an organization has already developed the competencies and assets
to identify who is likely to be most interested in a product based on
their behavioral characteristics, it's a small step to being able to identify
fraudsters based on their behavioral patterns.

Bottlenecks Destroy Scale

Reusing assets and skills creates cost efficiencies. However, this only
happens when processes *can* be reused. Bottlenecks can completely
derail an organization's ability to extract competitive advantage from
business analytics. One of the secrets that marks the difference
between an analytical competitor and a laggard is their ability to scale.
Although the boundary of what's possible keeps moving, it's useful to
highlight how significant these differences can be.

While it's a rough measure based on anecdotal experience, in
the absence of technology support, most analysts can handle up
to approximately six models at a time. This assumes they are following
appropriate hygiene processes such as benchmarking model degradation over time. By comparison, the most highly productive analysts are
able to achieve the same level of quality and outcomes for more than
three thousand models! Given this productivity difference, it is easy to
see *why* business analytics can enable competitive differentiation.

Skills play a role in driving this differentiation. However, there's far
more to success than just getting more people. Hiring more resources is
rarely the answer; every additional person needs time to get up to
speed, adds structural cost, and increases complexity.

The biggest enabler is focus; achieving this level of scale requires
understanding how individual activities impact the overall value chain.
By measuring performance and identifying bottlenecks, the team can
manage them, mitigate them, and move on.

Management Principles

Driving best practice in this space involves keeping the following
guidelines in mind:

■ Track your effort and optimize the right areas

■ Benchmark yourself and aim for the top

Measure Your Effort

Knowing where things can be improved and eliminating bottlenecks is impossible without knowing how long things take. Improvement requires a detailed understanding of where and when effort is being expended. If you can't measure it, you can't improve it. Improving the wrong area can carry expensive opportunity costs: Had that effort been spent eliminating real bottlenecks, the team would have achieved more with less.

Understand Your Strengths and Weaknesses

Knowing where bottlenecks exist is half the picture. The other half involves knowing what's possible. Bottlenecks always exist, but some are more important than others. Establishing a benchmark is critical in setting realistic expectations.

This is harder than it sounds. Understanding what's possible can be challenging, especially given the competitive advantage business analytics offers. Many organizations are reluctant to share their "secret sauce." Overcoming this challenge involves networking, leveraging the insights of vendors, and generating strong market intelligence, none of which is necessarily easy. Even so, the fact that it's hard doesn't make it any less essential.

▶ Related Solutions

■ Breaking bottlenecks

■ Scaling past the PC

■ Moving to operational analytics

■ Measuring performance

■ Measuring effort

■ Reducing time to recommendation

NOTES

1. F. Brooks, *The Mythical Man-Month* (Needham, MA: Addison-Wesley, 1975).

2. H. Sackman, W. J. Erikson, and E. E. Grant, "Exploratory Experimental Studies Comparing Online and Offline Programming Performance," in *Communications of the ACM* 11, no. 1: 3–11.

3. Robert L. Glass, *Facts and Fallacies of Software Engineering.* (Needham, MA: Addison-Wesley, 2002).

4. Kent Beck et al., *Manifesto for Agile Software Development* (Salt Lake City, UT: Agile Alliance, 2001).

CHAPTER **4**

Creating Assets

T he best teams don't just generate insight. Instead, they generate information assets that, when applied to business problems, help create repeatable and renewable value. This chapter focuses on five rules that, if followed, help organizations drive productivity, manage risk, and foster competitive differentiation.

DESIGN YOUR PLATFORM FOR USE, NOT PURITY

Things never go to plan. Make sure you have enough redundancy and flexibility to deal with whatever the world throws at you.

Some of the best insights are unexpected. Even when there's a well-defined goal, analytics usually has a heavy dose of the unknown. Unlike traditional IT systems, requirements are hard to define ahead of time. The target outcome might be improved fraud detection. Analysts rarely start from first principles; usually, they've got a good hunch on what's *likely* to work. However, it's not until they've finished their exploratory analysis and built their candidate models that they know what *will* work.

Their first step is to build a catalog of challenger models. To make an objective choice, they then need to work out which model provides the best predictions. This is a voyage of discovery; until they're at the end, they'll usually have no idea what will work. Quite often, the process itself will trigger new insights, which will, in turn, suggest new approaches. Uncertainty is the norm rather than the exception.

Because of this, it's hard to know the right number of people, the right platform size, or the right amount of data ahead of time. The answer they'd like to give for each is, "As much as we need." This answer rarely flies. Its cost is prohibitive. Processing power, storage, and bandwidth all cost money.

Few teams get the support they'd *like*. However, that doesn't mean that they can't have the support they *need* even as their requirements change.

Management Principles

To embrace flexibility, it's useful to embrace the following guidelines:

- Assume the worst and make sure you have a backup plan if things go wrong.
- Build your platform to support your use cases, not just what's architecturally attractive.
- Always architect for flexibility.

Plan for Redundancy

Enterprise-grade technology isn't cheap. Given the cost of mission-critical systems, it can be tempting to try and cut corners. Dropping backup systems or load-balancing technologies (such as grid or fabric processing) may seem like a low-risk way of reducing project costs. It isn't.

It's true that not every team needs strong systems redundancy and workload management. It's also true that more teams need this than usually budget for them. Systems are fallible and a bad patch or a clumsy cleaner can bring down a system in seconds. Inevitably, everything will go catastrophically wrong at the worst possible time. Unless there are multiple levels of redundancy, the organization may grind to a surprisingly costly halt.

A prime example involved an organization that thought their discovery platform was independent of their operational systems.

Because they believed they were decoupled, they didn't bother with any level of platform redundancy. If it went down, at worst they'd have to deal with some testy analysts.

About a year after they went live, they discovered that their apparently independent discovery platform was, in reality, tightly linked to their operational campaign management systems. Late one afternoon, their discovery platform went down because of a mis-applied patch. Seconds later, so did their campaign management system.

Despite the millions of dollars they'd spent building redundancy into their operational systems, their entire marketing engine halted because of an apparently unimportant analytics platform. Forty-eight hours and significant regulatory and marketing costs later, they agreed with the importance of having a truly redundant system.

Use Defines Architecture, Not the Other Way Around

Redundancy is important. So is getting the most out of your platform. A badly designed technology platform can create long-term growth problems. Getting this right is critical. A house and an office each needs a different fit and serves different functions. If one wants to live in a house, ending up with an office is going to be disappointing.

A key part of best practice involves getting the most out of one's tools. Technology isn't cheap, and bad design can reduce effectiveness. If one's using a hammer, holding a nail incorrectly can lead to a lot of smashed thumbs. If one's using an analytics platform, a bad design can significantly reduce processing throughput.

The platform should *always* be based on planned use rather than architectural attractiveness. This approach helps maximize asset use and avoids overinvestment. It's critical to have deep IT support through this process; getting things right involves technological subtleties.

As an example, one of the earliest decisions is whether to design the platform to scale vertically or horizontally. A vertically scalable platform focuses on sheer processing power. It revolves around increasing the processing capacity of every node as far as it will go. A horizontally scalable platform, on the other hand, focuses on distributed processing. It revolves around using multiple systems to balance processing loads across multiple machines.

Each has its own advantages, and each has its own limitations. The choice of approach is largely dependent on the problem to be solved. For example, having a platform with a small number of extremely high performance servers might make sense when the algorithms in use are mainly constrained by the central processing unit (CPU). Serial processes such as community detection in social network analysis often benefit in these situations. If, on the other hand, the processes can be parallelized or there are large numbers of simultaneous users, it might make more sense to adopt a horizontally scalable architecture and throw more nodes into the platform. Situations in which disk transfer rates are the primary constraint often benefit from this approach.

Another great example involves the difference between parallel processing and load balancing. To a neophyte, both look similar—every job is allocated across multiple nodes to increase overall platform utilization. There are, however, subtle differences. Parallel processing involves automatically dividing a task into multiple chunks, each of which can be processed by a different system. By contrast, load balancing may simply allocate jobs across different systems with no regards to each system's utilization. In the first case, a central controller makes sure each system is used roughly equally. In the second, one system may be operating at 100 percent capacity, whereas the others go fully unutilized.

Favor Flexible Architectures

A final point to keep in mind is the importance of building flexibility into complex environments. A moderately complex business analytics platform will span separate discovery and operational environments. It might also potentially have multiple staging environments covering development, test, and production-use cases, and, to provide redundancy, it might also have a number of hot or cold backup environments.

Setting this up in the first place represents a significant investment in technology. Because of this investment, it makes a great deal of sense to utilize it as much as possible. When these are logically *and* physically separate environments, organizations will often find they hit various processing bottlenecks.

Usage is hard to predict ahead of time. The reality is that most of the time, we'll get it wrong. The production operational environment may have been undersized, limiting the number of automated decisions the organization can process. Or the production discovery environment may not have been designed to accommodate greater than expected enterprise usage.

When these environments are logically *and* physically separate, the organization has no choice but to buy more hardware. Given that it's easy to predict that we'll often be wrong in our usage projections, the better approach is to design with flexibility as a key requirement.

Rather than base the architecture on physical *and* logical separation, a better approach is to establish a virtualization layer over the top of the physical infrastructure. Although the environments are still *logically* separate, they leverage a common *physical* layer.

This allows the organization to reallocate processing power as needed based on developing business requirements. If the production operational environment was undersized and the discovery environment oversized, fixing the problem can be as easy as adjusting virtualization settings. When these environments are physically separate, fixing the problem might involve six months of lead time along with a new business case to justify further capital costs.

Encouraging best practice in this context involves understanding that more often than not we get it wrong. Because of this, it helps to architect the platform in a way that allows managers to flexibly reconfigure the environment as needed. Although this isn't always possible, it helps to bear it in mind when designing the architecture.

▶ Related Solutions
- Keeping everyone aligned
- Staying mobile and connected
- Smoothing growth with the cloud
- Reducing time to recommendation

ALWAYS HAVE A PLAN B

You never know what you're going to need to solve a problem. Make sure you've got a backup plan in case you need it.

One of the great things about statistics is that there's such a rich variety of ways to solve what would otherwise appear to be insoluble problems. Do you have too much data and not enough horsepower? Use stratified sampling. Are algorithms taking too long to run? Fall back to the old standbys: logistic regressions and decision trees. Do you have too many variables and not enough observations? Use principle components or exclude highly correlated variables.

As effective as these solutions are, eventually all teams hit a problem they can't solve. Not because they don't have the chops, but because they simple don't have the technological horsepower to get a result in a reasonable amount of time.

Some problems are especially prone to this. Market-basket analysis and social-network analysis are notorious for requiring heavy-duty processing power, largely because it is exceedingly difficult to create a representative and robust sample. When sampling is impossible, the only option is to process *everything*, and that may require more processing power than the team has on tap.

This, obviously, is an issue; some problems can only be solved using these types of techniques. For example, it's hard to use viral marketing or identify loss leaders without doing this kind of analysis. If the team's opportunities require having access to more processing power than is available, and they don't have a backup plan, they're stuck.

Extending the existing platform can take anywhere from months to years. They need to find budget, source hardware, and potentially evaluate software. Sometimes this is an acceptable delay. Usually it isn't. In these situations, teams that didn't plan ahead are out of luck. Those that did, however, already have a backup plan to take advantage of "burst processing" when they exceed their platform's capabilities. They've already understood the provisioning challenges that go along with leveraging temporary platforms, either through their hosting providers, other external companies, or cloud vendors.

When they hit a problem they can't solve, they temporarily bring additional processing power and/or storage online. This additional capacity can be used to solve the short-term problem while a longer-term solution is investigated and eventually deployed.

Management Principles

Coping with otherwise impossible problems comes down to two things:

1. Know what your plan B is ahead of time.
2. Don't make them a habit.

Planning Means Thinking Ahead

Every team finds problems they can't solve. It's inevitable—there are so many opportunities in a typical business, it's simply a matter of time. The good news is that there are plenty of short-term solutions that overcome shortages in processing power and/or storage. The catch is that provisioning and negotiating these short-term solutions can take time. Usually, this is longer than the organization has.

Overcoming these challenges comes down to foresight and preparedness. Contracts should already be in place. There also needs to be defined processes for migrating data from the current environment to the temporary environment. Sometimes, this even requires anonymizing data to comply with international regulations on privacy.

Rather than wait until there's a problem, effective teams work through these challenges ahead of time. Even if they don't execute, they have the infrastructure and process in place to take advantage of a different approach when needed. When and if the problems appear, they simple execute on their plan B and deliver without disruption.

Stop-Gaps Aren't Solutions

The key thing to remember is that these should never be seen as a long-term solution. Whether because of the additional software licensing or for other reasons, short-term processing environments are usually fairly costly. If these environments are used more than infrequently, it's likely that the business analytics platform is under-specified. Temporary capacity increases should never be used to accommodate an underperforming platform. Instead, the team should solve the real problem and extend their analytical platform.

Related Solutions
- Scaling past the PC
- Smoothing growth with the cloud
- Moving to operational analytics

KNOW WHAT YOU ARE WORTH

Your time is valuable. Always be able to explain how much your work is worth.

Asset management can seem like a strange concept in a field largely focused on generating intangible items. In most situations, however, it's the difference between a team that knows what it is worth and one that does not. When the team can't explain their value, the perception is often that their time is worthless.

Effective teams drive toward continuous value creation. On the way, they'll generate a wide variety of intangible assets designed to manage, present, and predict information. For example, a marketing analytics team might develop a segmentation model intended to improve the effectiveness of direct marketing. By separating customers into two groups—those with a high propensity to buy and those unlikely to buy—organizations improve their conversion rates. After all, it makes no sense to send an offer to someone who's unlikely to be interested in it!

There's plenty of emerging research in this area, infonomics being one of the primary fields. Even though information is intangible, there are good arguments that suggest it should still be accounted for as an asset. Needless to say, this is a complex process. However, one doesn't need to be an expert to know their worth.

In most situations there's a simple solution. When insights drive valuable outcomes, it's a case of tracing the value chain back to the original assets. By doing so, it's possible to not only link specific fields within a warehouse to business outcomes, but also to weight the influence that these fields have on driving outcomes.

Value Changes over Time

The fact that value changes over time is logical. However, there's a simple problem involved: Most teams fail to treat these their analytical assets as the valuable items they are. This, simply put, is downright negligent. When it comes to managing capital investments, we understand the importance of monitoring depreciation, reasonable wear and tear, and understanding how effectively the asset is contributing to our bottom line. Despite this, few teams apply the same rigor to their own work.

When it comes to our own money, we'll normally keep a close eye on our returns whenever we invest. A rational investor wants to make sure they're getting the best return possible. Every asset has positive and negative growth cycles, and, at some stage, our existing investments may generate poor returns compared to what we could get elsewhere. When that happens, the smart things to do is to either reinvest to increase the quality of the asset (such as through renovating in the case of real estate) or liquidate the asset and put our money elsewhere.

Analytical assets such as models and other intermediary outputs are no different. They require investment. If they're working, they should be generating returns. All too often, organizations fail to measure the value-generating abilities of their business analytics assets, let alone understand how fast their assets are depreciating.

All analytics-based assets degrade with time if they're not updated or revised. As business contexts change and statistical variability inevitably sets in, the classification accuracy of predictive models drops. If left alone for too long, these assets eventually degrade to a point where they predict no better than random chance. Even worse, they may provide insight that's no longer relevant to the business.

Management Principles

A team that doesn't know what it's worth can't justify its value to the business. Quantifying and communicating a team's value comes down to the following:

- Always understand what you're worth in tangible, economic terms.
- Keep an eye on how fast your assets are depreciating.

Measure Your Value

Effective teams put a big emphasis on measuring their value-creating abilities. This applies to both direct *and* indirect benefits—many models actually drive positive benefits in more than one area. They explicitly measure the economic outcomes their assets drive by measuring those outcomes over time. This isn't a manual process—capturing this information is automated and used to aid investment decisions.

This isn't always easy, especially when assets are designed for insight and not operational execution. However, this is usually a flag that there's a deeper problem. If a team can't link an asset to an outcome that drives direct value, is there something else they could be doing that might drive better (and clearer) value? This somewhat confronting question can sometimes uncover deeper planning issues.

Alternatively, if it's currently impossible to understand the value created by the business analytics team, it might be a good time to start developing a framework that helps quantify the team's value.

Measure Your Asset Quality

Understanding the value chain is the start. The next thing is to track ongoing value. To be able to measure value over time, the team needs to keep a close eye on how assets are performing on an ongoing basis. The trick to making this process easier is to automate monitoring processes. These processes should measure both value as well as how quickly these assets are degrading.

For assets that provide insight (such as reports or dashboards), the main item of interest is often how frequently they're used. A decline in usage over time might indicate a lack of business relevancy. For assets that provide predictions or otherwise support operational activities, the main item of interest is often their predictive or classification accuracy. These ongoing measures should be used to drive process efficiency. This not only helps quantify value over time, but also helps the team drive economies of scale and scope.

 Related Solutions

- Breaking bottlenecks
- Encouraging innovation
- Opening the platform
- Measuring value
- Linking analytics to value

OWN YOUR INTELLECTUAL PROPERTY

Your differentiation is what makes you unique. Don't give away the keys to the kingdom.

Few if any teams have enough resources to do everything they'd like to. Between responding to ad-hoc requests for information, keeping track of their assets, and extending their scope of business analytics activities, it's unsurprising that most teams feel stretched.

Ideally, the team can hire more people when they need them. This is usually the exception rather than the norm. Most organizations operate under strong headcount constraints. Because of this, teams under pressure to deliver often have no choice but to take advantage of external resources.

Self-Interest Isn't Always in Your Favor

In principle, there's nothing wrong with this approach. It overcomes a short-term challenge and offloads a significant amount of risk. Whether this approach undermines the team's future success largely comes down to whether they manage to retain the intellectual property that is generated during the consulting engagement.

Ignoring strategic and advisory projects, most initiatives involve two key outputs: assets and results. The results are usually the item of highest interest. However, the asset's actually the critical element. It contains the logic by which the results are generated.

In the case of business analytics, the asset may be a collection of models or source code from which the final formulas or reports are generated. The difference between an asset and the results can seem subtle; it may be useful to think of these as the equivalent of a recipe and the finished good. The asset itself gives explicit instructions by which the final good can be created from scratch. The results, however, can only be consumed; having a cake doesn't make it any easier to cook one.

Keeping control of this intellectual property is critical for a number of reasons. First, like all assets, business analytics assets degrade over time. Recalibrating these assets and improving their accuracy usually comes down to rerunning the original modeling processes using current data. When the original assets aren't available, there's only one option. The team needs to rebuild these models from scratch; having the results from the initial run doesn't help. This takes substantial time and forces the team to create assets that they should already have.

Second, having access to this intellectual property substantially reduces the time needed to develop a new model from scratch. By knowing an already successful approach, teams get a head start on developing new models. Unfortunately, none of this is visible through the final results. Rather than having a process flow that guides the team through the actual process, all they have is a simple set of predictions.

The final issue is more subtle. Consultants make their margin by reducing their own internal costs. Much to the detriment of organizations that engage them, the fastest way for a consultant to drive margin is through reselling their intellectual property. In aggregate, this eliminates competitive differentiation. If everyone follows the same approach, everyone will probably achieve the same outcome. Those that find their *own* solution, on the other hand, magnify their competitive differentiation.

Management Principles

Without keeping control over the factors that drive competitive advantage, the best an organization can hope for is to be average. Managing this involves making sure to:

- Be crystal clear about what drives competitive advantage and what doesn't.
- Make retaining your intellectual property easy and explicit.

Understand Your Business Model

Although differentiation drives competitive advantage, it's not worth being different *everywhere*. Outsourcing makes a great deal of sense when it has little to do with competitive advantage and has everything to do with managing costs. Make sure to understand what's really important and what isn't before you define the terms of engagement for external parties.

Keep Your Intellectual Property

Engaging external parties isn't a bad thing. Often, it's the best option— sometimes, there's just too much work. The real trick is simply making sure the relationship is appropriately managed.

It's critical to understand what you do and don't retain ownership over. Be sure to make it clear that you own the assets generated as part of the initiative. Make this as easy as possible. Rather than forcing short-term staff to work independently, embrace them by doing things such as bringing them on onto your analytical platform. That way, the assets they generate will be transparently stored within the organization's asset registrar.

▶ Related Solutions
- Encouraging innovation
- Allocating responsibilities
- Opening the platform

MINIMIZE CUSTOM DEVELOPMENT

Don't be scared to build your own tools. Just make sure you're willing to carry the costs of them.

Innovation and invention are different. Innovation sometimes leverages invention, but not always. Sometimes, it's simply a case of doing something traditional in a nontraditional context. The medical field has been using survival analysis for decades to understand how much of an impact different treatments have on delaying death. Taking this same approach and using it to predict time to churn in telecommunications was a great example of innovation. Although the technique wasn't new, the application was.

Sometimes though, innovation requires true invention. Technologies such as Hadoop and Webkit were created and extended to solve problems that existing software couldn't. The act of invention enabled countless innovations. This applies equally to business analytics. Sometimes, off-the-shelf software isn't sufficient to solve specific problems faced by the business. To fill the gaps left by existing applications, the team might start developing their own applications or solutions using languages such as SAS, SQL, R, Hive, or countless others.

This *can* help establish competitive differentiation and drive innovation. However, this isn't guaranteed; not all inventions are successful. What it *does* always carry is significant overhead for the team responsible for maintaining the software. The team needs to spend time redeveloping software to meet changing conditions, providing support, and resolving boundary-case bugs as they appear.

The team ends up becoming a software developer in its own right, carrying all the management complexity that that implies. This isn't necessarily bad. If the innovations are sufficiently disruptive, this cost may be worth the benefit.

Inventions Don't Need to Remain Proprietary

Ideally, this is a temporary state. Over time, commercial off-the-shelf software inevitably catches up. Although it may not replicate the entire set of functionality offered by custom development, it will usually replicate a substantial proportion of the unique functionality. At that point, the team needs to make a pragmatic judgment about how much of their custom development is actually driving competitive differentiation and how much is there just because "that's the way we do it."

Too often, teams think that the answer *must* lie in maintaining their own routines and custom applications. It's an easy mistake to make. Custom development is like a tailored suit—it fits perfectly. Commercial software, on the other hand, is like a suit bought off the rack—it's designed to fit a variety of use cases.

Because of this, it's rare that commercial software will perfectly replicate a team's custom-built functionality. However, this doesn't automatically mean that the custom-built approach is better. Because that functionality comes with management and support costs, it's highly possible that the costs outweigh the benefit of tailoring.

Management Principles

In making a pragmatic decision about how much to invent and how much to leverage, it's helpful to consider the following guidelines:

- Be realistic about the costs of custom development.
- Focus on areas of competitive differentiation.
- If you're going to roll your own code, make refactoring a regular habit.

Factor in All the Costs of Invention

Few teams can actually afford to become a true software developer. Those that are willing to carry the operational costs that go along with this business model usually do so to establish a deep competitive advantage over their peers.

One can't underestimate the costs that go along with this approach. Maintaining well-kept code libraries is expensive; any team that doesn't believe it's carrying support costs is either not following best practices or is delusional. At a minimum, the team needs to control its source code and track differential changes (with full ability to roll back to previous points in time should additions break its applications), schedule regular incremental backups, and define and document feature requirements. Time spent following good management practices is a significant opportunity cost. That time could have also been spent driving economies of scope. If the benefits don't justify the costs, the team needs to be willing to compromise.

Invent Only If It Augments Competitive Advantage

It's also important to focus on the right areas. Not all areas drive equal returns. Best practice in code management often encourages extensive use of code profiling prior to optimization. Spending three weeks improving the efficiency of a library is a gross waste of time if that library only contributes less than one percent of total run time.

Business analytics is similar—maintaining large blocks of SQL-based code "just because" is pointless if using off-the-shelf ETL (exact, transform load) tools would substantially reduce asset management and documentation overhead, even if it has a minimal impact on run time. Equally, though, there will inevitably be specific activities that might benefit substantially from custom development. For a team interested in best practices, driving efficiency involves taking a frank and pragmatic look at what areas *actually* drive competitive differentiation (through efficiency, speed, or accuracy) and using off-the-shelf functionality everywhere else to minimize management overhead.

Culture Comes First

Finally, if a team decides to take the plunge into software development, it also needs to establish the right development culture. Too often, custom code devolves into a kludgy unoptimized mess. It's a constant truth in business analytics that it's hard to know requirements ahead of time. It's also a constant truth that the team's environment is usually under constant change. Data schemas change, source systems are migrated, and business problems shift.

Combine those with the constant pressure of a lack of time, and you've got a recipe for horrible code. Best practices require a team to periodically review this code and rewrite it to make it more logical, easier to maintain, and optimized. Unfortunately, this often requires the team to acknowledge the true cost of maintaining custom code. As a result of this, the team ignores best practices. This is an unacceptable practice and should be seen as such. Best practices require that all custom code be regularly reviewed and refactored as appropriate. If the team can't afford to do this, they can't afford to be writing custom code and should scale back their approach.

► Related Solutions
- Coping with information overload
- Moving beyond the spreadsheet
- Measuring effort
- Reducing time to recommendation

CHAPTER 5

Managing Information and Making Decisions

In a digital economy, organizations with the greatest information leverage are also those that unsurprisingly leave their competitors in the dust. This chapter focuses on five rules that, if followed, help drive maximum value out of your information assets and improve the odds of success.

UNDERSTAND YOUR DATA

Data isn't always what you think it is. Don't be surprised when it's wrong.

Guesswork can't replace insight and good decisions are easier to make when they're supported by good data. Without data, all we have are heuristics and experience, and for many organizations, this is simply business as usual. When there's a dearth of good data, experience counts for a lot. When there's nothing else to rely on, it might be the difference between success and failure.

Still, even those with decades of experience know the value of insight. It's hard to make an informed decision when one doesn't know what's going on. Comparatively, it's far easier to make informed decisions when one has ready access to high-quality information. If decisions are the engine behind outcomes, data is the fuel.

The only thing worse than having no data is having incorrect data. High-performance cars need high-performance fuel. Use the wrong fuel in a sports car and the engine is likely to seize. Data is no different—bad data drives bad outcome. Something as simple as customer profitability can have dire implications if incorrectly calculated. Bad estimates might channel investments to the wrong areas, causing massive losses.

This, fundamentally, is the key to understanding your data. Data quality is a subtle but powerful concept, one that all designers should be across. Data doesn't reflect reality; it's an imperfect record of what happened. Field staff may take shortcuts, tools may be inaccurate, or the assumptions on which it is based may be incorrect. These all contribute to the overall quality of the data.

Quality Data Is More Than Just Accurate Data

It's helpful to think of data quality across six key dimensions. High-quality data:

1. Accurately represents reality
2. Measures what it appears to measure
3. Presents the same measures if repeatedly captured
4. Is current
5. Is relevant to how it is intended to be used
6. Is missing few if any records

Business analytics requires high-quality data. It's impossible to drive high-quality outcomes when the data one relies on is inaccurate, out of date, and unreliable. Many quality issues are obvious—it's rare that someone would overlook old data with missing records. Some issues, however, are subtler, and it's these that usually trip teams up.

It's easy to miss issues with validity, accuracy, reliability, or relevance. Something as simple as a time stamp can be harmless or dangerous depending on how that data is used. For example, an analyst might want to predict what products customers will be most interested in.

To do this, they might develop a model that predicts customer-purchasing patterns over time. To a point, data currency has little relevance in this situation. Making sure transactions are correctly time stamped to the second will probably make little difference to their predictive models.

However, as the context changes, so does the apparent quality of the data. That same analyst might also want to use their data to synchronize systems as part of a real-time marketing and offer-management engine. In this new context, records that are off by a few seconds might crash the whole system. Mismatched records might cause processes to fail or incorrectly trigger.

Just because a field works in one context doesn't necessarily mean it will work in another. Data quality is a relative concept, and it's impossible to achieve best practice without intimately understanding your data.

Another common trap is assuming that data represents what you think it represents. Data validity can be hard to confirm; warehouses are complex and field names are not always accurate. Forgetting this can cause no end of headaches.

The Hospital with Invisible Patients

A health organization I knew illustrated the dangers associated with poor data quality. For years they had managed rosters and available beds based on a measure called patients. To the best of their knowledge, this represented the total number of patients within their hospitals on any given date.

After their forecasts were repeatedly incorrect over a series of planning periods, they started to wonder what was wrong. To get to the root cause of their problems, they peeled back the covers on how this particular data was captured. When they did, they realized their assumptions weren't entirely correct. It turned out that rather than being a measure that was updated when the patient was admitted to the hospital, it was actually a measure that was only updated when a patient *checked out* of the hospital.

Because of this, their measures always gave estimates that lagged the real number of patients in a hospital. By using this measure, they had regularly underestimated the true number of staff and beds they'd need to run their business. Bad assumptions led to their being constantly under pressure.

Management Principles

Encouraging best practice in analytical data management involves remembering the following guidelines:

- Never assume you know what data represents without confirming it first.
- Take charge of creating high-quality data and don't rely on someone else to do it.

Always Understand Your Data

First, make sure you know what you're working with. Data is data. Just because it exists doesn't mean it's necessarily relevant or useful, regardless of what it's called in the warehouse. Even though it might have the right name, that doesn't mean it's the right measure. Always validate how the data has been captured before you use it. If you don't, you're likely to discover that your assumptions were wrong, and when this happens, it normally calls into question your insights and assets.

Data Quality Is Everyone's Responsibility

Second, data quality doesn't magically happen; someone needs to own it. Ideally, everything in the warehouse is already high quality. Usually though, data quality varies across the warehouse. Some measures may be accurate and timely but are heavily incomplete. Contact-center staff may accurately enter data but may only do it sporadically. Other measures may be accurate and complete but lack timeliness. Third-party sales figures may be very accurate and audited to within an inch of their existence. That's great, but it is of dubious quality if they're delayed by three months.

Ideally, all data is cleansed before it hits the warehouse. Practically, this rarely happens. It's tempting in these situations to blame the organization. Unfortunately, this doesn't give the business analytics team a get-out-of-jail-free card for producing bad outcomes. Few people are closer to the data than the business analytics team. Because of this, the team needs to take responsibility to ensure the data they use is high quality.

That usually means they need to develop new skills, acquire new technologies, and spend time and effort fixing their data. They should still agitate for a better structure and be willing to engage with the rest of the organization to help drive general skills improvements. Explaining to field staff *how* the data is used to drive better outcomes can do wonders to improve data quality at the point of collection. However, if they need to spend time cleansing data, they shouldn't dodge responsibility. Driving bad outcomes because of bad data is, quite simply, unacceptable.

▶ Related Solutions

- Creating the data architecture
- Understanding the data value chain
- Creating data-management processes
- Capturing the right data
- Blending rules with models

IT'S BETTER TO HAVE TOO MUCH DATA THAN TOO LITTLE

Learn from history. Those who ignore it are doomed to repeat it.

To drive better outcomes, many organizations put specific focus on better decision making under the mistaken belief that, by forcing people to justify their decisions with data, outcomes will magically improve. The reality is that, of all possible benchmarks, data-driven decision making is probably the least impressive. Although it makes good copy, it's actually only a tiny step up from guesswork.

As far as insightful decision making goes, improving things to the point that decisions are made on hard data is a rather uninspiring achievement. If you're lost, it would be absurd to argue whether it's better to use a map or drive randomly using gut feel and intuition. Yet many organizations waste countless hours and resources debating this very concept.

Despite the value that obviously goes along with data-based decisions, many organizations aspire to achieve even this small improvement. Those that do may feel proud. It's better than nothing, but it's also important to remember that this is only the start.

Being Smarter Involves Being Predictive

More sophisticated organizations aspire to move beyond analyzing what *happened* and instead predict what *will* happen. Rather than be content with knowing *why* things failed, they prefer to be able to *prevent* things from failing in the first place.

Competitive advantage comes from outperforming one's competitors. One way of doing so is through making better decisions. The best organizations use their historical data to predict the future, giving them an edge over their less-informed competitors.

Getting there requires certain building blocks. The team needs the right tools. It needs the right skills. It needs good process. Essentially, it needs the right data. Somewhat counterintuitively, many fact-based organizations still lack this data. This can be a rude surprise given that they have usually invested millions of dollars in warehousing and data management!

As with many things, the devil lies in the details. Good warehouses have a broad set of high-quality information. However, without sufficient history, this information may be worthless for business analytics.

Statistical prediction relies on extracting patterns from large amounts of information. These patterns emerge in one of two ways. Either many people need to show similar behaviors *or* people need to show consistent behaviors over time. Detecting these patterns requires some degree of historical data. Without a history, it's impossible to see how things change over time.

Keeping historical data is an obvious use case, and most warehouses claim to retain some degree of history. The catch is usually that, in many warehouses, older data tends to become more and more summarized for efficiency reasons.

Being Predictive Requires History

Disk space costs money. To manage costs, many warehouses will often only store the minimum amount of historical, detailed data that's needed for operational planning. Beyond that point, all that data will be aggregated into rolling monthly averages, totals, or other derived measures. This helps reduce cost by minimizing storage requirements.

For example, a person's calls made over the prior two months might be summed into total calls per customer. This can reduce billions of records into a single record for each customer, substantially reducing storage costs. This aggregated data is then used for strategic planning, product management, and other higher-level processes.

This makes sense at an accounting level. However, it actively hurts the potential of business analytics. Granular predictions require granular data. To predict customer behavior, analysts need behavioral history. To predict how much a person is likely to spend over the next month, analysts need to link past behavior to future behavior.

To start with, it makes logical sense that next month's expenditure is likely to be similar to last month's expenditure. This is a relatively simple measure and only requires data from the previous period.

It also makes sense that their spending will be affected by how their purchases have been trending over the last few periods. If their expenditure has been progressively increasing from month to month over the last six months, it's likely that their spending will go up again next month. To find these patterns, the analyst needs even more historical data.

Pushing things even further, it *also* makes sense that the amount of their purchase will probably change, depending on season, going up at Christmas and down in January. This becomes more complicated and requires even more history. Getting any degree of statistical confidence may require many years of transactional history. Otherwise, it's unlikely that the model will be able to link season to expenditure.

Very quickly, the analyst goes from needing only last month's data to needing at least five years' worth of transactional data. If this data isn't available, they can't build the models they need. Even worse, it might take them another five years to capture the required information. If their competitors *don't* suffer from the same data retention issues, they'll be left further and further behind.

Management Principles

Encouraging best practice in capturing information involves emphasizing the following guidelines:

- Breadth is good; try to avoid letting your data disappear.
- Depth is also good; always capture more history than you think you'll need.

Capture Everything You Can

First, data is highly volatile; once it's gone, it's gone. You never know what's going to help increase model accuracy. Because of this, permanently sacrificing data is risky. However, this doesn't automatically mean that it needs to be stored in the warehouse; what is important is that it *is* stored.

Keeping historical data should always be a priority, especially if there is a high chance it will disappear. This is true even if it means that this data can only be stored off line. There's nothing worse than needing data that no longer exists or because of narrow-minded warehouse retention strategies.

The real trick is balancing retaining *everything* with retaining *what's important*. Part of the answer is to actively look for lower-cost storage solutions. Not every analytical datamart needs to be built on mission-critical (and costly) infrastructure. There are a wide variety of vendor-based and open-source solutions that offer creative ways to reduce total storage costs. Establishing a well-supported analytical datamart should always be a high priority, but even when a central datamart doesn't exist, letting this data disappear can cost a team greatly.

Things become a little more complicated when it comes to deciding what *should* be retained. On one hand, most analysts agree that we're generating more data than we have the capacity to store. On the other, Kryder's law suggests that our growth in storage capacity is unlikely to plateau in the near future.[1] Depending on whom you listen to, we need to either start selectively throwing data away *or* capture everything while capitalizing on falling storage costs.

Given these contradictory opinions, it can be hard to decide what to do. Making things worse is that there's no clear clarity on which answer is the correct one. However, there is one guiding principle that's unlikely to be proven wrong: Within reason, the team should still make every effort possible to keep more historical data than it is likely to need. It's easy to delete information, but it's impossible to re-create it.

Capture as Much History as You Can

Second, it's hard to know how far back one needs to go. Keeping data from disappearing is one thing. Equally important is building a rich history. Just as it's hard to predict what information will be useful in the future, it's hard to predict how much history is enough.

Rather than set an arbitrary year limit, the team should keep more history than it thinks it will need. There's nothing worse than trying to model the effect of seasonality on Christmas sales only to discover that one doesn't have enough history to do so.

▶ Related Solutions
- Encouraging innovation
- Scaling past the PC
- Smoothing growth with the cloud
- Creating the data architecture
- Understanding the data value chain
- Creating data-management processes
- Capturing the right data

KEEP THINGS SIMPLE

Complex decisions aren't necessarily better. Keep things as simple as they need to be but no simpler.

Complexity for complexity's sake is the bane of efficiency. On one hand, innovation comes from doing things differently. On the other, needless complexity is usually counterproductive. Complexity *always* creates costs. Sophistication is different from complexity and needs to be balanced against the benefits it brings.

It's rare that anyone disagrees with this: Managing complexity is one of the best ways teams can help drive productivity and efficiency. Unfortunately, this is harder than it seems. The most insidious thing about business analytics is a natural tendency toward complex processes.

Results Don't Require Complexity

Things usually start simply. The least engaged organizations treat all their customers exactly the same. Everyone gets the same offer at the same time and, unsurprisingly, customers consistently move to other organizations that better understand their needs. To become a more customer-centric organization, the organization takes the logical step of segmenting their customers and treating them differently. Even this relatively simple approach is likely to drive much better customer engagement.

This is a good starting point. However, improving things further requires knowing what to do with the outliers. Rather than focus on the norm, the organization needs to focus on the exceptions. Understanding how to deal with 80 percent of your customers is great. Usually though, it's the other 20 percent that drives 80 percent of net profit.

Growing and keeping these customers might drive real results. Unfortunately, every segmentation model has its limits. To handle the limitations of the original model, the organization starts defining additional rules. Over time, the organization creates more and more exception-handling rules to deal with these limits.

Alone, none of these exceptions are terribly complex. In aggregate though, they turn what was a relatively simple model-driven approach into a bastardized hybrid of models and rules. Originally, the process might have involved three simple steps: identify, classify, and act. Over time, though, all these exceptions and complex interactions end up forcing the organization to develop new supporting systems. Conflicting rules created by different groups need to be identified and managed. Authorizations needs to be built into the workflow to ensure all those different groups are comfortable with complex rule/modeling interactions. What started as a relatively simple approach ends up being tremendously complex.

On the face of it, it's easy to argue that this complexity is worth it. All these extra rules exist to handle a variety of exceptions, and if they were taken away, outcomes would suffer. However, this point of view ignores the real driver for the rules: a relatively limited segmentation model. Rather than fixing the limits of the original model, the organization ends up applying Band-Aid on top of Band-Aid, responding tactically when it should have responded strategically.

In the end, it ends up with a cumbersome process that is so complex that few truly understand how it works or how to improve it. Ironically, this usually results in more Band-Aids and more complexity!

The Impossible to Kill Model

One organization I knew highlighted how destructive this can be. Thanks to a very bright individual, they had coded a multistage modeling process that, given a target variable, statistically isolated key drivers from thousands of fields. It then took that reduced set of fields and applied a multistage modeling process. The results were then converted into SQL code that could be executed in the data warehouse.

In many ways, this was well ahead of its time. Pragmatically though, it was only marginally better than the simpler process it had replaced. Despite being far more complex, it drove only minor benefits. As far as solutions went, however, it had been tremendously overengineered.

On the face of it, it seemed like a good idea. It was highly automated and it offered significant process efficiencies compared to manually building models. However, it came with a key trade-off:

process complexity. The only person who understood how the end-to-end process worked was the person who coded it and, shortly after that individual finished their project, he left.

On the positive side, the process was so well designed that it ran for years afterward. On the negative side, the process was so impenetrable that it ran for years afterward. What started out as an apparent competitive advantage morphed into a constraint. Over time, the team ended up lagging behind their peers as other organizations caught up and eventually surpassed the team's approach. Because it lacked the skills to reengineer its process, the team's process ended up defining its business, all because its processes were more complex than was justified or manageable.

Management Principles

Encouraging best practice in decision making involves emphasizing the following guidelines:

- Build processes that will drive the right outcome in a manageable way.
- Efficiency comes from simplicity; don't make things more complex than they need to be.

Make It Work First, Worry about Sophistication Later

Value comes from outcomes, not complexity. Given the breadth of what's possible in business analytics, it can be tempting to aim for the heavens. This is a mistake. Effective teams understand the need to get things working first; sophistication can come second. The most advanced and complex processes are worthless if they delay the creation of real value.

At a statistical level, it's fun to debate the relative benefits of support vector machines over random forests. However, this is pointless if the organization can't drive an outcome. It's far better to use relatively simple techniques like decision trees and spend *more* time on getting the end-to-end process working than it is to use complex techniques but never get the process to work. Once the process is working and the team can drive better outcomes, there's plenty of time to focus on more sophisticated techniques.

Keep Things Simple

Second, maintenance is a lot more expensive than development. Those that develop a process may not always be around to maintain it. The more steps the process involves, the longer it is likely to take to execute.

Among other things, productivity comes from driving efficiency and limiting the amount of overhead required to maintain existing processes. Keeping things simple is a great way of driving productivity. Rather than making incremental fixes that increase complexity, effective teams investigate the root causes behind issues. Once these are understood, they try and find a parsimonious solution that reduces complexity while driving a better outcome.

They adopt a philosophy of almost Zenlike simplicity, constantly driving benefit with a minimum of complexity. Importantly, this rarely precludes sophistication; instead, it usually emphasizes it! Sophistication is fine as long as it eliminates *process* complexity. Adding more steps and rules is anathema to their goal. If a problem can be solved in one step in a maintainable way, it should be.

 Related Solutions

- Keeping everyone aligned
- Allocating responsibilities
- Moving beyond the spreadsheet
- Measuring value
- Measuring performance
- Measuring effort
- Creating data-management processes
- Reducing time to recommendation
- Enabling real-time scoring

FUNCTION SHOULD DICTATE FORM

 Trust the people who need to use your insights. You need their support.

Analysts often think that they know everything. This isn't a criticism; it's hard not to think that way when one works with data every day! Few people are as exposed to the inner workings of a business as analysts. However, because analysts tend to view the world through a data-centric lens, it's easy to confuse models with reality. Just because measures exist in a warehouse doesn't necessarily mean they're correct or useful to decision makers. Just because one believes one knows an answer doesn't mean that that answer's actually pragmatic or actionable.

Insights are worthless unless actioned. Even though analysts generate lots of insight, they rarely have the power to act on that insight. Normally, someone else needs to take that insight and act on it. To do this, the insight needs to be contextually relevant and useful. When it isn't, the insight will almost always be discarded, ignored, or incorrectly used. A big part of a business-analytics team's time is usually spent trying to convince front-of-house staff of the value of the team's recommendations.

Front-of-house staff is under constant pressure. As a main channel to the customer, their main concern is on getting their job done as efficiently and effectively as possible. Unlike most back-of-house and strategic services, they usually have little time for reflection. Their performance is normally based on processing volumes, conversion rates, or detection rates. More than anything else, they value concise and useful information.

Many business analytics teams make a simple mistake; they try to give *too much* information. Rather than wanting to see every single possible data point, front-of-house staff members often find it easier to see the bare minimum. Usually, they're more interested in knowing what to offer or high-level risk measures than overly complex statistical predictors. Simple, concise, and prescriptive measures are the order of the day. Front-of-house staff members may still be interested in a dashboard should more detail be necessary, but it's rare that they will prefer the detail over summarized information.

Management Principles

Encouraging best practice in designing measures involves emphasizing the following guidelines:

- Let the execution team dictate the form of the data they need.
- Make sure they still have access to other information if they want it.

Listen to the People Who Make the Daily Decisions

Rather than making a guess about what will be useful, the best thing a business analytics team can do is to engage directly with operational staff and understand their constraints. Let them define their needs rather than letting the data define their usage.

Give Them What They Want in Addition to What They Need

Always try and keep it as simple and relevant as possible. Brevity is the essence of efficiency and clarity. Having comprehensive dashboards is useless if decision makers don't have the time to review every measure. It's the role of the business analytics team to work out how to turn valuable data into something that's easily digestible and relevant.

Significantly, though, that does not mean that the team should hide information. It's not about keeping people in the dark; it's about making jobs easier and people more effective. If people are still interested in having access to the detailed information so they can understand the logic behind the recommendations, make sure it's available in some form. If you don't, it only makes the job of building trust harder.

▶ Related Solutions
- Coping with information overload
- Keeping everyone aligned
- Moving to operational analytics
- Linking analytics to value
- Enabling real-time scoring

WATCH THE DYNAMIC, NOT JUST THE STATIC

You don't know what you don't know. Try not to guess.

The world is a dynamic place; things change all the time. The only thing that's constant is that nothing's constant. That in itself isn't terribly insightful; dealing with change is a major part of doing business. What's more interesting is that despite this, many people try to run their business on static rather than dynamic measures.

It's almost impossible to run a business without having access to good information. When you're trying to understand your customers, knowing what products they have is the bare minimum. Knowing that money launderers follow certain money transfer patterns can help flag crime rings and prevent major losses.

Unfortunately, knowing how things *are* doesn't mean we understand how things *will be*. In the short term, being aware of these patterns helps drive value. Based on current data, the organization can improve offers and flag crime rings. Unfortunately, these patterns rarely remain constant, and it's usually the things we don't know that end up costing the most.

One of the biggest traps of decision making is that we make decisions based on what we know, not what we don't know. It would be great if we could just ask who was defrauding the company. Unfortunately, the smarter fraudsters would lie, making the data pointless. Having all negative responses in this case doesn't mean that fraud isn't happening—it just means that we don't yet know who is committing fraud.

The natural solution is to look for indicators that suggest fraud. Field reports might help establish a number of rules that identify potential fraud. Based on tape analysis, a casino might discover that certain dealers and players were colluding on blackjack tables. Through careful sleight of hand, fraudulent dealers might feed players extra high-value chips on their winning hands. Once their winnings have been banked, the partners in crime might then split the proceeds.

Knowing this trick helps establish new detection rules. These in turn help flag other cases. However, this is only one scam—there may be a large number of other cases the rule will fail to detect. Static rules limit business analytics to what's known. Dynamic rules overcome this constraint. More sophisticated forms of analytics take advantage of the fact that patterns dictate both *normal* and *abnormal* behaviors.

Knowing What's Abnormal Helps with the Unknown

Deviations from the norm are an excellent way of detecting that which we don't know. Rather than trying to create an exhaustive list of rules that detect every known scam, that same casino might instead start capturing and analyzing typical loss patterns over time. Assuming that relatively few tables are actually committing fraud, the casino can measure statistically normal dynamic behavior and use that to isolate aberrant patterns. These might include excessive losses over certain periods of time compared to the norm or dealer-based loss patterns that repeat at specific times of the day.

The real power is that this approach does not rely on the casino knowing what to look for ahead of time. Their detection shifts from having to find a specific scam (a relatively difficult task) to detecting changes from the norm (a relatively simpler task). In practice, this helps the casino flag the things it doesn't know for further investigation, thereby increasing the scope of what it *does* know.

This applies in every field. Another great example lies in driving better marketing engagement. A relatively unsophisticated organization might run their entire marketing engine on outbound campaigns. These are often driven by fairly simple selection rules such as "mail everyone between the ages of 18 and 24 who does not currently have our product."

This approach has obvious problems. The customer may not be interested in buying a new product because of an existing contract. They might not be interested in the product on offer. Or they might simply be sick of mail.

As the organization tries to become more engaged with its customers, it might consider other techniques. One approach might be using trigger-based marketing where offers are made based on a customer's interactions with the company. The organization might make the same offer, but rather than sending it on a fixed schedule, it might only send it if the customer browses that particular product on the organization's website.

Even this small change helps take into account the customer's behaviors, increasing relevance and driving better outcomes. By moving from a static approach to a dynamic approach, the organization can drive better outcomes.

Management Principles

Changing the team's point of view involves emphasizing the following guidelines:

- Model the dynamic, not just the static.
- Understand what is normal and what isn't.
- Wherever possible, use dynamic, behaviorally based measures rather than static, predefined rules.

Watch How Things Change, Not Just Their Current State

Static measures are valuable—knowing how much a customer has spent over the last few months helps determine a customer's value to the organization. However, knowing whether their spending patterns are going up or down provides another level of insight, one that helps drive better outcomes. Wherever possible, these dynamic measures should be used to understand behavioral patterns.

Understand What's Normal

Having these dynamic measures is a great start. Even better is being able to use them to understand what is typical for a given segment or account type. By understanding what normal behavior looks like, organizations can detect fundamental changes as they happen. Once detected, the organization can act on them.

In the absence of these types of measures, a decline in customer spend within a highly profitable (but small) customer segment may not be detectable until it materially impacts profitability. By having these measures, the organization may be able to act earlier and drive a better outcome.

Favor Behavioral Changes over Rules

Finally, organizations should bias their interactions toward behavioral measures over rules wherever possible. Because rules are static, they lose relevancy with time. Sometimes, this degradation may take years. Other times, it may only take a number of weeks. Because behaviorally based measures are inherently dynamic and reflect real-world context, they have a longer shelf life.

Taking this approach drives efficiency and value. An organization might determine that transactions over $1,000 have a significantly higher chance of being fraudulent. So, it establishes a rule that any transaction over $1,000 needs to be flagged for further investigation.

Unfortunately, as soon as the criminals work out that this rule exists, they'll limit their transaction to just under $1,000 to avoid triggering the rule while still maximizing their haul. In one deft swoop, they've eliminated the effectiveness of the rule and very likely left the organization with a false sense of security.

By using behavioral measures the organization could have avoided this. Compared to a person's normal account behaviors, processing a large number of nonpayroll transactions above a specific amount might be highly aberrant. Rather than looking for global patterns, the organization instead looks for changes in behaviors at an individual level. By basing their predictions on personal rather than general measures, the organization could have still flagged these transactions as being suspicious without knowing upfront the specifics of the fraud.

 Related Solutions

- Encouraging innovation
- Moving to operational analytics
- Enabling real-time scoring
- Blending rules with models

NOTE

1. C. Walter, "Kryder's Law," *Scientific American* (August 2005).

PART THREE

Practical Solutions: People and Process

Technology can be bought. Data can be captured. Building a high-performing team though? That's hard.

Building culture is like cultivating an orchard; it takes attention and time. There are few quick fixes and getting things right usually means putting in place the right philosophies and structures up front. When things go wrong, it can take months to unravel past mistakes.

The following chapters focus on how best to develop skills, define processes, and optimize activities. They cover developing competencies, automating processes, and how best to go about leveraging external parties.

CHAPTER **6**

Driving Operational Outcomes

D riving better outcomes involves improving accuracy, efficiency, or both. There are a multitude of ways of doing this. The hallmark of business analytics is that, for every problem, there are hundreds of possible solutions. However, despite this flexibility, teams tend to face a number of common challenges:

- Being constrained by inflexible operational processes
- Becoming a bottleneck because of a lack of enterprise investment
- Struggling under the overhead created by managing complexity
- Losing the ability to innovate due to systems constraints

The solutions described in the next section focus on techniques and approaches to overcome these challenges.

AUGMENTING OPERATIONAL SYSTEMS

CASE STUDY

WHY READ THIS?

When will this help?

Read this if you've made a large investment in an enterprise resource planning (ERP) system and you're struggling to see ongoing incremental returns from your investment.

How will it help you?

Using this approach will leverage your existing investment to drive continuous returns.

What are the guiding principles?

- Think about competencies, not functions
- Automate everything non-value-added
- Start flexible, become structured
- Design your platform for use, not purity
- Function should dictate form

What else should you read?

- Encouraging innovation
- Coping with information overload
- Moving to operational analytics
- Linking analytics to value
- Blending rules with models

The Background: In the Quest for Standard Processes, Flexibility Always Suffers

Standard processes help drive efficiency and efficacy. However, they also constrain flexibility and encourage a focus on functionally aligned applications. When it comes to leveraging intellectual property and assets across multiple problems, the biggest benefit of ERP systems can end up being their biggest liability.

ERP Systems Are Great at Driving Continuity and Efficiency

Business is complex and getting more so; without their ERP systems, most organizations would struggle to survive. A century ago, large companies dealt with a handful of products and thousands of staff. Today, a large organization can have thousands of products and tens of thousands of staff. If anything, this management challenge is growing with time; as complex as things are today, things are just starting. Everything's getting more complex; industries are merging, products are converging, and professions dividing. The only way to manage this complexity is through defining and sticking to standardized and highly repeatable operational processes. It's that niche that most ERP systems fill.

By using well-defined processes built on best-practice experience, organizations make it easier to manage risk and drive efficiency. Having experienced people may make it easier to drive better outcomes but unfortunately, experience is costly and scarce. Recipes are cheap, relatively speaking; as long as an organization can rely on a standard process, they can at least ensure continuity and a minimum level of performance.

ERP-based processes ensure operational continuity and efficiency through having highly defined activities, assigning clear ownership over outcomes and decisions, and enforcing strong governance and transparency. When outcomes are people based rather than process based, turnover can kill an organization. If the wrong people walked out the door, they might have to rebuild the company from scratch!

Efficiency is great. So is governance. Unfortunately, these speak primarily to process and not results; arguably more important is the quality of the outcome. Wearing the chief financial officer's hat, well-understood forecasting processes are good. A well-understood forecasting process that creates highly inaccurate forecasts, however, is *not*!

Standardization Implies Rigidity

The best processes are those that are standardized *and also* leverage insightful, relevant information. To get the best outcome possible, one needs to know what to do as well as have the ability to make better decisions. For a variety of reasons, most ERP implementations focus on the first with relatively little emphasis on the second.

ERP systems are designed to facilitate the flow of information between multiple business units and, by doing so, they drive better enterprise-wide outcomes. They emphasize well-defined processes and set their sights on consistency to target specific (rather than general) problems. This makes a lot of sense: From a process point of view, it's hard to generalize specific activities. For example, there's little overlap between inventory management and product development. The skills and activities that go along with identifying market needs aren't the same as those that help make sure the right products are ordered at the right time.

A key advantage of business analytics is its ability to drive innovation through progressive sophistication. The process of analytics ranges from largely historical reporting right through to advanced forms of optimization and predictive modeling. In many situations, an increase in sophistication (as opposed to complexity) can drive a corresponding increase in outcome quality. However, the key requirement to this is that analytical processes *can* be made more sophisticated over time. Although ERP systems emphasize effectiveness, their focus is heavily biased toward process integration and information management. This necessitates having a fixed way of doing business. Without rigid structures, it's impossible to bring a complex organization together.

When they do provide foresight, they usually emphasize ease of use over sophistication. Their advantages lie in delivering standardized end-to-end processes rather than enabling innovation. Once an organization has hit a minimum level of effectiveness, the answer doesn't lie in efficiency. Instead of trying to do the same things better, the only real solution is to actively find new approaches that deliver better outcomes with less investment. Unfortunately, most ERP systems actively prevent this approach. Instead, it's a case of running the business their way or choosing the highway.

Teams in this situation end up with a difficult problem. On one hand, they need to improve outcomes by innovating. On the other, they're constrained by highly efficient but strongly defined processes that allow little flexibility. Innovation comes from doing things differently.

Repeatability comes from doing things the same way. Each provides its own advantages. When combined, these present an apparently insoluble problem.

Why Should You Care?

Organizations suffering from these challenges tend to think that:

- They've made significant investment in ERP systems without any clear returns.
- They struggle to innovate.

ERP systems are great for establishing certainty. It's impossible for people to do their job without knowing what it is they need to do. However, certainty is only part of a good process—equally important is making the right decisions. Knowing *how* to do something is different to knowing *what* to do. It's the knowing *what* that helps drive returns.

Far too often, organizations pay more attention to process than they do to outcomes. *Standard* processes aren't always the same as *effective* processes. It's always interesting to ask the organization how much value standardized processes have actually delivered. If the answer is "not as much as we expected," it is usually because the focus has been biased toward governance and repeatability over driving better outcomes.

Another warning sign is the belief that innovation is hard. In some ways it is; disruptive innovation is always hard. Evolutionary (or incremental) innovation, on the other hand, shouldn't be. Taking things and making them incrementally better is the cornerstone of continuous improvement. Effective organizations should *always* be able to drive continuous improvement. Those that can't have a problem.

The value of a strongly defined process is in its rigidity. As Henry Ford worked out a century ago through mass manufacturing, it's easy to be efficient when one encourages focus and standardization. However, while standardization drives efficiency, efficient processes don't necessarily result in accurate predictions or valuable outcomes. By definition, the most efficient process in the world is the one in which people do nothing at all! When it becomes too hard to try different approaches, most people simply give up. Continuous improvement slows and the business suffers.

What Not to Do

The obvious answer is to make processes smarter; rather than rely on people power, organizations redesign their processes around accuracy and efficiency. Contrary to many other examples in this book, this is actually the right solution. It's the execution that makes the difference.

Making better decisions is easy when one has access to better information. When ERP processes don't give enough insight to allow someone to make a better decision, there are only two choices:

1. Insight can be generated outside the system.
2. The system can be modified to provide better insight.

Hardwiring Insight to the Individual Undermines Continuity

Blaming bad data never justifies inaction. Decisions still need to be made, even if the systems don't help in making those decisions. When the processes themselves don't provide enough insight, people do their analytics elsewhere. Right or wrong, that's simply reality. There's a reason so many people find themselves addicted to Microsoft Excel. It's the only way they can get the insight they need to do their job.

In these situations they'll pull whatever information they can get their hands on onto their desktop. They'll analyze it to the best of their skills, get whatever insight they can, and make the best decision they're capable of. It's not great, but it's better than nothing.

Assuming their analysis is reasonable, it can't be denied that this is better than the alternative. There are still countless issues with the approach, but at least their decisions are based on better information. The key flaw with this approach is that it all comes down to the person. Without having specific skills and knowledge, it's impossible to achieve the same outcome.

This makes general enablement impossible. Short of cloning an individual, no one else can do what they do. Even worse, if and when the individual changes roles or leaves the organization, everything that person has achieved disappears. Success is transitory, and over time, the organization inevitably regresses back to where it was: making bad decisions because of bad data.

Hardwiring Insight to the System Undermines Reusability

The other option is to hardwire analytics into the process. Most ERP systems offer some level of in-built, already configured analytics. At face value, this is attractive; the smarts are integrated into the process and all it takes is turning it on. In some situations, this may actually be the right decision. Most of the time, however, it ends up limiting differentiation, constraining innovation, and preventing reuse.

Differentiation is impossible when everyone does the same thing. Looking purely at the costs, using out-of-the-box approaches to analytics seems cost effective. This discounts the importance of being unique, and, unfortunately, having an out-of-the-box approach to analytics is totally replicable. At best, the organization can only ever achieve the same results as every other organization using the same process and technology.

Using out-of-the-box techniques also hurts innovation. Because ERP systems rely on standardization, the process almost always takes front seat. If the in-built analytical functions are a "black box" and can't be tailored to the organization's unique characteristics, the best that can be hoped for are acceptable outcomes. Innovation disappears and the organization ends up being, at best, a lackluster me-too company.

These are bad enough. Even worse is that functionally aligned business-analytics applications actively prevent organizations from turning business analytics into a competitive advantage. Business analytics help drive economies of scope by allowing organizations to apply specific competencies to solve multiple problems across the business. When the tools are hard-coded to a single, functionally aligned process, this becomes impossible. Every new process needs new technology. Because every process ends up leveraging a different approach with different technologies, there's usually little hope of generating economies of scale or scope.

Separate Problems Can Have Common Solutions,
Assuming You Can Take Advantage of Them

A great example involves demand management and network planning in telecommunications. Every Telco needs to know how many phones and services they're going to sell if they're going set effective sales targets, invest in the right products, and allocate the right resources. Equally, every Telco needs to know where they need to extend their network; if they don't have enough tower or trunk bandwidth, their services will suffer.

The processes and supporting systems behind these use cases are normally different. However, both can be improved through the use of analytical forecasting. Societal trends and product launches can be used to forecast handset demand. Data usage and land-development patterns can be used to forecast network bottlenecks. The beauty of analytics is that analytical forecasting can help drive accuracy across both planning processes.

Fitting with a process-centric paradigm, most ERP systems offer specific modules to support each of these operational activities. These modules often offer embedded forecasting capabilities. Unfortunately, these capabilities are usually module specific. Although this helps improve the return on investment associated with a functionally aligned project, those same capabilities rarely carry across to other processes.

Hard-linking technology to process impedes reusability. Just because an organization has solved demand management problems doesn't mean it can apply the same skills to solve its network-planning problems. This undermines competitive advantage. Every improvement comes with high incremental investment.

The How-To Guide: Run It in Parallel and Reuse It

The real answer isn't to tear apart processes. Although flexibility is valuable, so is efficiency. It's hard to drive change when you can't fall back on clearly defined processes. However, it's equally true that structure shouldn't constrain innovation; when it does, it undermines competitive advantage.

By its nature, analytics is a largely unstructured activity. Although it's possible to work to high-level milestones, it's extremely hard to create a recipe for insight ahead of time. Not until the team has found the answer can it define the activities that led to that insight. This doesn't fit well with well-defined processes. With no specific activities to define, standardized processes lose their relevancy.

Because of this, flexibility is both a blessing and a curse. The organization needs it to facilitate innovation. On the other hand, having too much flexibility makes running the business impossible. The real trick lies in blending structure with flexibility—the answer isn't to reengineer and hardwire insight into the process. Instead, the answer is to augment ERP processes with operational analytics.

Superficially, this might seem the same as externally generated insight. In many ways it is, but with one key difference: Operational analytics from a common enterprise platform helps drive competency, technology, and data reuse. This allows the team to reuse their resulting assets and drives cost efficiencies and specialization by taking reusable skills and applying them to solve multiple business problems.

This enterprise analytical platform is loosely coupled with the ERP system, usually through web services, simple data exchange, or real-time execution calls.

The main benefit of this approach is that it helps drive efficiency *and* innovation. Activities that can be standardized are. Those that require innovation have the flexibility they need. Organizations maintain the flexibility to innovate and experiment on the analytics front without having to do expensive process reengineering. By blending the best of both worlds, the organization drives better accuracy *and* efficiency.

Augmented Case Management

Consider, for example, how some organizations manage ongoing customer contact. Client-level interactions require deep insight. Whereas patterns at an aggregate level are useful in driving broad improvements, predicting the actions of a specific individual based on their specific characteristics is hard. Experience counts for a lot, and good case management is critical in creating better outcomes. This is especially true in the public sector where customer relationships can last for decades. A child growing up in a bad environment may need government support for two decades or more.

Good case managers understand the individual. Unfortunately, even good case managers occasionally miss things. In some situations, a single case can draw from tens of thousands of words of historical notes. Given that it's not uncommon for case workers to be responsible for a hundred or more cases at any point in time, it's easy to see why building a useful picture of client-level interactions can be difficult.

Excellent case managers can uncover the patterns behind every previous interaction. Unfortunately, this takes more than just having the right experience. Analytics makes this job simpler by providing risk indicators, free-text pattern identification, or network analysis. Having access to this information helps case workers make better decisions. They know how likely an individual is to regress and can profile the client's exposure to other high-risk individuals. By being supported by an effective ERP system, they can act on this insight.

Benefits and Limitations

This approach offers a number of benefits as well as a few important limitations. The major benefits revolve around:

- Driving strategic use of business analytics
- Building toward competitive differentiation

Business Analytics Enable Strategic Outcomes

Improving one process drives tactical return. It's always possible to continually improve any given process. However, when it comes to improving a process, it's usually the first major improvement that delivers the greatest return. Something as simple as moving from naive forecasting to analytically based forecasting can drive significant improvements in accuracy. In some cases, this can be as high as a 50 percent reduction in forecast error! At some point though, diminishing returns kick in and the rate of gain slows.

On the other hand, improving *many* processes can help drive strategic return. By taking the skills and technologies that enabled those incremental gains and applying them to multiple business problems, organizations magnify their return on investment. Execution is a key part of the picture. However, by making sure analytics skills are portable and can be applied to multiple problems, organizations move toward using business analytics strategically rather than just tactically.

Business Analytics Enables Competitive Differentiation

Another major benefit is differentiation. True differentiation comes from aligning business analytics to an organization's unique characteristics, environment, and objectives. This is impossible when one uses the same approach as every other organization in the market.

ERP systems are based on standardization. By definition, they stifle flexibility in favor of repeatability. It's rare that they allow the creative innovation that helps fuel competitive differentiation. This doesn't mean they're bad: It's just that this isn't their strength. By loosely coupling analytical capabilities with ERP processes, the organization gets the best of both worlds. They gain the ability to drive creative innovation without having to sacrifice the benefits that go along with standardized processes.

Business Analytics Shouldn't Drive Inefficiency

This approach provides many benefits. Equally though, it's important to remember that it's not a silver bullet—inappropriate use of this solution can easily lead to bad outcomes.

Large-scale systems *require* standard processes. When it comes to enabling a field staff of thousands, freedom carries real costs. Without some degree of standardization, efficiency is hard to deliver; push things too far, and the process falls apart into chaos. Analytics needs to *augment* the process rather than *define* the process. In the end, the greatest insight in the world is worthless if it cannot be actioned and repeated by the rest of the organization.

Another limitation to be aware of is that just because it's analytically based insight doesn't mean that it is automatically right. Depending on an organization's ability to capture key information, there can be many situations in which the data being analyzed doesn't include the real drivers behind outcomes.

Intuition and experience are critical in these situations. Because of this, processes have to allow decision makers the ability to override the system's recommendations. However, it's equally true that this freedom to override the system requires balance. If unmanaged, it can lead to overconfidence. When someone is given the option to make changes, the default preference is often to take advantage of the opportunity. If left unchecked, good predictions can suffer from continual overrides. This leads to situations in which the supposedly analytically driven outcomes are no different from the original outcomes.

Business Analytics Shouldn't Drive Complexity

A final important point to remember is that just because it's possible to separate out analytical activities doesn't mean that it's always the right thing to do. A major advantage of many enterprise solutions is their integrated approach; they include all the processes and assets necessary to solve a given business problem. Taken to an extreme, this solution would require every ERP system to be strictly separated into two parts: the workflow component and a bespoke analytics component that covers everything from information management to reporting to advanced and predictive analysis.

Augmenting integrated solutions only makes sense when it's directly linked to driving economies of scope and competitive differentiation. If information management is seen as plumbing, it makes little sense to re-create existing data management processes "just because." Augmentation needs to drive better outcomes, more relevant insight, and competitive advantage. If it doesn't, it is needless cost.

BREAKING BOTTLENECKS

WHY READ THIS?

CASE STUDY

When will this help?

Read this if your team is overworked to the point of being unable to deliver.

How will it help you?

Using this approach will help shift the team from being seen as a constraint to being seen as an enabler.

What are the guiding principles?

- Automate everything non-value-added
- Eliminate bottlenecks
- Know what you are worth

What else should you read?

- Coping with information overload
- Allocating responsibilities
- Moving to operational analytics
- Measuring effort

The Background: Every Gateway Becomes a Bottleneck Given Enough Traffic

Good business analytics teams excel at generating actionable insight. Unfortunately, there are always more problems than they have time to answer. Inevitably, some questions are left unanswered, and insight gets delayed. When these delays become excessive, other groups often start looking for alternative solutions. In the worst case, these other solutions can actually lead to the destruction rather than the creation of value. Despite still being tremendously valuable, the team becomes the bottleneck.

Delays Harm a Team's Credibility

Business is dynamic and things change daily, inside and outside the organization. Coping with this change involves understanding what's happened and predicting what will happen next. The best way to do this is by rapidly analyzing large amounts of information and providing insight to those who need it. The business analytics team is best suited to this task.

When things are in balance, the organization's need for insight is matched against the team's ability to generate insight. Every request is met with a quick and accurate response, questions are answered, insights are actioned, and value is created. However, this balance is fragile—demand for insight can easily exceed the organization's ability to generate insight. When this happens, things rapidly spiral out of control.

Ideally, the people who need answers can comfortably turn to the business analytics team for help. However, there are times when this doesn't work; despite their best intentions, sometimes the team just can't give the organization what it needs. If it's a skills issue, it's simply a case of getting the right training. When it's a workload issue, however, there's no recourse. Short of turning someone *else* away, the team is stuck. When this happens, it's usually for one of two reasons:

1. The team has had too much success—good answers lead to greater trust, which drives more questions.
2. The team is undergoing cost-cutting—organizations under financial pressure will often cut staff and slash budgets.

When demand outstrips a team's ability to deliver, the team has a problem. Although its delays are fair and justifiable, no one cares. If and when the team fails to deliver, it runs the risk of the organization questioning its value and business relevancy.

Unrestricted Analytics Can Be Dangerous

As bad as this is for the team's credibility, it's even worse for the broader organization. Questions still need to be answered, and if the business analytics team can't deliver, it may seem logical to bypass them entirely. By giving everyone the ability to do their own analysis, the team stops being a bottleneck. An overenthusiastic chief financial officer might even start considering at this point how best to rationalize the team!

It's a logical approach, but it rarely works as well as planners would hope. Regardless of the field, efficiency and effectiveness are directly linked to specialization, and hiring the right people involves matching skills to the job. A great accountant isn't necessarily a great marketer. Although there's some overlap, many of the skills involved are very different.

Being good at analyzing data requires a variety of skills ranging from the simple to the advanced forms of statistically driven modeling. Even though domain experts may be able to ask the right questions, they don't always have the technical skills needed to find the right answers. They're often unfamiliar with business analytics tools and may lack the technical skills and experience needed to generate insight. They usually have little knowledge of where the information they need resides.

More importantly, they're rarely aware of the dangers associated with making specific assumptions about their insights. These risks are rarely obvious, and some are more dangerous than others. When it comes to extracting data, the risks are relatively low. A job might run for too long or a person might misinterpret data. More advanced forms of analytics, however, can carry substantial risks.

The Narrowly Avoided Multimillion-Dollar Loss

I remember one occasion when a colleague of mine knew enough to be dangerous but not enough to know how dangerous he was. At the time, his major problem involved trying to work out which opportunities would drive the greatest revenue. To do so, he decided to use statistical drivers to identify which projects would drive the best return. On building his model, he came to the conclusion that certain projects offered far better opportunities than others. His model suggested that by investing in specific projects, he'd help the business generate hundreds of millions of dollars' worth of incremental returns.

Just before he ran to the board to present his findings, I offered to have a quick look over his analysis to make sure it was robust. It was lucky I did—I then had to explain how:

- Using a sample of 10 historical projects probably wasn't the most robust approach.

- When taking into account his margin of error, his investments might make anywhere from $200 million return to a $400 million loss.

In all fairness, neither of these were obvious issues to someone who had self-taught himself to use a modeling toolkit in Excel. He wasn't a foolish or ignorant person; he'd simply fallen into the trap of using skills outside his domain. Needless to say, he took a few steps back and re-evaluated his approach.

Why Should You Care?

When the insights team becomes a bottleneck, organizations:

- Take longer to make decisions
- Miss opportunities
- Experience increased turnover

Organizations that lack insight struggle to make timely decisions. They spend more time debating the merits of information than making decisions. They end up being slower to respond to market changes than their peers.

These delays lead to missed opportunities. Sometimes, the organization is simply too slow to capitalize on them. Sometimes, the organization never even realizes that the opportunity existed in the first place! Regardless of the outcome, these missed opportunities cause the organization to underperform relative to its more analytically aware competitors.

The final and most damaging outcome is usually team turnover. When the demand for insight and the supply of people are mismatched, it creates pressure on the analytics team. It's rare that a team can survive this pressure without suffering attrition. Every time the team loses a skilled individual, its ability to answer questions drops further. This exacerbates the problem and creates a vicious cycle.

What Not to Do

The obvious solution is to hire more resources. If the problem is a lack of people, why not hire more people? As with many simple answers, taking this approach can create complex problems. In practice, it usually introduces:

- Further delivery delays
- Increasingly complex management

New staff members typically have very low productivity. They need to become familiar with the organization's tools, processes, data structures, and business model. Even worse, the productivity of experienced staff will fall as they bring the new staff up to speed.

Hiring additional staff allows a team to scale, but this scale comes with a cost: bureaucracy and complexity. As teams grow, they need more and more management overhead. At some stage, this overhead mitigates or eliminates the returns associated with more staff.

Another solution is to move to a defensive position. Instead of solving the problem, the team raises the drawbridge. Information is power and when a team feels under threat, it sometimes start consolidating its power bases by staking claim over specific information repositories. They'll then enforce its role as the guardian of that data, blocking others from accessing it directly. It's not a pretty solution, but it *is a* solution; becoming the information gatekeeper helps keep the wolves at bay, even if it's only temporarily.

This is only ever a short-term solution. Eventually, the team makes too many enemies and in the long run, the organization is forced to either work around it or outright disband the team.

The How-To Guide: Become an Enabler, Not a Gatekeeper

The better solution is a somewhat counterintuitive one. Rather than delivering more insights, the team focuses on delivering less! Much like the parable of the fisherman,[1] rather than be the source of all answers, the analytics team shifts into being a group that helps others find their own answers. The team:

- Transitions from being a pure insights team into an enabling team
- Provides mentoring and quality control services over analytical activities
- Focuses on raising the organization's overall skill in business analytics

Fully covering this topic could easily take a volume in its own right. Getting started, however, involves creating or enhancing the following enabling components:

- **Self-service analytics.** The organization needs a common platform that allows individuals to do their own analytics. This usually includes creating their own reports, establishing their own dashboards, doing their own simple analytics, and otherwise managing their own information needs.

- **A simplified semantic layer.** Warehouses are unfriendly places, especially for relatively unsophisticated users. Trying to access the full set of data available within most organizations can be extremely confusing. Many warehouses include thousands of unique variables, most of which have highly arcane titles! To make this easier to interpret, the analytics team usually creates a simplified information layer. This acts as a filter to provide a subset of commonly used data along with nontechnical definitions.

- **Single source of quality data.** Clarity comes from starting with the same information. Most of the people who need to access data are not specialists in analytics. Because of this, it's critical that the data they use be of consistently high quality. The analytics team has a critical role in facilitating data quality and creating a single source of value-added information.

- **A community of practice.** Raising an organization's general abilities in business analytics comes from sharing information and mentoring. The team can help drive this by creating a virtual group that meets on a regular basis to share experience and advice.

- **Quality control.** Letting everyone have the freedom to do whatever each one wants helps drive scale but comes at a cost: As discussed in the example, bad analysis can lead to staggeringly bad decisions. When these decisions are automated, organizations can destroy a great deal of value in a very short period of time. To prevent this from happening, the analytics team needs to provide quality control services, checking models and reports for logical or statistical errors before they are put into production. Although they don't necessarily need to develop them, they *do* need to cast their specialist eyes over the results to provide some level of governance and confidence.

Putting in place a structure to support these outcomes takes more than just technology. Coming up with a strategy for these is complex.

It requires a strong communication strategy, effective change management, and a very clear and simple engagement model. People need to know about the change in approach, why the team is doing it, and how to leverage the team's new capabilities.

It is a huge mistake to assume that self-service analytics is a technical problem. Meeting the business's needs always trumps technical efficiency, and even the best initiatives can still end up as white elephants if the organization doesn't buy into them. No matter how good the technology, it will still end up being heavily underutilized if insufficient attention is paid to change management, enablement, communication, and engagement. Without a specific focus on mentoring, assisting, and change, the best efforts of the team in charge of the rollout will usually go to waste.

Benefits and Limitations

The biggest benefit of a self-service platform is that it makes it easier to generate and distribute insight. The analytics team ceases to be the bottleneck and instead becomes a catalyst for improved organizational decision making. However, it's not without limitations. A common mistake is to make the platform more sophisticated than it needs to be. Although it is tempting to include as broad a set of functionality as possible, unsophisticated users actually find this overwhelming.

The best self-service platforms are based on greatly simplified analytical tools that provide a subset of all possible functionality. If and when specific users outgrow the capabilities of this self-service platform, they should look for other toolkits that provide greater levels of functionality, flexibility, and power. Trying to make the self-service platform solve *every* problem is normally a recipe for an underutilized investment.

Another limitation is the need for governance. Users are often given too much flexibility to generate their own data, and without appropriate governance or review, the platform ends up being an unwieldy mess of duplicated data. Instead of providing clarity through common access to information, it runs the risk of actually making things even more confusing! Managing this usually comes down to starting with a single source of high-quality data and establishing data governance champions who are responsible for identifying potential efficiencies and providing cross-group oversight over data creation.

OPTIMIZING MONITORING PROCESSES

CASE STUDY

WHY READ THIS?

When will this help?

Read this if you don't know whether your assets are performing *or* if you're spending too much keeping an eye on how they're performing.

How will it help you?

Using this approach will help increase the time you have to create value and reduce maintenance and monitoring costs.

What are the guiding principles?

■ Automate everything non-value-added

What else should you read?

■ Measuring value

■ Measuring performance

■ Measuring effort

■ Creating the data architecture

■ Linking analytics to value

The Background: Maintaining Value Takes Time Away from Creating Value

Whether it's due to relevance or predictive accuracy, every analytical asset slowly loses its ability to generate value as time passes. Fixing this is easy: Reports can be restructured to be made more relevant and models can be rebuilt to become more accurate. Unfortunately, keeping an eye on these assets takes time away from creating other value-generating assets. All things being equal, every team eventually ends up in a situation in which all its time is being spent maintaining value rather than creating value.

Assets Require Stability to Stay Valuable

Generating value from data isn't a quick process. Rather than making one giant leap, it usually involves taking lots of baby steps. Teams need to source their data and get it into the right structure. They need to develop assets that leverage that data. They need to deploy those assets and make sure they're used, and they need to quantify the value they create. Although the goal is value, most of the team's time is spent creating and managing all those intermediary assets. This creates a surprising amount of management overhead and eats into their ability to drive additional incremental value.

Like their real-world counterparts, analytical assets lose value as things change. Predictive models lose accuracy as the populations they model evolve. As technology improves, products change, and as products change, their target markets also shift. These external changes degrade the relevancy and usefulness of analytical assets. Unless managed, this general degradation reduces the ability of those assets to continue delivering economic value. To maintain the value that they've delivered, the team needs to monitor and maintain their assets.

External Change Can Destroy Assets

This rule applies everywhere in business analytics, regardless of whether you are in the public or private sector. For most commercial organizations, customer demographics can change substantially in as little as a few years. New customers replace old and, given enough time, an organization can actually end up servicing an entirely different market from the one it started with.

The conflicting forces of customer attrition and customer acquisition give an excellent example. Once upon a time, the gold standard for smartphones was a BlackBerry. Although it was the benchmark to beat, it was also relatively expensive compared to its alternatives. As the technology became a commodity, the cost of smartphones dropped. Apple, Samsung, Nokia, and HTC all launched their own take on the smartphone, many of which were powered by Apple's iOS and Google's Android.

Over this period, most telecommunications companies saw significant changes in their traditionally product-defined marketing segments. Smartphones were no longer primarily business phones, and as costs dropped and functionality increased, many of the models they used to predict who would be interested in which class of phone became inaccurate.

This external change forced internal change. Telcos needed to rebuild their analytical assets (often from scratch) to restore predictive accuracy. They needed to capture new data to support changing market requirements and behavioral patterns. As warehousing teams modified their storage schemas to accommodate this new data, analytics teams' data-management process failed and needed to be rebuilt.

Even small market changes can significantly damage the value of existing analytics assets. Closely monitoring a team's assets for issues is the only way to manage this risk and ensure consistent value creation. Sometimes, this is easy; changes to schemas and architectures can break assets outright.

Assets Must Be Reviewed but Time Is Always Limited

Monitoring assets for degradation is a critical function of a competent team. Without it, the team can't guarantee that it is sustaining value. Unfortunately, most teams are drastically short of time and the time they spend *maintaining* value is usually perceived as being less important than spending time *creating* value.

Business analytics teams face a variety of internal and external pressures. Internally, they know what needs to be done to maintain robust and reliable assets. Externally, however, there's constant pressure to develop new value-creating assets. No matter how important sustaining value is, most organizations want to see growth, and maintaining value doesn't help the organization grow.

Reviewing assets carries a big opportunity cost. The time the team spends reviewing existing assets is usually perceived, fairly or not, as time taken away from creating new sources of value. This creates obvious tension. Most teams are time poor. However, they still need to demonstrate and measure the value they create. Failing to do so is rightly seen as a serious breach of good governance.

Over time, this problem only gets worse. By generating more and more assets, they increase the value they create. Unfortunately their time remains limited and they eventually hit a point where, using their preferred approach, it's impossible for them to review all the assets they've deployed into production. Usually, they simply give up and hope for the best.

They stop reviewing their assets at all unless something outright breaks. It's a calculated risk, but it's also an absurd one. If we took the same approach to servicing our cars, we'd constantly suffer from seized engines because of a lack of oil. Rather than prevent the problem, many teams are content to try and absorb the costs when things go catastrophically wrong! It's not that they're unaware of the importance of tracking asset-based value creation or robustness. It's simply that they don't have enough time to do so.

Why Should You Care?

Taking the easy approach and ignoring the problem creates two issues. The team:

1. Increases their exposure to operational risk
2. Needlessly sacrifices value

Ignoring risks may make the job easier. However, it doesn't make them disappear. Ignoring asset validity isn't an option, especially when they're used in an operational context. Doing so exposes the organization to significant operational risk.

On one hand, bad targeting can actually violate government regulations. Governments around the world tend to frown on privacy breaches. In many countries, organizations can be fined after the fact for marketing to customers who have opted out of direct communication. In some cases, these fines can be extremely punitive. In other situations, these outcomes can actually cost the organization real money at the time the recommendation is made. For example, inaccurate fraud models can be extremely costly, especially if they miss significant issues. Sometimes, this can cost millions in direct losses.

The costs of poorly performing assets don't stop there. Bad assets create opportunity costs. Although usually not as significant, it is also important to remember that the more accurate and relevant an asset, the greater its ability to create value. When assets are allowed to degrade beyond an acceptable threshold, those assets could have been driving better value had the team taken the time to recalibrate it.

These opportunity costs don't only apply to predictive models; the same principle applies to reports. An accurate report provides relevant insight and drives better decision making. Over time, though, the business inevitably changes. Products may be reallocated to different units or territories may change. As assets lose business relevancy because of these changes, they tend to harm more than they help. Instead of making decisions easier, they create confusion and delay decision making.

Teams that haven't solved these problems usually have no idea how accurate any of their predictions or insights are on any given day. They have no idea how frequently their reports are actually used, and they have no idea whether the organization actually finds value in their insights. That this may be seen as business as usual by some teams is a sad commentary on how deeply they're trapped by these issues.

What Not to Do

Ignoring the do-nothing-and-hope-for-the-best option, most teams try to spend more time reviewing assets. They'll allocate time to review asset use and performance on a regular schedule, and where assets fail the health check, they'll recalibrate, redevelop, or retire them. Although this is better than nothing, it still creates a variety of problems. The team:

- Wastes time they could have otherwise spent creating value
- Mitigates fewer risks than they would have otherwise been able to

Every time an asset is examined and nothing is wrong, the team wastes valuable time. There's an opportunity cost; they could have spent that same time building new assets and driving further value. This loss of productivity may seem like a necessary evil. In reality, the opposite is true. There are better solutions that do not involve wasting constrained resources.

The other issue is that risk management becomes driven by time. A review will pick up many risks. Unfortunately, those same risks existed regardless of whether the review took place. Using this approach limits risk identification to when the review takes place. Given that models are usually reviewed on a set schedule, risk mitigation becomes dependent on how frequently the team can afford to spend time reviewing assets. If they underestimate the speed at which a particular asset is degrading, they run a very real risk of having underperforming assets in production. Predictions *could* have been more accurate.

The How-To Guide: Automate the Monitoring Process

The better solution involves moving from manual to automated monitoring. Rather than check assets on a fixed schedule, the team creates automated operational monitoring process, thereby shifting effort from the individual to the system.

Most measures of interest to a business analytics team are quantitative in nature. The team will often be interested in whether models classify things correctly. It will want to know whether assets are being accessed or used, and it will want to know whether jobs failed to complete and whether the results were expected.

Rather than arbitrarily deciding the best time to review these assets, automated monitoring processes continually assess these assets against expected or desired outcomes. Should any asset degrade past an acceptable threshold, the system notifies the relevant owner. This has the dual benefit of reducing operational risk and driving productivity. More importantly, it gives the team that much more room to scale activities. All that time it spent manually reviewing assets is now free to reallocate to value-creating initiatives.

Getting this working involves ensuring that, at a minimum, the following are put in place:

- Process automation
- Management by exception
- Dashboards and profiling tools
- A common measurement framework

Without process automation, productivity gains are impossible. The system itself needs the capability to schedule regular monitoring jobs that apply various business or statistical rules to identify bad outcomes. These don't have to be complex—a common example involves establishing a trigger that monitors model classification accuracy. If that measure degrades by more than 5 percent in a two-week period, the system will notify the asset owner. The important thing about this approach is that the processes and measures are generalizable to *every* similar asset. Rather than re-invent the wheel every time the team develops a new asset, it can simply select from a standard shopping list and replicate existing measures.

Automation is important, but it's only part of the picture. The process also needs to notify the asset owner when triggers fire. The trick is that these notifications need to be visible across any preferred notification channel. The owner may prefer to use e-mail, SMS, or even social-media tools like Twitter or Facebook. If the asset owner has to manually check a dedicated portal every day, the owner has lost the benefits of automation; the time needed to check in undermines the point of the productivity gains.

Once a trigger has been fired and the appropriate owner has been notified, they need to quickly profile the reasons behind the trigger. The easiest way to do this is through dashboards. Trying to have a trigger for every exception is complex. Having a single trigger that lets owners know that something is wrong is easier to implement. Dashboards gives owners the ability to quickly flag why things are going wrong and drill through to the real issues—they can focus on the important and ignore the trivial.

Finally, productivity comes from having a consistent set of business, analytical, and technical measures. These get applied to every project, irrespective of the target outcome. Common measures of interest include classification accuracy, report usage, user satisfaction levels with the relevancy of the insight provided, or business outcomes.

Benefits and Limitations

The biggest benefits of automated operational monitoring lie in risk mitigation and driving productivity. By automating the process, the team can make sure assets are continually monitored for quality. Continual monitoring helps prevent assets from staying in production beyond their usable life. As soon as the asset's value-creating potential drops below an acceptable threshold, the team knows. They reduce operational risk. They also drive productivity. Rather than having to repeatedly check for asset performance, the team can direct its attention to value-creating activities.

However, it's also important not to overengineer the measurement framework; it's easy to go overboard. If inappropriately managed, the measurement and monitoring framework can become an end in its own right! Trying to track too many measures can inhibit efficiency. When this happens, it usually becomes too hard to make sure every project implements every measure. Operational monitoring ends up being inconsistently applied across different initiatives and assets.

ENCOURAGING INNOVATION

CASE STUDY

WHY READ THIS?

When will this help?

Read this if you spend all your time driving continuous improvement and not enough time driving disruptive innovation.

How will it help you?

Using this approach will help encourage incremental *and* revolutionary improvements.

What are the guiding principles?

- Think about competencies, not functions
- Drive outcomes, not insight
- Know what you are worth
- Own your intellectual property
- It's better to have too much data than too little
- Watch the dynamic, not just the static

(Continued)

What else should you read?
- Augmenting operational systems
- Breaking bottlenecks
- Keeping everyone aligned
- Smoothing growth with the cloud
- Capturing the right data

The Background: Success Creates Inertia

To be successful, teams need to transition their discoveries into operational execution. Otherwise, all they'll ever create is insight, not economic value. Doing this requires taking their often ad-hoc and flexible processes and rationalizing them into standardized, repeatable processes. This structure drives efficiency but also hinders creativity and experimentation. Intentionally or otherwise, teams end up emphasizing continuous improvement over disruptive innovation.

There's More Than One Type of Innovation

Doing things better lies at the heart of innovation. Sometimes, it's as simple as being able to achieve the same outcome with fewer resources and in less time. Sometimes, it's as powerful as creating a new market from scratch.

The worst-kept secret of innovation is that there's more than one type of innovation. Sometimes, innovation is revolutionary. It's disruptive, and it changes markets. Five years ago, the iPhone didn't exist. Today, the old incumbents are on the ropes. More often, though, innovation is evolutionary: It takes an existing activity and makes it better. Analytics and big data help enable innovation. Looking at things from a new perspective can uncover new opportunities. Getting into the detail can reveal patterns masked by broader trends, and acting faster than your competitors can be a point of differentiation in its own right. It's often this need for innovation that leads organizations to look into business analytics.

Acting on Insight Requires Repeatability and Standardization

Most organizations follow a fairly typical trajectory. They start out with lots of data and little insight. Without knowing the simple stuff, they can't innovate. Eventually, someone decides that they're missing out on a prime opportunity to make better decisions by using this data, and, using whatever tools they can, they generate insight to the best of their abilities. Relative to where they started from, they use business analytics to drive a revolutionary change in the way they do business.

From here, the emphasis shifts from a lack of insight to an inability to scale their insight. Functionality focused groups create functionally focused insight. Rather than trying to solve *every* problem in the organization, they answer their own questions, helping themselves but not the broader organization. To deal with their own information vacuum, other groups develop their own skills and leverage their own tools and over time, the organization ends up with highly fragmented, functionally separated business analytics skills. They're inefficient, but they're still able to innovate. Because their use of business analytics is still so organic and flexible, they're still able to drive disruptive innovation.

At this point smarter organizations realize that this is tremendously inefficient. Rather than duplicate their skills and tools across the organization, they decide to encourage economies of scale and scope. Assuming all goes well, they establish an enterprise platform that supports a broader analytical center of excellence. They achieve best practice in operational analytics. This is a critical step, but it comes at a cost: By driving efficiency, the organization loses the ability to drive disruptive innovation.

Standardization Hinders Disruptive Innovation

To see how this trade-off happens, it's important to follow the steps that lead there. Following best practices, organizations build separate discovery and operational environments, giving them the ability to deploy insights and manage the business analytics value chain. They define clear handover points between the business, IT, and the analytics centers of excellence. They use consistent data models between the two (discovery and operational) environments and create well-governed and well-defined asset migration processes that cover developing, testing, and deploying assets into production.

Given this complexity, efficiency comes from defining and streamlining handover points. It's simply impossible to manage the resulting process and platform complexity without strong governance. What works in a functional, ad-hoc environment can fail catastrophically in an operational context. This shift from chaos to structure involves trading off flexibility for efficiency. More than anything else, this helps drive scale. The most efficient organizations can move from developing models to validating them to deploying them operationally in a matter of days, if not less. Needless to say, that requires an impressive level of coordination!

Standard processes have many benefits, some of the main ones being that they're highly repeatable and simplify team coordination. They also make it easy to deliver evolutionary improvements and incremental returns. What standardization *can't* help with is disruptive innovation. This type of innovation comes from doing things in a fundamentally different way. Rather than follow the standard process, it involves reinventing it, often from scratch.

When It Comes to Disruption, Organizations Are Their Own Worst Enemy

When disruption's the goal, everything's open for review. Coming up with radical improvements might come from applying different skills, new technologies, or mashing up data from many different sources. It requires experimentation, risk, and, above all, flexibility. It's also the antithesis of highly efficient processes.

Efficiency requires repeatability. It requires well-defined activities. It requires total confidence that the platform will work reliably. Assets, technologies, processes, and data sources need to be well defined ahead of time. This is the exact opposite of the characteristics that allowed the very same organization to drive disruptive innovation at the start of their journey!

Given this trade-off, it's not surprising that organizations consistently struggle to foster disruptive innovation once they've achieved a certain level of success. Most end up charging people with the responsibility to drive both evolutionary *and* revolutionary improvements. Usually, this is doomed to fail. Disruptive innovation would require the team responsible for business as usual to reject their current approach for highly risky, uncertain outcome. Evolutionary innovation is far easier. When the system is geared to support structure and efficiency, it's easier to take current processes and activities and make them better. As would be expected, most teams end up focusing almost exclusively on evolutionary innovation.

Why Should You Care?

Organizations suffering from these challenges tend to stagnate and struggle to do things differently. When asked, there's no shortage of ways things could be improved. Unfortunately, good ideas tend to die a painful death. Even when visionaries try to innovate, the systems themselves undermine success.

By far the most common symptom is that teams find it near impossible to try new things without substantial lead times. In some cases, it may take them half a year or more just to test a new approach. This in itself highlights how destructive this situation can be; when it takes over half a year to even start considering to do things differently, why bother?

Improving Results through Augmented Models

A great example involves stopping people from canceling their services in telecommunications. To combat churn, most organizations develop and deploy attrition models. These predictive models calculate the odds of an individual canceling their service within a given time period. For operational reasons, this is usually two to three months in the future.

These models are then scheduled and deployed. Their scores are sent to the organization's customer relationship management system and outbound calling systems to help target people with the highest likelihood of churning. Most of the time, the major focus is on making things work as efficiently as possible. This drives the usual suspects, namely, process standardization, operational analytics, and strong governance.

Continuous improvement becomes a question of how to drive granularity. The more the organization can differentiate treatments, the better its retention rates. Some customers prefer to be contacted out of hours, whereas others prefer to be contacted via e-mail. To drive this differentiated treatment, the team usually focuses on building more models and increasing the frequency of scoring runs. The team will try to go from one to ten to hundreds of models, each trying to model a different customer segment.

This approach is powerful but has limitations. It's great in predicting *who* is likely to churn in a given time frame. What it *doesn't* normally do is predict *when* they will churn. Inherent in the model is an assumption about how quickly the company in question can actually act on that insight. Given the way their processes are normally designed, it's useless knowing who will churn tomorrow if it takes a month to contact them!

This is a major oversight; knowing *when* someone is likely to churn opens up entirely new contact strategies. If someone is likely to churn in six months, the organization could take advantage of multistage campaigns that use progressively more expensive contact strategies as they get closer to the likely churn date.

Six months prior to expected churn, the company might send an SMS to see whether people are happy with their service. Three months prior to expected churn, they may offer a service bundle at a minor discount on the condition that the customer renews their contract for another 24 months. Finally, on the month that they are most likely to churn, the company might make direct contact via the call center. They may even up the stakes by making an even more attractive offer.

The potential for innovation doesn't stop there. Even better, this approach could be augmented to take into account personal relationships. We all know people who have canceled their phone services. Usually, we'll also find out *why* they canceled and how much better their other offer was. If we see them as being influential, we might also churn. Viral churn, the situation in which customers churn because their family and friends have found a better deal, is very real.

The Challenge of Disruptive Change

Taking advantage of time-based information and social network information is disruptive innovation at its best. When the competition follows the same core process, these augmentations can enable comparative quality advantages and increase retention rates. The challenge is that because of the way organizations operate, taking advantage of these disruptive innovations is near impossible. Extending their processes to include these approaches usually requires new technologies, new competencies, and new ways to deploy the resulting assets.

Every change carries some degree of risk, and few organizations are willing to invest in new technologies and skills without having some level of confidence that the results will provide real return on investment. Making sure that change will be positive requires experimentation, and the easiest way to build this confidence is to test the approach using the organization's own data.

Unfortunately, this is easier said than done. When the same group is charged with driving disruption *and* business as usual, something has to give. On one hand, there's usually not enough time to experiment. On the other, there's also not enough time to develop the new skills that are needed! Even worse, new approaches also require new technologies, and these technologies are rarely part of the team's analytics platform. Getting things up to specification is a harder process than one would think.

Upgrading existing environments requires substantial lead time. Resources have to be coordinated and should an upgrade fail, the business may start losing real money. One cannot underestimate how significantly this limits agility and innovation. Coordinating resources is so hard, it's not uncommon to schedule platform upgrades up to six months in advance!

Despite being highly capable, most teams simply give up. Their need for efficiency and standardization eventually cripples their ability to drive creativity through flexibility. In the end, the analytics team focuses almost exclusively on evolutionary innovation. This still drives incremental returns, but it rarely enables truly disruptive sustainable competitive differentiation.

What Not to Do

Organizations in this position usually start by trying to relax governance. Logic suggests that the problem must be rooted in process. If things take too long to do because of excessive constraints, why not simply relax constraints?

Fix the process while using the same platform and the company can improve without any real need for change or investment. At its simplest, the team may relax its testing and validation checks when it comes to temporarily testing new technologies and approaches. If these temporary changes deliver real value, normal migration and upgrade processes kick in. Things move back to a strongly governed process model.

Intuitively, this makes sense—it reuses existing technology investment and requires only process change. Even better, it doesn't require any real investment. It must be said that this does help in some situations. If effectively managed, organizations can overcome various process and data challenges. It's also ideally suited to champion/challenger situations in which competing processes are benchmarked against each other. In these cases, strong governance only applies to the champion model. Every challenger model simply requires a best effort approach until it's likely to replace the champion model.

Unfortunately, this solution doesn't always work. Often, the most innovative approaches require cutting-edge technologies that may be highly unstable beta releases. Making sure that these new technologies play nicely with existing technologies isn't easy and requires extensive testing and validation. There's good reason for this: Software conflicts can bring down the entire analytical environment! An outage of this nature introduces unacceptable interruptions to the business, and, if it happens on the operational platform, it ends up costing real money as operational processes grind to a halt.

Managing these risks requires a staged testing process, something that costs money and takes time. Coordinating the teams necessary to test technologies can take weeks or months, and, if the new approach does not succeed, the same technologies often have to be uninstalled from the environment. This drives a second round of testing, validation, and cost. Often, this is seen as throwing good money after bad. It does nothing to help the perception of the analytics team.

With all these risks, it's not surprising that most organizations that take this path let risk dictate their innovation. They end up scaling back their creativity to "innovations" that only ever leverage what they already have. Anything else is just too risky!

The How-To Guide: Establish an Innovation Lab and Separate Disruption from Continuous Improvement

The better solution is to bypass the problem entirely and establish a separate (but linked) innovation lab focused on creative destruction. Unlike a traditional Skunk Works,[2] the group is tightly integrated with the rest of the organization. Formalizing the innovation process is a large topic, one that deserves a book in its own right. The cultural aspects alone are worthy of at least a few chapters! Because of this, we can only review a small set of the factors that lead to better outcomes.

To help grant flexibility without losing the ability to commercialize their findings, innovation labs:

- Are granted significant architectural flexibility and a separate, virtual (or parallel) processing platform
- Leverage the same data and systems as the rest of the organization but are responsible for driving disruptive/cross-functional innovation
- Operate with significantly relaxed governance

Parallel Processing Platforms

IT groups often standardize on a small set of operating systems and hardware platforms. Good IT management involves rationalizing an organization's technology portfolio as much as possible. This isn't to constrain creativity but, rather, it's to help drive economies of scale in support skills and licensing negotiations. This standardization reduces the number of skills the IT department needs to maintain and helps create leverage with vendors through sheer purchasing power.

These constraints drive operational cost efficiencies but also constrain flexibility and, in many, cases limit innovation. Within this context, the main issue is that cutting-edge technology often only runs on specific platforms. Although mature applications usually support multiple operating systems and hardware architectures, emerging software tends to only support a small set of specific configurations, and these configurations may not be supported by IT—they may require a particular flavor of Linux or be limited to specific hardware architectures. If the platform is an unsupported one, the team may hit an impasse: IT may simply refuse to support the application.

It's important to remember in these cases that IT is there to support the business. The key caveat is that the returns need to justify the incremental investment necessary to support a niche application. Unfortunately, this also means that the business case needs to become even more positive! Luckily, there's an easier solution: Organizations often take advantage of virtualization to support their innovation labs.

Servers are created as virtual images in a larger, sometimes cloud-based platform. These can include anything from mainframe-based platforms right through to private clouds, such as Amazon's EC2. When effectively managed, they allow significant flexibility.

Operating systems can be created, modified, and archived as needed with processor and memory allocations changed on the fly. Should a problem prove to be too large for the deployed environment, allocating more memory can be as easy as a few mouse clicks! Should the approach prove unsuccessful, the image is simply brought down and deleted. Unlike physical hardware, this instantly frees up resources for other uses.

Operational Integration

Innovation is only the start: If the organization is to benefit economically, it needs to commercialize the innovation. In this context, this means being able to transition to operational analytics. This is only possible when the team does two things.

First, it needs to use the same data as the rest of the organization. Doing so requires two fairly obvious connection points. One is to the information needed to generate the insight. The other is to the systems that will act on the insight. An effective innovation lab has both of these. It maintains strong links to the common analytical datamart and to whichever operational systems are responsible for execution. This applies in both directions, too. Extensions made by other groups become available to the innovation lab, and extensions made by the innovation lab become available to everyone else.

Unfortunately, this need for data-level integration is often over-looked during architectural definition. Because the system will be leveraging untested technologies, it can be tempting to host the innovation lab *and* its data in a hardened zone, separate and secure from other enterprise assets. When this happens, commercializing innovation becomes that much harder.

Second, the team that's responsible for disruptive innovation isn't always responsible for execution. It makes little sense to bypass expensive contact channels "just because." Therefore, the innovation lab still needs to maintain close ties to other groups in the organization. Rather than working independently, they simply focus on different tasks. As the innovations are defined and commercialized, they're transitioned into business as usual, and the innovation lab moves on to the next problem.

Management Model

Finally, the innovation lab is granted a significantly reduced level of governance. Because its focus is on agility over repeatability, many controls are no longer applicable. For example, exhaustive testing is no longer necessary—unlike most enterprise systems, environments within the innovation lab only need to work for the duration of the project, not for the life of the asset.

This applies to security controls as well. Third parties often need far higher levels of access than they would normally be offered. Rather than try and triage platform issues, IT support in these situations is usually better off by simply opening the platform to those who developed the software. To support the innovation lab, IT may need to shift from a support team to a facilitation team.

Benefits and Limitations

The biggest benefit of the innovation lab is that it allows an organization to drive evolutionary *and* revolutionary improvements. Jointly, the organization can improve all aspects of people, process, data, and technology without sacrificing the ability to operationally test the results. This helps enable innovation without sacrificing value measurement or creating needless disruption. Teams can play to their strengths rather than trying to achieve the impossible. Innovation is challenging enough without having to fight against needless internal constraints!

As with everything, though, this solution still has limitations. One of the greatest lies in persuading the IT department to change its operating model. Creating the platform as described can run counter to many governance-based IT cultures and may require the IT team to develop new management skills. Simply convincing the organization to adopt this approach can be a major argument in its own right!

Another limitation is that, although the innovation lab helps with the pioneering stage of innovation, it rarely helps with the harvesting stage of innovation. Fast turnaround and relaxed governance almost inevitably lead to highly nonstandard processes. Just to make things work, processes are held together with duct tape and string.

In the right context, this is not a bad thing. If it's enough to demonstrate returns, the lab has served its purpose. However, turning these jury-rigged outputs into a standardized process usually requires starting from scratch. It's for this reason that the team needs to retain close links to other groups in the organization. Innovation without commercialization is like a car without wheels: It may still look good, but it won't go anywhere.

Finally, simply having access to an innovation lab does not guarantee success. The lab is only an enabler that provides the flexibility needed to create disruptive innovation. The organization still needs to do the hard work of defining the value, communicating it to stakeholders, delivering the initiative, and measuring the resulting successes to help justify the business case.

NOTES

1. Give someone a fish and they'll eat for a day. Teach someone to fish and they'll eat for the rest of their life.

2. The original Skunk Works was Lockheed Martin's Advanced Development Program, a semiautonomous business unit that operated with significantly reduced governance and oversight. It conducted advanced research and development work on multiple secret projects and led to the creation of the SR-71 Blackbird, the F-117 Nighthawk, and the F-22 Raptor. It's famous for delivering staggering advanced work with a surprisingly small team and based its name on the Skonk Works, a factory just outside Dogpatch in the comic *Li'l Abner*.

CHAPTER **7**

Analytical Process Management

A cting on insight requires alignment, coordination, and transparency. This requires balancing flexibility with standard processes. Understanding how best to go about managing transparency and standardization isn't easy. Most organizations struggle with:

- Having too little or too much insight
- Minimizing the time they spend doing non-value-added activities
- Finding ways to continuously improve processes
- Engaging external parties without losing ownership over the resulting processes and outcomes

The solutions described in the next section focus on techniques and approaches to overcome these challenges.

COPING WITH INFORMATION OVERLOAD

CASE STUDY

WHY READ THIS?

When will this help?

Read this if your organization makes decisions on gut-feel *or* things go wrong because you use too many black-box systems.

How will it help you?

Using this approach will help you leverage experience *and* analytics.

What are the guiding principles?

- Drive outcomes, not insight
- Automate everything non-value-added
- Minimize custom development
- Function should dictate form

What else should you read?

- Augmenting operational systems
- Breaking bottlenecks
- Keeping everyone aligned
- Allocating responsibilities
- Measuring value
- Linking analytics to value
- Blending rules with models

The Background: Having Too Little Insight Is as Bad as Having Too Much

Most organizations are worried about their lack of insight. Despite having large data repositories, they lose sleep over their inability to generate answers. Therefore, they invest heavily into acquiring the skills and technologies needed to drive data-based decisioning. The true irony is that having too much insight is just as paralyzing as having too little: After spending significant amounts of time and money into generating insight, organizations end up in equally bad situations.

Indecision Only Leads to Pain

Business has never been easy. However, it's hard to argue that things have become easier over the last few decades. One of the biggest side effects of the information revolution has been complexity and a very real (and constant) risk of information overload. Even though we have better access to information than ever before, that same information can actually drive bad decision making!

Every day, we generate more data than has been available in the last decade: Where we go, what we do, who we interact with online, and what we buy all contribute to the world's ever-growing data stores. To someone charged with making daily business decisions, this data growth presents a myriad of opportunities and challenges. On the positive side, it's never been easier to answer a question. On the negative side, it's never been harder to actually *find* the answer.

Sometimes, it just seems easier to go with experience and ignore the problem. Experience can help guide us to better outcomes, but as with everything, it has its limits. One of the biggest of these is our ability to consider *everything* put in front of us, not just what's obvious or recent. Over the last decade, we've gone from hundreds of records of information to, in some cases, trillions.

Information complexity is easy to appreciate but hard to handle. Bad analysis easily leads to bad decisions. When a private-sector organization can't run its business, it often goes bankrupt. When the public sector can't act in a coordinated manner, the public suffers. Neither is a good outcome.

Too Many Choices Can Lead to Information Paralysis

To drive better outcomes, organizations need to make decisions. They need to focus their attention in the right place. They need to engage correctly with customers. They need to profile risks and act appropriately. They need to make and act on these decisions in a timely manner.

Unfortunately, with complexity comes an ever-increasing number of decisions that need to be made. When an organization only has one outbound channel, it's easy to decide how to contact customers. Choice adds delay: When that same organization has many outbound channels, it needs to work out which one will drive the best outcome.

On a daily basis, any given organization makes thousands, if not millions, of microdecisions. These can be as simple as deciding what product to offer given an inbound customer contact or deciding whether to respond on a social-media site like Twitter or Facebook. When decision makers can't consider everything they need to, one of two things happens. They either become trapped by information paralysis or they satisfice and make the best decisions they can, given their limitations. This may be good enough but not ideal—by satisficing, they're inevitably creating a suboptimal outcome.

Prioritization Is the Answer but with Experience Alone, It Can't Scale

The reason behind this sacrifice is that not all areas of the business are equally valuable. There's a general rule that says 80 percent of an organization's profitability is driven by less than 20 percent of the products they sell. Working out which products fit into that 20 percent is easy when things are simple. Ideally, decision makers already know this and priorities accordingly.

When things are simple, prioritization is straightforward. Many planners and decision makers simply start from the top and review each item individually until they hit the bottom of the list or run out of time. Unfortunately, this approach doesn't scale. As things become more complex, experience becomes an increasingly important contributor to efficiency. Having prior knowledge about what is likely to be important and what isn't helps direct focus to the right areas. However, this only goes so far; not every decision is similar to the prior one.

Decision makers usually end up:

- Making decisions through rules of thumb and heuristics
- Spreading themselves too thin and not spending sufficient time on the important things

The Good: Analytics Can Enhance Prioritization

Rules of thumb are only effective as long as our assumptions remain accurate. When presented with a new situation, decision makers are forced to give everything equal focus, and, inevitably, unimportant things get more focus than they should while important things may go unnoticed. Business analytics offers an obvious solution. Organizations can take advantage of statistics to uncover patterns and create predictions. Because analytics relies on repeatable algorithms, it's also extremely scalable; making one or a million decisions is simply a question of hardware.

Although analytics can't replace experience, it helps by making decision making easier. Having the right insight at the right time can eliminate hours of investigation. Unfortunately, this same benefit can be a curse, because, when inappropriately used, massively scalable processes tend to contribute to information overload.

The Bad: Too Much Analytics Can Lead to Even More Information Overload

It's technically feasible to calculate and present the profitability of every individual transaction, one by one. Although it's a great example of business analytics' scalability, it doesn't necessarily make decision making any easier. Having access to information isn't enough—insight needs to be relevant and focused.

Buyers may be interested in understanding which products are the most profitable in different regions. Having access to transaction-level profitability information is a great input, but until it's aggregated, it doesn't make their decision making any easier. In fact, having access to this low level of detail can actually make it harder for them to do their jobs! Those who are responsible for making decisions tend to be extremely time limited. To make better decisions, they need to either exhaustively review every single piece of information *or* spend time they don't have processing information to make it more relevant.

Given their lack of time, neither option is palatable. This creates a very strange situation. Paradoxically, decision makers continue to try and run their business through heroic effort and gut-feel decision making, despite actually having access to all the information they need to make better decisions.

Why Should You Care?

The most common symptoms of an organization suffering from information overload include:

- Immediate access to an abundance of data in every possible form imaginable
- Rushed decision making and planning cycles
- A fire-fighting rather than fire-preventing culture
- Relatively high numbers of operational management staff compared to their competitors

Microdecisions usually need to be made quickly. Pricing, inventory management, or buying decisions are often reevaluated daily (sometimes hourly in certain industries) based on up-to-the-minute sales information. Working out which offer is the right one may need to happen within the span of a phone call.

Given this need for speed, it seems to make sense that decision makers should have access to every possible piece of information they *might* need. Unfortunately, this rapidly becomes overwhelming. Rather than making their decision making easier, it actually creates a metadecisioning problem. To make a better decision, they need to decide which information is going to be useful! In practice, they usually don't bother and just go with whatever feels right.

Timely decisions always feel rushed. However, there's a difference between speed and haste, and even though time frames may be tight, decisions shouldn't feel rushed. Organizations that struggle with either too much or too little information constantly question their decisions. When there's not enough information, they worry that they may not have known what's really going on. When there's too much information, they worry that they may have missed something. Although not always overtly communicated, there is often a tacit lack of confidence in the decisions that were made.

This lack of time and information uncertainty reinforces a culture of heroic effort and fire-fighting. Because decisions are rushed and made on an experience-based ad-hoc basis, it encourages a hero mentality. Success is intimately tied to overcoming the odds. Poor decisions are fixed after the fact, usually through overbuying or overallocating capital within supply chains. Rather than encourage efficiency, repeatability, and getting it right the first time, recognition is given for fixing problems.

This fire-fighting culture usually leads to organizations hiring far more resources than they actually need. Poor operational decisions usually cost real money. Because of this, it's relatively easy to put together a business case to hire staff to fix the resulting problems. Over time, bad microdecisions usually end up creating needless structural cost.

What Not to Do

Making better and faster microdecisions is the clear solution. In practice, organizations try to improve through either:

- Acquiring more experience
- Targeting hyperefficiency

Both approaches provide short-term advantages. However, these come at the expense of scalability in the first case and risk in the second.

To Hire People, First You Need to Find Them

Hiring more people might seem like the obvious solution. Having more people means there are more people to make decisions. Unfortunately, this rarely works as well as one would expect.

Many organizations have capital constraints that prevent them from hiring people in the short term. Headcount increases need to be budgeted well ahead of time. Even when an organization can hire more people, this approach assumes that suitable resources can be found. Depending on the industry, organization, and product set, it can sometimes be near impossible to find a suitably qualified individual at the price the organization is willing to pay. When they cannot, they are forced to take a risk and compromise by hiring lesser-skilled people. Having more people may make it easier to make more decisions. However, this doesn't mean that the decisions will be good ones.

Active Decision Making Always Hits a Point of Diminishing Returns

The problems don't end there, either. Assuming suitable resources can be found, the organization eventually starts hitting a point of diminishing returns. Most decision makers are under constant pressure. Because of this, most are constantly on the lookout for ways to narrow their focus on the factors that will have the greatest impact on their business.

Although it won't necessarily be perfect, most competent decision makers have prioritized their work to focus on the important stuff. Adding more people into the mix can help improve the granularity of planning and decision making. However, the returns associated with driving granularity aren't indefinite.

Not everything contributes equally to overall margin or profitability, and as the organization moves down the list, the proportional impact of better decision making or planning also declines. Given diminishing returns, hiring more people is an expensive way to scale in the long run. Because of this, hiring more people should be seen as a short-term fix, not a solution.

Totally Automated Decisions Are Rarely Robust

Given the limitations of trying to acquire more experience, it may seem logical to go the other way and focus purely on scalable and repeatable analytics. Because of this, it can be tempting to try and fully automate *all* microdecisions. This doesn't work anywhere near as well as one might expect.

It's possible to make decisions about stock allocations or rostering automatically with no human intervention. Models can predict stock is out and identify the best time to reorder. They can also identify the ideal allocation of resources to minimize staffing costs while maximizing service. Given this, why *not* eliminate the human factor and simply automate everything?

In some situations, this works extremely effectively. However, as a general rule it often exposes the organization to an extremely high level of risk. Statistically based models always incorporate some degree of uncertainty, and unless the data is perfectly stable and completely independent from external shocks, analytically based predictions are a best-guess based on all the information that is available. It might be a very good best guess, admittedly, but still one that has inherent uncertainty.

As events occur that were not expressly incorporated into the original models, the predictive accuracy of the models will decline. Fads can render a reordering algorithm almost totally ineffective. The underlying demand for a given product may be low for a substantial period of time. However, effective product marketing might suddenly drive demand to unprecedented levels.

Without the experience of an effective product manager/planner, the analytically based demand forecasts may be highly inaccurate until the point where they are reestimated, taking into account this exogenous shock. During this time, the organization is sacrificing either significant opportunity cost or incurring very real operational costs.

Relying on full automation increases efficiency at the expense of risk. It has the potential to significantly reduce planning cycle time as well as structural cost but only at the risk of being catastrophically wrong when the organization's environment changes rapidly. This is a dangerous trade-off to make, especially given that it's arguably impossible to predict *when* things will change.

The How-To Guide: Automate the Majority, Review the Important

The better solution involves blending the two approaches, capitalizing on both experience and efficiency. Automation is used to generate baseline decision-making recommendations. This leverages a variety of analytical techniques including predictive modeling, forecasting, and optimization. Rather than just presenting insight, these processes create specific recommendations.

On one hand, this allows an organization to scale to the most granular level possible. On the other, it also usually results in a substantially improved level of aggregate predictive accuracy. One of the key advantages of statistically based models lies in their ability to incorporate a wide variety of factors ranging from seasonality to the impact of promotional activity.

This information is then merged against outcomes-based measures such as cost, profitability, contributing margin, or revenue. This blended view of decisions is used to automatically priorities which decisions are the ones that will make a real difference. These are then flagged for further consideration.

By having accurate recommendations for the majority of items that have a proportionally smaller impact on outcomes, organizations can automate many of their daily microdecisions. This frees decision makers to focus their attention on those decisions that have the greatest contribution to target measures, thereby minimizing organizational risk and driving improved outcomes while still capitalizing on their deep industry experience.

Benefits and Limitations

The major benefits of this approach revolve around efficiency, risk, and scalability. Automation creates a baseline approach that usually provides an acceptable level of accuracy. This accuracy is then further improved through experience-based planning, allowing the organization to take nonquantitative factors into account. It also helps mitigate risk: Predictions can be adjusted to take into account recent occurrences that might make the baseline models inaccurate.

Rather than taking a piecemeal approach to driving granularity, organizations can immediately scale to the most granular level. They can do so without needing to substantially increase staff levels. The need for fire-fighting resources also declines, further improving structural costs.

The major limitation of this approach revolves around cultural change. Overcoming the hero culture associated with many operational decision-making and planning processes can be a very real challenge. Because it is self-reinforcing, there is generally a strong distrust in any form of automation. Experience is seen as the major driver behind success, and there's disbelief that anything could be as effective as the existing approach.

Even worse, people sometimes see eliminating fire-fighting as an active threat. Individuals in these environments are often able to build an entire career out of solving problems that shouldn't exist in the first place. As such, although the process, technology, and data aspects of execution are usually quite straightforward, the human dimension can pose serious challenges. However, the benefits are worth the effort.

KEEPING EVERYONE ALIGNED

CASE STUDY

WHY READ THIS?

When will this help?

Read this if you struggle to coordinate the activities of multiple teams.

How will it help you?

Using this approach will help you reduce transaction costs and drive efficiency.

What are the guiding principles?

- Start flexible, become structured
- Design your platform for use, not purity
- Keep things simple
- Function should dictate form

What else should you read?

- Allocating responsibilities
- Scaling past the PC
- Moving to operational analytics
- Creating data-management processes
- Reducing time to recommendation

The Background: Too Many Answers and Not Enough Time

Business analytics is about doing things better. This inevitably means that existing processes need to change. Unfortunately, making sure everyone's aligned isn't as easy as it might seem. Although there might only be one team that needs to act on any given insight, the business analytics team needs to be able to engage with *all* of them. There's simply not enough time in the day to meet with them all.

Business Analytics Is a Team Sport

Somewhat counterintuitively, most successful business analytics teams spend the majority of their time managing change rather than generating insights. Some teams choose to start small by picking a project, exhaustively testing a new approach, and seeing whether it makes a difference. They use their results to justify the change. If and when it works, they pick a new project and repeat the process.

Other teams drive large-scale change with the support of a very top-down approach. Their leadership team mandates that business analytics will henceforth be a core part of the business. Anyone who disagrees is free to find a new job!

Most business analytics teams fall somewhere in the middle. They rely on a more organic approach to applying business analytics—one that scales with time. Projects are considered independently, but every successful project justifies further projects. The team starts with one project, moves to two when it's successful, and moves to four when those are successful. The returns from successful projects are channeled into future initiatives, creating a cost-neutral business model.

Self-funding models have a number of advantages. One of the most obvious is risk management—by starting small, the organization limits its exposure to the size of the initiative. This is often instrumental in getting a project across the line. Change is scary and many decision makers favor a gentle approach to doing things differently.

Regardless of the approach the team chooses to use, it can't realize value without support. One of the ironies of business analytics is that those who are responsible for generating insight are rarely responsible for acting on that insight or maintaining the systems they use. Those responsibilities instead fall to other groups.

Everyone Has a Role to Play

Getting an initiative up and running requires the coordination of three groups of people:

1. Those who are responsible for generating insight.
2. Those who are responsible for acting on the insight that has been generated.
3. Those who are responsible for managing the underlying data and systems.

In principle, all these people could be part of the same group. In practice, though, they tend to be separated across the organization. Due to their close relationship to technology, information-management functions tend to exist in the IT department. Business units will often separate their insights and execution teams.

The way most organizations manage fraud provides a great example. The insights team may have specialist knowledge spanning social-network analysis, predictive modeling, and anomaly detection. What they don't usually have, however, is the time to investigate suspicious events or maintain their IT and enterprise data systems. Those jobs fall to the investigations team and the information-systems department.

Once the value of an initiative has been identified, embedding the new process requires alignment. Everyone needs to be aware of the role he or she will play in both the initial rollout as well as ongoing execution. If not, things get delayed while people try to work out who is responsible for what.

Everyone may agree that a new, behaviorally based anomaly detection routine is better than the organization's current approach. Putting that new process into production requires clear direction about who is responsible for what. Someone needs to maintain the process. Someone needs to act on the resulting recommendations. Someone needs to make sure the process is taking advantage of current behaviorally based data. These roles and responsibilities need to be defined, communicated, and agreed on.

Taking into account the three groups of people, the final extended team size might be between 5 and 10 individuals spread across the organization. Given this size, coordination is relatively simple: All it takes is making sure that everyone gets together on a regular basis, usually through a checkpoint meeting or the like. These checkpoint meetings are enough to maintain momentum, drive alignment, and keep track of progress.

Over time, though, coordination ends up crowding out the time spent creating value. Initiatives spawn initiatives and eventually, what was a small-scale approach to business analytics becomes a larger-scale transformation. What was manageable with 1 or 2 projects becomes impossible when the team expands their scope to 10 or 20 projects. This complexity rises frighteningly fast.

Poor Coordination Creates Delays

The best organizations are able to develop, test, and operationally deploy their insights in three days or less. Any given initiative will usually have 1 champion model or process and up to 10 challenger models or processes. Each of these needs to be benchmarked on a rolling basis to understand how better or worse it is at driving value than the current champion process.

Efficient analysts are capable of managing hundreds of models. This gives them the scope to work on anywhere from 10 to 20 initiatives simultaneously. Although teams vary substantially in size, a typical team might have between 6 and 10 analysts reporting to an insights manager. Simple multiplication shows that a high-performing team can be involved in two hundred or more different value-creating initiatives at any point in time, and they might be managing thousands of models behind the scenes. That's a lot of insight!

To get these insights into production, the team needs to engage with business representatives, a few architects, a few operational-systems managers, a few field staff, and so on. Even if one takes into account overlapping areas of responsibility, coordination is a complex process. Organizations at this level of sophistication have to coordinate 30 to 80 people for each initiative, and this excludes the field enablement necessary to help educate operational staff on how to use this insight!

The problem with checkpoint meetings is that they can't scale. If the organization is trying to move from insight to execution in three days or less, four one-hour meetings consume over 15 percent of the total time available! Trying to manage this complexity by getting *everyone* together on a regular basis is clearly impossible.

Why Should You Care?

Organizations that struggle to coordinate their projects tend to:

- Constantly experience delays
- Feel unsure about who's responsible for what

Meetings are an essential evil. Without them, teams lose alignment and find it hard to coordinate. Unfortunately, every meeting consumes some of the finite time that's available, time that could have otherwise been spent on productive work. Good project management maintains a balance between team alignment and actually doing the work. However, as complexity and scope increases, so does the need for coordination.

Given unlimited time, this isn't a problem. Unfortunately, time isn't unlimited. People only have so much time in their week, and as that time gets filled up, meetings end up being delayed. As the business analytics team scales their scope, it becomes increasingly hard to coordinate calendars. Eventually, initiatives get delayed not because of technical challenges but because it is simply too hard to maintain momentum.

This lack of alignment manifests as uncertainty. This is a subtle, yet highly destructive force in business analytics—because business analytics involves change, it requires trust. When people are uncertain about who is responsible for what, how things will change, or how the insights will be actioned, it can be extremely hard to generate the trust necessary to change the way things work.

What Not to Do

Organizations often gravitate toward the obvious solution of scheduling checkpoint meetings well in advance to make sure everyone is available when facing these challenges. Unfortunately, this limits future efficiencies. Initially, this makes sense: If the problem is that people aren't available when they need to be, the answer must be to organize meetings even further in advance! By setting up a fixed meeting time on a regular basis, the extended team can plan around that meeting and ensure all members of the team are available.

At first, this usually works. However, it comes at a cost: It establishes a lower limit on how quickly the teams can execute. A key objective of these checkpoint meetings is normally to communicate handover points and establish what needs to be achieved before the next meeting. Although these meetings may occur every two weeks, the tasks may only take a matter of days to complete.

If the next step requires a handover to a different team, progress stops for the remaining 12 days until everyone can get together again. Teams try to manage these handover points through phone calls and e-mail, but these have varying levels of effectiveness. The golden standard is usually the meeting that explicitly defines responsibilities and outcomes for the upcoming two weeks.

Therefore, despite initial success, teams that adopt this solution usually find that they struggle to drive continuous efficiency improvements. They hit a limit on how quickly they can execute, and, short of scheduling more frequent meetings, they struggle to improve efficiency beyond that point.

The How-To Guide: Move from Meetings to Workflows

The better solution comes from establishing systems-based workflows to help coordinate teams. This approach is heavily used in other fields, such as software development, project management, and engineering. Roles and responsibilities are explicitly defined and workflow-based technology is used to keep track of progress. The system keeps track of high-level milestones (as defined by the business analytics team) along with the processes necessary to deliver the target outcomes. As individuals finish their work, they notify the system, which then automatically notifies downstream participants of their responsibilities.

A simple example lies in developing and deploying models. Minimally, these models normally requires the roles and activities described as follows:

- Business Stakeholder: Define requirements
- Advanced Analytics Modeler: Develop model
- Team Leader: Review and validate model assumptions and outputs
- Business Sponsor: Validate approach and projections
- Advanced Analytics Modeler: Deploy model into data warehouse and validate scoring outputs
- Operational IT Manager: Schedule and operationalize model
- Field Support Execution Manager: Brief field on applicability and use of operational model

This process has obviously been heavily simplified for brevity. However, it still provides a useful example on how roles and dependencies can be defined and notifications automated.

Benefits and Limitations

The biggest benefits of this approach are that it:

- Enables continuous efficiency improvements
- Reduces uncertainty in the extended team
- Makes it easier to identify bottlenecks

By decoupling delivery from checkpoint meetings, teams can move as fast as they want. Objectives can be iterated in a matter of hours rather than having to wait for the next get-together to work out what needs to be done. In practice, delivery cycles can be reduced from months to days.

Another major benefit is that documenting the overall process helps reduce uncertainty. This assists greatly with change management—the extended team can see how their individual activities are working toward a final outcome. This actively eliminates one of the major drivers behind checkpoint meetings: the need to make sure everyone is still aligned and moving in a common direction.

A side benefit of this approach is that it greatly simplifies the team's efforts to capture quantitative data on bottlenecks. Because individuals explicitly complete each activity in the overall process, every activity has an explicit start and end date. By analyzing this information, the team can better identify where bottlenecks exist and, through investigation, understand whether those bottlenecks are being caused by technical, resourcing, or other constraints.

Although this solution provides substantial advantages, it still carries a number of limitations to be aware of. One of the biggest of these is the temptation to define activities at an excessive level of detail. Every activity that needs to be checked off creates additional overhead, and being overly granular can actually start creating, rather than eliminating, inefficiencies.

Another limitation is that, although a workflow-based approach to managing analytical activities helps drive efficiency, what it does not do is provide guidance on what that workflow should look like. Organizations have different structures, different focuses, and different goals. Because a workflow is so intimately tied to how an organization does business, only the most generic workflows are generally applicable. To get the most value out of this pattern, organizations still need to make the effort to define their own approach.

ALLOCATING RESPONSIBILITIES

CASE STUDY

WHY READ THIS?

When will this help?

Read this if your team spends significant time duplicating effort across different activities.

How will it help you?

Using this approach will increase productivity and magnify differentiation.

What are the guiding principles?

- Think about competencies, not functions
- Start flexible, become structured
- Own your intellectual property
- Keep things simple

What else should you read?

- Breaking bottlenecks
- Keeping everyone aligned
- Opening the platform
- Measuring effort

The Background: Local Improvements Rarely Drive Global Efficiencies

At a minimum, every process needs to generate value. It makes a great deal of sense to make someone specifically responsible for this value. It also makes sense to charge them with driving continuous improvements. The challenge is that most processes are made up of many highly specialized activities, each of which requires different skills. Unfortunately, few people are experts in everything, and confusing the responsibility for the outcome with the responsibility to do the work behind the outcome inevitably leads to suboptimal results.

Insights Give Answers, Value Chains Drive Outcomes

In many ways, analysts are like miners. They extract insight from data, refine it into a valuable resource, and, by ensuring the right party capitalizes on it, drive economic returns. This value chain involves a series of specific activities. The team needs to source the right raw data. They need to transform that data into a form that allows them to analyze it. They need to apply a variety of techniques to interpret the data and generate insights.

Once they've found the answers they're looking for, they need to ensure that insight gets to the right people, and they need to track the results of using that insight. Teams that assign responsibilities based on these individual activities usually find that they struggle to create value. Benchmarking someone on their ability to develop a model is putting the cart before the horse; what's important is the outcome, not the asset.

Because of this, it makes sense to hold people accountable for outcomes, not assets. One team member may be given the responsibility of using customer lifetime value measures to help grow profitability. Another may become responsible for targeting cross-selling opportunities to grow share of wallet.

Behind the scenes, these value chains are still based on the same activities. The main difference is in the way their success is measured. In this context, it usually boils down to two types of measures:

1. Effectiveness

2. Efficiency

Ideally, these value chains are more effective and drive better outcomes. Analytical assets, if designed and used appropriately, should drive better operational and strategy decision making. By measuring the difference business analytics has made, the team links their effort to value.

The other side of the equation is the team's efficiency and the amount of effort the team had to expend to get there. Logically, every one of these activities carries a time cost. Developing a model may take hours or days. Structuring data could take days to weeks. In driving continuous improvement, the other major goal of the team is to minimize the amount of time it takes them to do their job.

Value Chains Are Rarely Perfectly Efficient

When starting out, teams build their value chains as efficiently as they can given time, tools, and knowledge constraints. Deadlines are never ideal. There are always better tools out there. Hindsight is always 20/20—it's easy to know what you should have done *after* you have finished the project.

Given infinite amounts of time and resources, teams would have all the time they want to refine these activities and make them as efficient as possible. In practice, relative inefficiency is the norm. Quick fixes and temporary solutions usually become permanent. When a deadline is fast approaching, spaghetti code may not be attractive but at least it'll get the job done!

Imperfect Value Chains Require Ongoing Attention

Initially, inefficiency isn't a problem. Despite relying on inelegant solutions, the team still gets the job done. It is productive, it is seen as supporting the business, and it is driving real value. Unfortunately, over time the weight of inefficiencies starts to constrain the team.

Inefficient and inelegant processes tend to be fairly brittle. Small changes in upstream systems or environmental data can create large disruptions, and fixing these issues can take significant time. When processes are hard-coded and complex, it can take a team days to unpick the process and understand why it's failing. Even worse, because these processes may span a wide range of activities, simply testing the process to see if it's fixed might take hours.

The difficult thing is that, even though there is little incremental value in repairing existing processes, the team really has no choice. A broken process creates negative value; it forces the organization to sacrifice value that it *used* to have. The more time or computational horsepower a team spends maintaining or running an existing process, the less it has to invest in new growth initiatives.

Because of this, driving continuous efficiency improvements isn't really an optional activity for a well-performing team. They *have* to do it if they're to scale their productivity and maintain existing value-creating activities. When the data sets are small and the assets few, picking things apart and optimizing them can be almost fun. When things become complex, however, these processes can become a nightmare to fix.

The Quick Fix That Took Two Weeks

One team I worked with decided that, by integrating all its data extraction and transformation routines into one massive job it would be able to greatly reduce the amount of time it needed to manually interact with its processes. Rather than having a bunch of small jobs, the team refactored its process so that the more efficient processes took approximately 36 hours to complete. Unfortunately, the warehouse's data schema had changed and, because of this, the team's newly built process would crash approximately 10 hours into the job.

Every time the team wanted to try a fix, it needed to rerun the process from scratch. Finding the right fix took quite a bit of time. In total, it took them around two weeks to fix what should have been relatively simple, not because the problem was overly difficult but because of the amount of time they spent waiting while testing.

The unfortunate side effect of this was that they were totally unproductive for all this time. Because this particular process updated their analytical datamart, the entire team had to put down their tools until they could start getting data again.

Why Should You Care?

Teams at risk of these delays usually have:

- A high proportion of undocumented or opaque processes
- Inflexible processes that prevent the team from trying different approaches
- Significant delays when processes fail

One of the classic signs of a team trapped by inefficiency is an almost total lack of understanding about what some of their processes actually do. This might seem like a gross lack of management oversight, but it's surprisingly common.

As a team experiences turnover, the people who originally developed the process move on. Some of these processes can be extremely complex and involve thousands of lines of code. Depending on their technical skill and the time they spent documenting their code, it's easy for a team to end up with a process that's automated, robust, and useful, but almost totally incomprehensible.

Monolithic processes also limit flexibility. They often cover the end-to-end value chain of information extraction, insight generation, and operational deployment. Because of this, changing something relatively minor may require profiling and debugging the entire process. Something as simple as benchmarking a decision tree against an existing logistic regression model might take two weeks' effort to profile the existing process, make the changes, and debug the results!

This complexity creates delays whenever processes fail. Understanding *why* the process failed can be an extremely time-consuming task, even if the person who originally developed the process is still employed by the team. Revisiting old work can be daunting, especially if it was never documented in the first place.

What Not to Do

The obvious solution is to go through each value chain and progressively refactor each of them. In effect, someone is given responsibility for reengineering each process. Initially, this works; even though the person has to put his or her existing work on hold to get there, he or she still normally manages to reduce the process's operating complexity. Unfortunately, over time this complexity almost always re-emerges, sometimes worse than before.

Different People Have Different Strengths

The reason behind this is simple: Similar to how doing the dishes doesn't stop new dirty dishes from appearing, reengineering existing processes does nothing to prevent new processes from being designed badly. Teams have an uneven distribution of skills, and where some people might be more sophisticated at data management, others may be better at modeling.

Because of this uneven distribution of skills, everyone ends up taking a different approach to solving problems. Given that every business-analytics value chain spans a variety of different activities, some solutions will naturally end up being more efficient than others. Unfortunately, because each value chain is owned and optimized by a different person, the quality of optimization for each activity will vary based on the individual's personal skills.

Two similar processes may be refactored independently by two different people. One of those people might be good at data management. The other may be good at building highly accurate and parsimonious models. Given these different skills, you would reasonably expect that the first process would end up with more efficient data-manipulation activities. You would also reasonably expect that the second process would end up with a more sophisticated (and hopefully accurate) model.

The catch is that, because these processes were refactored independently, it's extremely hard to replicate the best aspects of each *globally*. Instead, every process ends up with *local* optimizations aligned to the skills of the person who refactored them. Trying to cross-pollinate skills through scrums and other information-sharing sessions can help, but only to a degree. The global efficiency of any individual process is still fundamentally limited by the skills of the person refactoring it.

The How-To Guide: Allocate Responsibilities across Outcomes *and* Functions

The real solution is to separate the work from value-chain ownership. Just because someone is responsible for driving an outcome doesn't mean that the individual needs to be responsible for delivering every activity in the value chain. Instead, everyone takes ownership over two distinct responsibilities: outcomes *and* activity specializations.

The team moves from a purely outcomes-based responsibility model to a matrix of responsibilities that includes outcomes *and* functional activities. Those members of the team who are extremely knowledgeable about data management start working across *all* value chains that involve data management. Those who are highly skilled in model development start working across *all* value chains that require models.

Using this model allows people to identify and leverage commonalities between processes rather than focusing on optimizing any single process. Although SQL experts may still be responsible for specific initiatives, they'll also get involved in every project that involves data management. If they need to generate reports, they'll leverage the reporting experts. If they need to develop models, they'll leverage the modeling experts rather than try to build their own. They'll still be responsible for the outcome, they just won't be responsible for actually doing the work associated with every activity behind that outcome. By assigning activities ownership based on functional strengths, every value chain benefits from the team's efficiencies.

Benefits and Limitations

The biggest benefits of this solution lie in reusing experience and driving operational efficiencies. Best practices can be easily replicated across all activities rather than being tied to a specific value chain. This raises the bar across the board, driving global improvements rather than local improvements.

The biggest limitations usually involve management complexity and the effort needed to pick apart existing processes. Taking this matrix model of responsibilities *does* introduce additional management overhead. People need to be managed based on their ability to drive an outcome *as well as* their ability to support cross-process work.

Without the right set of performance measures, it's quite easy to direct focus too heavily toward one or the other. Too much emphasis on outcomes and people will only focus on their own processes. Too much emphasis on assets and people will forget about the importance of driving an outcome. Getting the balance right isn't easy and sometimes takes a few iterations.

There is almost inevitably some degree of reengineering that needs to occur before a team can capitalize on this approach. Existing processes are rarely functionally separated enough to make the transition easy, and simply refactoring a truly monolithic process into a more modular approach can take days or weeks! Depending on the complexity of existing processes, the effort required may be substantial. Regardless, in the long run the team rarely has any other choice if they're legitimately interested in driving global efficiencies.

OPENING THE PLATFORM

CASE STUDY

WHY READ THIS?

When will this help?
   Read this if you constantly leverage external resources instead of developing internal skills.
How will it help you?
   Using this approach will help foster competitive differentiation through business analytics.
What are the guiding principles?
- Know what you are worth
- Own your intellectual property

What else should you read?
- Encouraging innovation
- Keeping everyone aligned
- Allocating responsibilities

The Background: Outsourcing Intellectual Property Rarely Leads to Competitive Advantage

All teams face skills shortages at some point. Leveraging consultants and contractors is a great way of overcoming shortfalls and getting access to specialist know-how but it comes at a cost: Teams are rarely interested in up-skilling the members of the teams they are working with. Organizations are only ever as good as their people, and when external resources are left unchecked, their people walk off the job every time their work is finished.

There's Always More Work Than Resources

Managing a business analytics team is possibly one of the most challenging jobs out there. The skills are diverse, the problems often ill-specified, and resistance to change is a constant threat. When so much is dependent on discovery, it's hard to know what's going to work ahead of time. Guidelines are useful, but they rarely give the specificity needed to set a due date!

Largely due to this inherent uncertainty, most managers struggle with resource planning. Depending on data and the skills of the person in question, developing a model can take anywhere from three days to three months! Even worse, much of this depends on the unique characteristics of the organization. What takes days in some organizations can take months in others due to nothing more than cultural differences. Without deep, painfully won experience, it's *always* hard to translate demand into accurate resourcing plans. Take on too much, and the team will fail to deliver. Take on too little, and the team may lose relevance to the broader organization.

This combination of opportunity and uncertainty leads many teams to take on more work than they can realistically deliver. Even worse, even the best teams suffer some degree of attrition. Some people find new jobs, some people are internally poached, and some people simply aren't right for the role they're in. Although attrition may be for good reasons, it still makes this tension worse and introduces even more stress on the team.

External Resources Offer Advantages

Faced with immediate resourcing shortfalls, teams only have three options. They can hire someone new. They can leverage another resource from elsewhere in the organization. Or they can engage an external resource on a short-term basis, such as a contractor or consultant. All are pragmatic but in practice, only one is usually feasible.

Hiring more resources requires budget and headcount. If the new hire is to replace a person who left, this budget may already be available. If not, getting budget involves building a business case. This takes time, and in the meantime, the team keeps suffering. Once things are approved, hiring new staff still involves significant search costs. Depending on industry, requisite skills, and regulatory constraints, finding and hiring the right person can take anywhere from months to a year. Because of this, growing the team is usually a strategic solution rather than a tactical play.

Given these delays, it makes sense to try and use other resources within the organization. They may carry a transfer price, but they'll probably have good cultural fit. The main problem is that, although this is attractive to the team with the shortfall, it's rarely as attractive to the team that owns the resource. Using other internal resources is often blocked for political as well as pragmatic issues. In many organizations, poaching resources is seen as reducing a team's power base. Even if that's not the case, most teams are already under some degree of workload-related stress. It's a rare manager who's willing to let one of their valuable resources go and help someone else!

In practice, there's often only one option: The team needs to engage an external party. In principle, there's nothing wrong with this—one of the biggest advantages is that, by doing so, the team will get access to skills and know-how that might otherwise be difficult to source. If the team lacks operations research skills, engaging a consultant may help the team meet their commitments in the short term. In the long term, they can still look to develop optimization skills in parallel.

Unfortunately, the consultant's self-interest often undermines the potential competitive advantage of business analytics. This isn't because of malice; even the best consultants still need to put food on the table!

External Resources Are Also Self-Interested

For most consultants, their market worth is tied to their unique tools, skills, and assets. Because of this, many are unwilling to hand over their intellectual property. Although they may develop the models the organization needs, they'll rarely hand over the models themselves. Instead, they'll often only deliver the code and routines needed to score new customers or transactions.

It may seem a fine distinction, but it's an important one. On the positive side, the organization can still take advantage of operational analytics. All that's needed to deploy a scoring process are the scoring rules, not the model itself. Unfortunately, this doesn't allow future modifications. If all they have are the scoring processes, the organization loses all ability to know *how* the routines were developed in the first place. This prevents them from recalibrating or redeveloping the original models.

This is a very real and serious problem. All assets degrade with time. As things change, the predictive accuracy of all models decreases. Eventually, the predictions degrade past an acceptable level and the models produce a result no better than the best alternative. Without having access to the original model, the organization has no way of knowing *why* the predictions are degrading. If they want to profile and recalibrate the model, they need to reengage the consultant.

Obviously, this is great for consultants—it assures them of a future revenue stream! For the organization though, this costs money. If the organization has since made a significant investment in developing the competencies required to build their own models, this can seem like a waste.

There's also a second, deeper issue. Profitable consultants increase their margin by reusing assets and processes. When something works, they can magnify their profitability by reusing that same approach across multiple clients. For the organization, this negates any form of true competitive differentiation—when everyone uses the same modeling approach, everyone moves toward an average outcome.

Therefore, organizations are trapped in seemingly unresolvable situations. Short-term pressures mean that they *have* to engage external parties to deliver. By doing so, however, they lose the ability to develop any truly competitive differentiation. Even worse, they run the risk of losing access to the intellectual property they've paid for. In the end, they usually sacrifice the competitive advantage of business analytics. Instead, they regress to vendor and project management rather than driving differentiation through their use of business analytics.

Why Should You Care?

Organizations suffering from this challenge usually carry higher operating costs than organizations that have in-sourced business analytics. Their strategy ends up being dictated by their constraints rather than their opportunities. In extreme cases, this can degrade almost to the point of organizational blackmail. One organization I knew discovered this the hard way.

The Project That Turned into Corporate Blackmail

Because of a combination of a lack of skills and time, the organization had engaged an external party to develop its customer-segmentation models. This initial piece of work had been seen as a rousing success. Despite being quite expensive, the project costs were seen as being reasonable in comparison to hiring a specialist resource. Even better, the consultants had been able to turn around the work in record time. For the first year, everyone was happy.

The real issues started to crop up in the second year. The organization noticed that due to ongoing changes in its customer base, its segmentation model was no longer as useful as it once had been. All the evidence suggested that a simple recalibration would fix this. Unfortunately, the consultants had declined to hand over the internal logic within the segmentation model. Instead, they had only delivered the code needed to score and segment the organization's customer base.

The organization was a bit unsettled when it realized it had never actually acquired the intellectual property it thought it had paid for. However, the organization understood that the consultants had a business to run and so decided to go back to them.

What started as a minor issue quickly became a major one when the organization asked for a quote to recalibrate the model. Citing resource constraints and increased operational costs, the consultants came back with a project estimate that was almost double the original project!

The organization was trapped. By this time, its segmentation model had been totally embedded in their operational customer relationship management processes. Unpicking these processes wasn't an option—it would not only disrupt outbound marketing activities but it would also negatively impact the effectiveness of their marketing.

Disengaging with the consultants also carried significant costs. Replicating the existing segmentation model would have involved developing a new one from scratch. All the gains the organization had made by hiring an external party would quickly evaporate—it needed to hire the staff it had originally deferred. Even worse, this wasn't even an option. By the organization's best guess, hiring new resources was going to take longer than it had to solve their immediate issues.

In the end, the organization had no choice but to pay the exorbitant rates and sink even more money into establishing a team to try and defer the next year's gouge. Instead of managing costs, they doubled them. They had learned a very costly lesson into why outsourcing intellectual property is such a dangerous exercise in business analytics.

What Not to Do

The obvious solution is to take a hard line and never use external consultants. In practice, this is usually counterproductive. Some competencies may not generate sufficient returns to justify the team developing them. Consultants are extremely valuable *because* of their specialization; often, they can provide skills that would be otherwise impossible to affordably source. Making a blanket rule that external consultants should *never* be used only hurts the organization.

The How-To Guide: Treat Everyone as if They're Part of Your Team—Even Outsiders

The better solution is to establish an open platform and embrace external parties into the fold. Everyone, regardless of whether he or she is internal or external, follows structured processes. Rather than having everyone work independently, all resources must use a standard set of tools and ensure that their assets are registered and tracked in this central repository.

Accepting a contract to work in this environment means agreeing to follow this approach. Any external providers unwilling to register their work in the open platform should be avoided. Although this solution is staggeringly simple, it helps avoid what can be a tremendous amount of exposure.

Benefits and Limitations

The biggest benefits of this approach are that the organization retains its intellectual property, ensures it can capitalize on it in the future, and maintains the opportunity to drive competitive advantage through its use of business analytics. Even though its models may initially be very similar to those used by other organizations, it retains the ability to develop differentiation through innovation and creativity.

The biggest limitation of this approach usually involves resistance from certain consultants unwilling to sacrifice what could otherwise be a lucrative revenue stream. Although there may be valid reasons to resist using the centralized platform (such as a lack of specific functionality), these complaints should generally be viewed with skepticism. A good consultant knows that strong relationships do more to drive an ongoing business partnership than blackmail.

PART FOUR

Practical Solutions: Systems and Assets

A business analytics team without the right tools is a like a carpenter without a saw. It can still get the job done; it will just take a lot longer than it should.

Getting appropriate tools isn't hard. It just requires investment. Rather than make the required investment, many teams are willing to compromise and do what's easy rather than what's right. Not only does this hinder their efforts to scale, it creates an upper limit on the level of sophistication they can apply.

Driving higher-quality outcomes requires organizations to take a structured and appropriate approach to platform architecture and asset management. Without this, they run the risk of creating too much or too little structure. The following chapters focus on how best to leverage purpose-built tools, how to manage the resulting assets, and how to establish a measurement framework that covers value, performance, and effort.

CHAPTER 8

Computational Architectures

Making the most out of one's technology requires aligning use to context. Not everyone needs the most powerful tools in the world. Everyone, however, needs purpose-built tools if they're to succeed. Using a motorbike when one needs a truck is a recipe doomed to failure.

Technology can be baffling even to those comfortable with advanced analytics. Most organizations struggle with:

- Using inappropriate tools simply because they're available.
- Getting access to the processing horsepower they need to solve increasingly hard problems.
- Working in environments in which they need to be mobile but share their work with others.
- Driving down platform maintenance costs.

The solutions described in the next section focus on techniques and approaches to overcome these challenges.

MOVING BEYOND THE SPREADSHEET

WHY READ THIS?

When will this help?

Read this if your analytics capabilities are tied to spreadsheets.

How will it help you?

Using this approach will help you start the journey toward being an analytical competitor.

What are the guiding principles?

- Drive outcomes, not insight
- Automate everything non-value-added
- Minimize custom development
- Keep things simple

What else should you read?

- Scaling past the PC
- Staying mobile and connected
- Moving to operational analytics
- Understanding the data value chain
- Creating data-management processes

The Background: What's Easy Isn't Necessarily Right

Analysis has never been easier—tools such as spreadsheets have become commodities. Unfortunately, being available isn't the same thing as being effective; spreadsheets, when inappropriately used, generate more problems than they solve. Although it's tempting for a team to leverage what's easily available when they're getting started with business analytics, taking the path of least resistance runs a significant risk of future pain and expensive mistakes.

Spreadsheets Have Transformed Business

Spreadsheets are a blessing and a curse. When VisiCalc launched in 1983, spreadsheets became a business killer app. By providing a table-based structure with none of the rigidity of a traditional database, they made it easy for millions of analysts to analyze data. They were the first tool that made it possible for a relatively nontechnical user base to pull structured information together, do analysis, and share the results visually. It's an interesting commentary on the flexibility of modern spreadsheet software that people have successfully demonstrated that many are actually Turing-complete in their own right![1]

If anything, the flexibility of spreadsheets has actually increased over time. Scripting and programming languages have only made it easier to do even more advanced forms of analysis. If an existing function isn't available, developers can add it to their library of favored functions by coding it themselves.

Given this flexibility, apparent power, and ease of use, it's not surprising that most businesses run on spreadsheets. It's telling that one of the first things drilled into newly hired graduates is usually learning how to use spreadsheets! Given the prevalence of skills, sheer availability of commodity software, and breadth of options when it comes to analytical functions, why *not* use them as the primary desktop-analytics tool?

It's a good question. The first thing to remember is that there's a difference between analytics and business analytics. If the goal is analytics, spreadsheets might be the right tool—the decision about whether a spreadsheet is a good fit becomes one largely based on functional requirements and available skills.

If, however, the goal is business analytics, the answer is a little more complex. The general consensus is that, in the main, they're a poor substitute for dedicated tools and often create more problems than they solve, but it's rare to find a reason for this. Given that spreadsheets offer so many advantages, it's not always immediately apparent why they're good for analytics in some situations but almost never for business analytics.

Spreadsheets Are a Poor Fit for Business Analytics

There are many reasons that spreadsheets drive poor outcomes in business analytics. Their advanced analytics algorithms aren't always implemented correctly. They have no in-built ability to keep track of different document versions and revisions. They introduce typographical errors and can introduce transposition errors, and historically they have been relatively inflexible when it comes to presenting information. These are major limitations, but the real reason not to use them for business analytics goes deeper.

Spreadsheets are a poor fit because more than anything else, they limit scalability. Because of that, they destroy one of the key competitive advantages offered by business analytics. Their inability to scale stems from three limitations—they:

- Introduce needless complexity
- Create significant management overhead
- Limit an organization's ability to automate processes

The beauty of spreadsheets is that anything's possible. That's also their main problem. If you are simply playing around, there's no issue. If, however, you are making recommendations that will impact operational activities, those recommendations need some form of oversight. Flexibility with limited governance is a recipe for complexity and risk. In principle, spreadsheets could be as highly governed as any other strongly defined process. The problem is that they require a disproportionate amount of active oversight compared to their alternatives.

Although it's possible to do an exhaustive audit, this rarely happens in practice with any consistency. The sheer cost needed to prevent issues usually creates an unrealistic burden on the team; auditing a complex spreadsheet can take days of cross-checking calculations and cell references. Even when they *are* audited, it's depressingly easy to miss simple logic errors.

Instead, development is left unchecked, and, almost inevitably, the result is a mess of undocumented data and processes that are virtually impossible to pick apart. For most organizations, this is business as usual. Many have tremendous amounts of intellectual property locked up in spreadsheets, most of which represents truly lost knowledge.

One of the most extreme examples I've seen involved hundreds of sheets spread across tens of files stored on a network drive, each of which was linked by cascading calculations. It was bad enough that it was realistically impossible to audit these calculations. Even worse, simply opening them up successfully needed a good hour, lots of knowledge about where to start, and more than a little bit of luck! The worst thing of all was that the person who had originally created this mess had since found a new job. He had left the organization with a large number of assets, all of which had unknown worth and arguably could no longer be used by the organization for which they had been designed.

Spreadsheets Are Hard to Audit and Reuse

The best way to manage risk is to make processes repeatable and auditable. A key prerequisite is defining standard processes and ensuring compliance to those processes. The easiest way to do this is to hard code it into the system; rather than tell everyone what to do, simply make it impossible to do anything that isn't allowed. For this reason, databases do data validity checking prior to updating their master data store. This also applies in most operational systems; they conduct basic to advanced forms of data assessment to ensure information is correct prior to execution, and, most organizations extensively use workflows to make sure appropriate sign-offs are obtained before decisions are executed.

Inherently, spreadsheets offer none of these systems-based controls. Although some provide the basic toolkits to develop them, it's up to the users to create them. This forces one of two approaches. Either the team needs to invest time developing these controls *or* they need to invest time to audit the results before they're executed. In practice, neither usually occurs, again largely for reasons of cost and time.

Another horror story involved a company I worked with that had based multimillion-dollar investment decisions on a series of highly complex spreadsheets. These spreadsheets incorporated everything from custom code right through to Monte Carlo simulations for boundary testing. In isolation, this wasn't a problem. It's very possible that the calculations were correct. However, the company hadn't been willing to invest the staggering amount of time that was needed to audit the spreadsheet and ensure the results were accurate.

When I foolishly took on this unenviable task, I eventually found out that a variety of calculations had been incorrectly entered. This had generated a result that was orders of magnitude incorrect. Luckily, I discovered the error before they had committed the money. I imagine they would have been rather disappointed to find out that their investments would have been underperforming against expectations by tens of millions of dollars!

Spreadsheets Can't Easily Be Automated

Time and cost are great reasons *not* to use spreadsheets for business-analytics purposes. The final reason is that spreadsheets rarely support automation. This, more than the other two issues, is the most damaging. Effective business analytics involves turning discovery-based insights into operationally executable insights. These need to be integrated with other decisioning and activity management systems.

Spreadsheets can't do any of this in any meaningful way. They don't inherently support automation or offer the ability to integrate with other operational systems. Because of this, their use regresses business analytics into simple analytics, thereby nullifying any potential for competitive advantage.

To understand the significance of this, it's important to make a distinction between automating activities and creating an automated process. Most spreadsheets offer varying levels of support for automating activities. Highly repetitive tasks such as copying and pasting information from one sheet to another can be recorded and replayed. This can make a complex task as easy as clicking on a button.

Unfortunately, this is only half the picture. The more important part is the ease with which the entire process can be embedded within another process and used noninteractively. This may seem somewhat confusing; after all, most spreadsheets can automate a great deal!

A good practical example lies in estimating customer profitability levels. Knowing a customer's profitability is often a key input into working out which customers should receive higher attention. Rather than throwing more money at nonprofitable customers, it makes a lot more sense to try and make the more profitable customers happy.

These profitability estimates are usually based on a number of complex calculations. Common inputs include the cost of the services they use, the margins they provide from the products they've purchased or used, and the total volume of products the customer currently holds.

As behavioral patterns change with time, the results will change on a regular basis as customers change their product holdings.

This information is extremely valuable at an operational level. By including this information in the organization's customer-relationship management systems, call-center operators can make better decisions about how aggressively they should try to retain different customers. A highly profitable customer thinking of leaving is probably worth more effort than a customer that costs the company money! This, in turn, drives differentiated treatment. For example, it might be worth offering them a higher discount than normal.

To make this process work, it needs two things. Firstly, it needs to be integrated with the operational system. Secondly, it needs to handle constantly changing source data. This is where spreadsheets fall apart. Few (if any) spreadsheets offer native integration into operational systems. The same goes for using a push-based approach to refresh data automatically as source data changes. Instead, the spreadsheet needs to be reopened, the data refreshed, and the results exported to a predefined location. The operational system can then pick up the latest recommendations.

This presents a major problem. Because the process can't be automated, insight-generating processes inherently can't scale. To run it more frequently, the team needs more people, and people are generally expensive.

Organizations that rely on spreadsheets as their insight-generating toolkit may generate useful insights. However, they normally struggle to move from analytics to business analytics. When they base their approach on spreadsheets, they inevitably find that they create cost, increase risk, and eliminate one of the major sources of competitive advantage from business analytics.

Why Should You Care?

Diagnosing a firm suffering from spreadsheet hell is almost comically easy: Ask anyone where a particular number came from and if they struggle to answer, they're usually relying on spreadsheets to generate their insights. If you're feeling cruel, ask how they manage their assets. If they point to the shared network drive and talk about file-naming standards, they probably have a problem.

Another common symptom is infrequent asset review and maintenance. Once created, spreadsheets are usually left to stagnate with no defined retirement point. This creates cruft and adds cost. Once they are creating negligible value and are at the end of their lifecycle, spreadsheets should be retired and archived or deleted. Usually though, they continue to exist on shared drives indefinitely, like the zombies they are, consuming storage and breeding confusion.

Over and above the irritations just described, this creates some very serious problems. Spreadsheets substantially increase operational risk. Unless everything is exhaustively audited, it's frighteningly easy to make bad decisions on bad data. This can cost very real money and, in some cases, lead to criminal liabilities.

They also increase cost. When everything needs to be created from scratch, even the simplest things can take far longer than they should. This carries both an opportunity cost as well as a real cost. On one hand, that time could have been better spent elsewhere. On the other, organizations will often invest good money after bad, hiring temporary staff or additional permanent staff. This may help resolve the *perceived* problem, one of having too much work to do with too few staff members. It rarely helps solve the *real* problem, though: The organization is using inappropriate tools.

A final problem to be aware of is that spreadsheets create artificial constraints on what's possible. What works well with hundreds of records might not scale to deal with hundreds of thousands or even billions of records. Although the core approach may be logical and appropriate, the tool itself becomes the limitation. This prevents the organization from delivering what it should otherwise be able to do.

What Not to Do

The most obvious answer is also the wrong one: Buy additional modules that extend the functionality offered by the spreadsheet! The logic seems sound. If the spreadsheet can't do something, why not upgrade the spreadsheet by extending it?

In a small set of situations this makes sense. If the goal is research, the answer may be as simple as having the right algorithm. In this case, the spreadsheet is largely irrelevant. Once the analysts have the answer they need, their work is largely throwaway.

If the goal is business analytics, however, updating the spreadsheet is a major misstep. In the long run, it drives little (if any) real competitive advantage. Even though the spreadsheet can now do even more forms of advanced processing, it still lacks automation, governance, and effective information management capabilities.

Even worse, this additional functionality is normally only understood by the person who implemented it. If that person writes the documentation they should be writing, this isn't a problem. Unfortunately, spreadsheets rarely get this level of process control, which is to say, the knowledge ends up with the person, not within the asset. When that person leaves or moves on to a different role, the organization's ability to leverage their approach normally disappears with them.

The How-To Guide: Use the Right Tools for the Job, Not Just What's On-Hand

The better solution involves using purpose-built tools. The best tools support tactical requirements *as well as* those characteristics that foster competitive advantage. More specifically, the tools at a minimum need to:

- Separate data from logic
- Solve today's as well as tomorrow's problems
- Support automation

One of the ways that spreadsheets simplify analysis is by blending data with logic. Broadly speaking, calculations and raw data are treated the same. Every sheet can include raw data, calculations, charts, and even programming code.

This blending has a number of advantages. For one, it makes it easy for nontechnical people to manipulate information. Because everything is extremely flexible and largely unstructured, users can throw things together however they wish. Planning overhead is kept to a minimum and there are few rules to learn. This makes it easy for *anyone* to get started.

Another advantage of blending data with logic is that it's very easy to come up with a solution to many problems. Faced with a problem and armed with a spreadsheet, there's always more than one way to solve it. It's just a case of doing whatever you are most comfortable with, even if it's not the most efficient approach. Getting the right answer may be as manual as copying and pasting numbers into adjacent cells to make a comparison. Or it may be as complex as writing a series of macros that do automatic comparisons across multiple sheets.

This flexibility starts as a blessing but ends up a curse. It tends to strongly discourage reuse of existing data assets: Because data and logic are usually combined into one inseparable asset (the spreadsheet), it's hard to reuse existing data for a different analysis. Instead, the data will usually be copied into a new spreadsheet, duplicating information. Over time, this substantially increases the risk of getting bad results as spreadsheets proliferate. If numbers for a previous period are adjusted, hundreds of spreadsheets may need to be updated.

Although it's technically possible to establish links between spreadsheets to ensure referential integrity, this creates complexity and rarely works perfectly. In many ways, it's similar to trying to bolt multiple trailers onto a car to increase its ability to carry passengers. It may work, but it is better just to use a bus in the first place.

Separate Data from Logic

The first step in picking the right tools involves choosing those that deliberately separate data from logic. Raw and processed information should be stored in tables that can be reused across multiple problems. The business logic needed to solve each problem is then separated from these tables.

This drives a major point of efficiency: information reuse. The net results are substantially reduced complexity and risk. Because information is only stored once but reused multiple times, the odds of any single person incorrectly duplicating data drop significantly.

Use Scalable Tools

The tools also need to be able to scale with the problems being considered. This doesn't mean that everyone needs super-computer-grade software from day one. Depending on the problem, this is probably overkill!

What it does mean, however, is that the team members need to make an informed assessment about how much their processing requirements are likely to scale over the next few years. Without some degree of foresight, it's very easy to become trapped by your tools. What works well today may not scale to deal with tomorrow's problems.

This may not seem like an issue worth considering today. It's tempting to think that if at some point the tools no longer perform adequately, it's just a case of moving to tools that do at that point in time. This is a mistake. In theory, tools are substitutable. In practice, function often defines form. Over time, everyone develops their own approaches to make their jobs easier. Because processes and tools are tightly coupled, these processes become defined by the tools that were used to create them.

When the wrong tools are selected at the beginning, a team's assets and processes eventually become a serious constraint. Because they're based on tools that no longer scale, migrating to new tools requires extensive process reengineering. Every asset and process often needs to be re-created using the new tools.

This takes time and costs money. Unless there's a pressing need to fundamentally change the way people do their jobs, it's usually the path of least resistance to keep doing business as usual. Rather than treat the tool's constraints as a fixable problem, the team gives up and assumes the constraints are hard limitations. The better solution involves picking tools that offer enough scalability to deal with current as well as future problems. This applies both in terms of scale and scope. The team members need to be able to scale as the information they'll be processing increases. Otherwise, no matter how good they are, they will only ever be working on stop-gap solutions.

The tools also need to offer sufficient functional breadth to solve new problems as they emerge. Different problems may require different techniques if they are to be solved and ideally, the tools in use should support both current and future requirements. Otherwise, the team ends up with "one of everything" to cover their breadth of problems. This application creep increases complexity and risk.

Build around Automation

The final thing to remember is that effective tools need to support process automation. It matters little whether this is through metadata-aware assets, recording tasks, scripting, or fully developed programming languages. The important thing is that the people doing the analysis can translate their activities into an asset that can be run unattended.

This is essential in driving economies of scale. Because it also encourages structured processes, it also reduces overall risk. Structured repeatable tasks are easier to audit. If and when the people move into different roles, the processes they've built can continue to operate until other individuals come up to speed with their jobs.

Benefits and Limitations

The biggest benefit to getting off spreadsheets is that the organization significantly reduces both complexity and risk. Their total asset volume declines substantially and the currency of their assets improves. Most important of all, their information accuracy tends to increase.

The major limitations revolve around training, capital investment, and cultural change. New tools require new skills, and without adequate training, people will gravitate back to what they're familiar with. Furthermore, those new tools may or may not be free. Open source offers a variety of free options, but if they don't meet the organization's required use cases, they have no choice but to source commercial software. This obviously comes at a cost and needs to be budgeted for.

Finally, this often represents the first step toward developing a competitive advantage through the use of business analytics. As such, it requires change. The team may need to be convinced that the new approach is better than the old. This can be met with cultural resistance. If this isn't managed, the team will regress to business as usual, nullifying any hope of competitive differentiation through an information advantage.

SCALING PAST THE PC

CASE STUDY

WHY READ THIS?

When will this help?

Read this if everyone in your team uses different tools and struggles to share their knowledge.

How will it help you?

Using this approach will help you drive economies of scale and scope.

What are the guiding principles?

- Think about competencies, not functions
- Start flexible, become structured
- Eliminate bottlenecks
- Always have a plan B
- It's better to have too much data than too little

What else should you read?

- Augmenting operational systems
- Coping with information overload
- Staying mobile and connected
- Smoothing growth with the cloud
- Moving to operational analytics
- Creating the data architecture
- Capturing the right data
- Reducing time to recommendation
- Enabling real-time scoring
- Blending rules with models

The Background: Scale Takes More Than Just Making Sure Everyone Uses the Same Tools

As teams grow, their scope of operations increases. This increase in coverage offers many more opportunities for the team to reuse their know-how and assets. The catch is that, unless all members of the team work off a common framework, it's often just too hard to try and reuse one another's work.

Growth Comes with a Need to Scale

Insight is addictive; the more the organization knows, the more it wants to know. However, insight doesn't magically appear. Someone needs to create it. This puts a lot of pressure on the people responsible for generating insights. The demand for their time greatly outstrips their availability and, almost inevitably, they become completely saturated. They become overworked and stressed.

They fight for more staff and, eventually, their requests are granted. At this stage, the team's enthusiasm is often sky-high: They have a common purpose, they're growing, and the organization is fully behind them. With investment, however, comes obligation and the team needs to start creating value as quickly as possible.

Despite having tremendous momentum, this is a challenging time for many teams. Because it's so new, there's no business as usual to improve on. Instead, team members need to define their operating procedures from scratch. They need to acclimatize to a new cultural environment and become familiar with the organization's business model. They need to establish an operating model that incorporates more than just support. Ideally, it needs to establish how to engage skills, drive technology reuse, and leverage common data.

Groups Are More Than Just Collections of Individuals

An immediate priority is usually getting access to appropriate tools. To keep things simple, all team members are often given the freedom to choose their own tools. This seems to make sense; after all, if they've been hired for their experience, it makes sense to capitalize on their existing knowledge as much as possible.

Despite seeming to be a safe decision, this is actually a costly mistake. At first, everything seems fine. All members of the team choose their own tools and they get to work. Admittedly, there's little overlap between these tools, but that doesn't seem to matter—productivity levels increase, the team gets results, and everyone is happy.

These short-term results, however, usually mask a very serious problem: The team's manager has no idea what their team is up to. Because everyone is using different tools and following different processes, it becomes extremely hard for the manager to understand what the team is working on or how well the team as a whole is keeping up with planned delivery schedules. In a perfect world, this isn't a problem—the team is professional enough to manage its own time and deliver to schedule. The problem is that when things start to fall behind, the first time the manager will know about it is usually just after a critical milestone was missed.

This operational risk is bad enough, but what's even worse is that the team ends up spending far too much time managing information. Despite significant overlaps in the information generated and used by the team, team members reuse little. Instead of generating insight, the team spends almost all its time manipulating data.

Desktop processing almost inevitably drives inefficiency. Because everyone works totally independently, information-management processes end up being linked to the PC, not to the system. The processes are stored on individual PCs or in arcane folders on the shared network drives. Because of this lack of cohesion, it's a frustrating and time-consuming exercise for team members to work out where the information they need is stored.

Rather than make the effort to reuse assets, team members will ignore what is there and regenerate what they need from scratch. It's just too hard to try anything else. This wastes valuable time and consumes needless storage.

Why Should You Care?

The most common symptom of this problem is an almost total lack of process transparency. Everyone does his or her own thing and there's little, if any, commonality in approach. Even worse, everyone uses different tools for the same activity. Even if two people realize they are reinventing the wheel, the fact that they are using different tools means they can't reuse each other's assets. This makes it almost impossible to drive continuous improvement—if everyone uses different tools, the only way to reuse processes is to re-create them in each tool. This is extremely resource-intensive and inefficient.

The problems don't stop there. Using a wide variety of different desktop tools usually increases the team's operating costs. Because data needs to be duplicated in a variety of different file formats, the team ends up carrying excessively high storage costs. The team's choice of tools also leads to high support costs or, even worse, no support whatsoever.

If that wasn't bad enough, everyone ends up developing his or her own approach. Because of this, the insights and skills of one team member are almost totally nontransferable to other team members. Rather than having to learn one tool, everyone needs to learn as many tools as there are team members. This makes skill improvement extremely difficult and stifles innovation.

What Not to Do

The most obvious solution naturally involves making sure all team members are using the same tools. On the positive, this at least reduces support costs and capitalizes on the skills and processes that have already been developed. Even though it's a small step, rationalizing tools does actually drive some efficiencies. Unfortunately, it does little to help with driving economies of scale. Because processing still occurs on the desktop, the team still carries significant transaction costs. Desktop PCs and operational analytics do not mix well.

Although team members might be able to automate some of their personal activities, their desktop PCs lack sufficient reliability to integrate with the organization's operational systems. The only way to schedule a job is to make sure their PCs are left on. This is somewhat less than ideal. Something as simple as a cleaner accidentally knocking out a power cable with a vacuum cleaner overnight might delay a job by over 24 hours!

Another major limitation is that assets are still linked to the individual. Although purpose-built tools may make it easier to transform insights into assets, the use of desktop PCs means that these assets are inevitably distributed across a number of different file systems and environments.

Some members of the team may store their assets on their personal PCs. Some may store them on the shared network drive. Some may store them in the enterprise knowledge-management system. Without creating and maintaining a manual asset register, it's almost inevitable that some of these assets will be lost over time.

Desktop PCs also carry relatively high support costs. If anything goes wrong, it's up to the individual to solve the problem. Although this may provide a level of comfort, it can also introduce significant delays. A colleague of mine once spent over a week trying to determine why his PC would crash every time he ran a certain job. After extensive testing and investigation, he finally determined that it was due to a faulty RAM module in his PC. Although I'm sure he got a great deal of satisfaction out of his masterful investigation skills, you could probably argue that that might not have been the best use of a highly skilled mathematician's time.

The Desktop Catastrophe

Overall, the team suffers because members can't learn from one another and, even when they can, they can't move to operational analytics. There's no better example than a colleague of mine who didn't believe me when I suggested that he might want to reconsider his approach. He had been using some specific tools for almost a decade and, while he was extremely comfortable with them, they had only ever been designed to run interactively on a PC. Every time he wanted to refresh his models, he needed to open up his application and manually rerun his projects.

When I checked in with him a few weeks later, he had a smug look on his face. Through some highly inventive scripting, he'd managed to automate his work. He'd exhaustively tested it on his PC. Somehow, he'd even convinced IT to pick his results up from a shared folder at a specific time and have them delivered straight into the organization's planning systems. More than anything else, I think he was looking forward to proving me wrong.

The concept was good. Sadly, the execution wasn't. He did a great job taking care of the things under his control. Unfortunately, he'd forgotten to take into account the things he *couldn't* control.

His process was supposed to run overnight. In the morning, their planning systems should have had the latest forecasts. This didn't quite go as planned. Over the first month, his process failed because:

- His PC went to sleep and his job failed to start.
- The network connectivity between his PC and the server degraded because of an overnight data management run.
- The janitor turned off his PC while trying to help the company save money.
- His network mappings disappeared and his jobs failed to start.
- The data created by his systems was incorrectly formatted, causing the planning system to abort the import.

After a month of intermittent failures, IT pulled the plug on the project and started looking for other solutions.

The How-To Guide: Drop the Desktop and Move to a Common Platform

The true solution is very straightforward. It involves moving from a desktop processing model to a client/server processing model. The team establishes a dedicated environment with established support structures.

This centralizes processing, assets, and information storage. The team then interacts with this server through the use of one or more purpose-built desktop clients that do little to no processing locally. The personal computer becomes an entirely replaceable dumb terminal with no local data storage whatsoever. This helps on a number of fronts beyond simple risk management and support.

Benefits and Limitations

First, it helps drive economies of scale. Because the environment can be designed with high availability in mind, the team can confidently leverage automation and start integrating their insights into operational systems. This reduces the effort and time needed for business-as-usual activities. Usually, this simply involves automatically delivering results and predictions into the enterprise warehouse where they can be exposed to other downstream systems.

Second, it helps centralize assets in one location. Most server-based tools support some degree of asset management, whether in the form of a true asset register with check-in/check-out functionality or simply a shared metadata-driven repository. Rather than being spread across numerous file and content management systems, the team can establish a mandate that all assets and data must be registered in the central environment.

Finally, using a common platform helps drive data reuse. By having access to a shared storage environment, the team can establish a true analytical data mart. This the first step in the ongoing process of minimizing time spent managing information.

A key limitation is that this approach requires giving up some degree of freedom. The team needs to start interacting with other groups and formalizing activities and relationships. One of the attractions of running software on a PC is that it requires little to no involvement with other groups such as IT. The team is effectively free to do whatever it wants as long as it has the technical skills to support it.

Moving to a client/server environment is often where transaction costs first become apparent. Acquiring the software and provisioning the platform is often the first real experience many business analytics teams have with formalized IT systems, and their experience is usually not a positive one.

The simple reality is that, left unchecked, business analytics tend toward ill-defined and flexible processes. Although this may work within the context of insight generation, it rarely works when it comes to building bulletproof processes and systems.

Coming to terms with this level of formality is an essential step for teams looking to generate a true competitive advantage through business analytics. Certain activities, such as operational analytics, require this formality if they are to avoid breaking operational systems. As such, giving up these freedoms should not be seen as a problem. It's the necessary price of entry to turning business analytics into a competitive differentiator.

STAYING MOBILE AND CONNECTED

CASE STUDY

WHY READ THIS?

When will this help?

Read this if you have some people who need to stay mobile but can't guarantee network reliability.

How will it help you?

Using this approach will help you keep them productive without having to sacrifice reuse.

What are the guiding principles?

■ Start flexible, become structured

■ Design your platform for use, not purity

What else should you read?

■ Opening the platform

■ Scaling past the PC

The Background: When the Job Runs Up against Systems Architecture, Architecture Always Loses

Centralizing processing helps drive reuse and cost efficiencies. Unfortunately, it assumes that everyone using that central environment will have consistent access to it. This isn't always the case, and when this core assumption breaks down, even the best analysts can become totally unproductive if they don't have an alternative option available.

Mobile Resources, Centralized Facilities

The move to client/server computing fundamentally revolves around sacrificing control for productivity. Making this change is rarely easy. When people have to sacrifice control, they usually react with fear and uncertainty. Eventually though, things settle down and the world moves on. In most situations, this is the end of it; under the guidance of a leader with a clear vision, the team progressively moves toward best practice. However, there are a few specific situations in which this pure model doesn't quite fit, and resistance, rather than being based on fear, is actually justified.

In order to be effective, the client/server model needs constant and reliable network connectivity. In many situations, it's simply a case of setting up a virtual private network (VPN) and using a local network connection as if it were directly connected to the organization's network.

This works well when connectivity can be guaranteed. However, this isn't always the case. To minimize overhead given a mobile workforce, some organizations hot-desk or hotel, and depending on their network configuration, not every seat may have adequate connectivity. Some organizations force their workers to telecommute and, depending on where they live, it may be hard to guarantee sufficient bandwidth for certain applications or data transfers. Some people simply can't connect at all: people working with highly remote clients often can't even get access to a mobile signal!

Because the client computer is effectively a dumb terminal, network interruptions are more than inconvenient. When they occur, they render all remote resources unproductive. High-speed cell-phone technologies such as third and fourth generation (3G and 4G) standards usually offer sufficient speed and coverage for most applications. However, these come at a high cost, especially if there is substantial data transfer to and from the server. To those unaware, these costs can be nasty trap.

The Trauma of Bill Shock

A great example lies in a colleague of mine whose job involved extensive international travel. Because of the nature of his work, he needed to be able to guarantee voice and data connectivity on his travels.

Normally, he tried to manage this with a mobile Wi-Fi hotspot paired with a SIM card from the country he was in. Although this generally worked, it required a great deal of effort and coordination. When his mobile phone was upgraded to a 3G smartphone with the ability to tether with his laptop, he thought all his problems were solved.

Before he left for his first week-and-a-half-long trip after getting his new phone, he gave his provider a call and enabled international roaming. In retrospect, this wasn't the greatest idea. When he returned, he came back to a phone bill around $10,000. Although he *could* tether his phone with an international 3G-grade connection, actually using it wasn't quite as affordable as he thought it would be!

This presents an interesting dilemma. On one hand, people still need to be able to process and analyze information with their standard tools, regardless of where they are. Unfortunately, regressing back to a pure desktop-processing model is clearly a step backward. On the other though, the classic client/server model clearly does not work. It may be too expensive or it may even be totally infeasible. As hard as it is to believe, there are still quite a few areas around the planet where the only high-speed communication options are still expensive satellites!

Why Should You Care?

The symptoms are highly straightforward: Staff members struggle to access the server environment reliably. This impacts their productivity and prevents them from achieving their targeted objectives; even the best analysts become ineffective when they are prevented from accessing their tools! Notably, this does not apply to local staff, even if they are remote to where the server is hosted. If connectivity is an issue for local staff, this solution does not apply—there are fundamental network connectivity issues that should be resolved first.

What Not to Do

The default solution is simply to regress back to desktop processing. This *is* actually half of the solution. If staff cannot work because of network connectivity issues while remote, the only realistic answer is to give them the ability to do local processing. Critically, though, going back to the old approach will actively undermine many of the advantages offered by client/server computing. Assets are linked to the person/PC, and it is hard to drive efficiency or economies of scope.

The How-To Guide: Allow Desktop Processing, but Grant It with Conditions

Ideally, people working remotely still connect to the server using virtual private networks (VPNs) or the like. If this is impractical, there is only one real solution: Give them the ability to do local processing. Significantly, though, a key restriction is that they have the ability (and are mandated) to migrate their assets and data sets back to the server environment as soon as they gain local connectivity. Because this creates overhead, it is usually ignored. However, it is an absolutely critical activity if organizations are to drive economies of scale.

This is often more complex than it might seem. It's obvious that the models need to be migrated back into the server environment. What's sometimes not so obvious is that all the data preprocessing also needs to be migrated back into the server environment. This often involves remapping data sources from the local PC back to the warehouse, an activity that takes time and effort.

Benefits and Limitations

The major benefit of this approach is that the organization sacrifices none of the advantages of client/server computing, despite giving specific individuals the ability to do local processing.

On the other hand, the major limitation of this approach is that it creates additional overhead on those doing the work. They not only need to generate the right insights but they also need to migrate all their processes back into the centralized environment. This creates a very real need for management oversight. Unless good processes are enforced, the team will sacrifice many of the advantages of centralized processing.

SMOOTHING GROWTH WITH THE CLOUD

CASE STUDY

WHY READ THIS?

When will this help?

Read this if upgrading your processing and storage platform is consistently too expensive to justify.

How will it help you?

Using this approach will help you scale as you need, rather than wait until you have a crisis.

What are the guiding principles?

(Continued)

- Design your platform for use, not purity
- Always have a plan B
- It's better to have too much data than too little

What else should you read?

- Scaling past the PC
- Reducing time to recommendation

The Background: Platform Upgrades Are Costly and Disruptive

As teams scale their activities, they need increasing amounts of processing power. Eventually, their needs surpass their processing capacity and they are forced to upgrade their computational platform. Unfortunately, this isn't an easy process—by the time they've solved all the issues that go along with extending their platform, they may be too late.

Processing Requirements Eventually Outstrip Capacity

Formalized systems require strong governance to work effectively. Without governance, they regress back to chaos. This governance implies greater cost—it requires more management and greater administration costs. Strongly governed systems have another major disadvantage: They limit flexibility and changes need to be planned well in advance. Every change to a well-governed process or system needs an extensive impact analysis. Each one needs to be reviewed to make sure it doesn't conflict or undermine other activities or applications within the process or system.

This is especially true within a common analytical platform. A simple patch can bring entire processes down if that patch disables functionality already in use. Making sure that every patch, upgrade, or modification is safe requires teams to go through extensive unit, integration, and systems testing. These tests can't happen overnight—they must be planned well in advance. When business analytics is limited to a single specific problem, this is rarely an issue. Functionality is limited and the team's needs are both well understood and easily predicted. When their scope of operations expands, however, things become more complicated.

Each team that comes onto the environment increasingly overloads the server. More people lead to greater contention, which, in turn, leads to performance impacts. At first, this may not be an issue, especially if the server was designed with sufficient overhead to handle problems that were out of the ordinary.

However, as the number of problems being solved on the platform increases, this contention eventually reaches an unacceptable level. Jobs take too long to complete, and the business starts to lose agility. Even worse, some problems may be so large that they can't be solved by the existing platform. At some stage, this reaches a point where there's no longer a choice: The organization *needs* to upgrade the environment if it's to keep driving value from business analytics.

Managing this migration creates a whole host of challenges that carry significant risks. However, not all of these are a foregone conclusion—smarter organizations are able to mitigate some of these challenges through effective design and intelligent architecture.

Platform Migration Is Risky

Although processes vary by organization, migrating from one environment to another usually involves five high-level activities:

1. Designing the new platform
2. Deploying the new platform
3. Migrating to the new platform
4. Testing the new platform
5. Retiring the old platform

Designing the new platform carries significant risks—the architecture team needs to make a best guess about how big the environment needs to be. This estimate not only needs to support the current known requirements but also any future requirements. If they underspecify the platform, the pains will reemerge in a relatively short period of time. If they overspecify the platform, they'll carry excessive opportunity cost and may even run over budget. Because Moore's law[2] says that hardware costs will come down over time, they probably would have achieved a more cost-effective outcome had they waited and upgraded at a later date.

Deploying the platform takes time. One consideration is the amount of time needed to provision new hardware and software. This, relatively speaking, is usually fairly fast. The more challenging consideration is the time needed to coordinate all the parties that need to be involved. Depending on the size and complexity of the organization, this might include the business (for user acceptance testing), the IT department, the outsourced platform support team, and the outsourced application support team, not to mention all the vendors involved with the change. In some cases, this can take up to a year of advance notice!

Once the platform is up and running, all the organization's existing assets need to be migrated from the old to the new. This can be a challenging and time-consuming process, especially in complex environments. Not only that, but the organization is also forced to carry double the support costs for as long as the two platforms operate in parallel. Every asset on the platform then needs to be validated and tested before it can be used operationally. Migration is usually an imperfect process, and, more often than not, some assets will fail to work on the new platform. This testing process again takes a sub-stantial amount of time and usually diverts attention away from value-creating activities.

Finally, once everything has been validated and the new platform is considered to be safe for operational use, the organization needs to spend even more time retiring the old platform. For many people, this may seem like a strange concept. If the hardware is no longer in use, surely it would be as easy as simply turning the system off and getting rid of the old hardware?

Simplistically, this is true. In practice, however, this is more complicated that it would first appear. Most data centers are highly secure environments, and removing hardware requires the right people to be given access at a set point in time. This takes coordination and usually involves multiple parties, especially for situations in which some facets of IT support are outsourced.

There's also no guarantee that the team doing the migration suc-cessfully identified and retired all the old environment's operational processes. As staff members change teams or leave the organization, they often fail to fully document everything they have built. Turning off the system can sometimes cause unexpected process failures, necessitating another round of testing and resource support as the server is decommissioned. Finally, getting rid of an old server is rarely as easy as taking it to the dump. Many contain hazardous materials that need to be appropriately managed and recycled.

Needless to say, going through this upgrade process is time consuming, risky, and expensive. Few organizations are eager to embark on this journey. Instead, they'll delay as long as they can. However, there eventually comes a time when organizations *need* to make the jump to a new platform if it's to drive ongoing competitive advantage. This dynamic creates a highly challenging situation—they *need* to upgrade the environment on a fairly regular basis but they may not be able to afford the disruption that each of those upgrades involves.

Why Should You Care?

The most common symptom is an underperforming platform. The team experiences regular delays not because of a lack of skills but because jobs take too long to complete. A simple test is this: If a major determinant of the time needed to develop insights is time spent waiting for results, the platform is probably underspecified.

This applies to both big and small jobs. On the larger end, users may be waiting days for data extracts to finish. If this needs to happen once a week, they probably have an issue. On the smaller end, users might need to wait a few minutes for reports to run. If they run these reports 20 times a day, they also probably have an issue.

There are two notable exceptions for which this may not actually be a problem. The first is when delays occur within an operational process. As long as the process still completes in the time frame desired by the business, everything is fine. It's only when the length of delay forces people to wait that it's a real problem.

Second, some problems are legitimately large, especially when they involve big data. Delays are inevitable in these situations. Trying to analyze petabytes of information takes time! However, it's important to temper this with a healthy dose of skepticism. Although delays may be inevitable, the real question is usually whether the delays are reasonable. Doing things differently or having access to a better platform might reduce the length of these delays.

What Not to Do

The standard approach is usually to move to a bigger server. This solves the short-term problem but simply creates a longer-term one: If the organization makes real steps toward driving economies of scope, the new platform will also eventually need to be upgraded. When it does, the organization will need to carry all the same costs over again.

The other approach is the ostrich. It usually involves the organization burying its head in the sand and ignoring the problem. Needless to say, this undermines any real competitive advantage. Existing benefits will continue to accrue but the organization is bottlenecked. Without having access to additional supporting technology, they become limited to simply doing business as usual.

The How-To Guide: Put the Extra Work into the Platform and Make It an Enterprise Cloud

The real solution is to move away from a classic client/server model and toward an enterprise cloud. Many of the concepts in this model are exactly the same as client/server processing: Users still access a shared environment using clients on their personal computers and do little to no processing locally. Assets are still managed and shared in a central repository.

The key difference is in how processing occurs. Rather than having one server do all the processing, jobs are distributed across a network of servers. One or more master servers normally coordinate process management. Unlike a classic server-based model, users neither know nor care where their job is actually executed. Although rooted in distributed computing, this approach often leverages grid, fabric, or parallel computing and offers obvious scalability advantages. Rather than being constrained by one server, users have access to a very large processing environment, sometimes even with a shared memory pool.

This approach helps drive maximum performance out of an organization's technology investment, significantly increasing platform utilization and user satisfaction levels. However, it requires up-front configuration. Although it has many similarities to client/server computing, it often requires additional software. Going from a stand-alone server to a true private cloud with effective workload management usually takes more than dropping in a few more servers.

Expand Out, Don't Migrate

On its own, performance is an important benefit. Even better, this approach solves another problem: It greatly simplifies platform upgrades. Rather than having to move to another platform every time the organization needs additional performance, the organization can simply configure and deploy another node within the grid. Given that these nodes are normally based on a standard configuration, this can be a straightforward and relatively rapid process.

Because the existing platform continues to operate as is, there is no need for migration or server retirement. Testing is limited to reliability and availability tests. Because the technology and assets remain as is, users rarely need to go through user acceptance testing.

Other advantages lie in risk and cost management. Much of the guesswork associated with sizing disappears. If the organization needs more processing power, it simply adds more nodes. Because it no longer needs to operate two highly functional platforms in parallel, it also reduces the need for additional support costs during the upgrade process.

Finally, the project-management team also simplifies their resourcing challenges. Normally, coordinating all the right resources would require months of advance notice. When upgrades can be scheduled around individual availability rather than common availability, the critical path becomes easier to manage. Each node can be provisioned and configured independently and integrated into the environment when ready.

Benefits and Limitations

The benefits are obvious and significant. The organization reduces its risk, creates a simple and straightforward process for increasing performance as needed, and reduces much of the complexity and disruption that's normally associated with a platform upgrade. However, there are limitations.

The biggest limitation is cost. The initial configuration can sometimes be quite expensive, largely due to the level of redundancy needed.

By definition, grid-based environments need multiple servers. Logically, this often also means that they can easily start out being three or four more times more expensive than a single client/server environment. However, this disadvantage needs to be balanced against its equivalent increase in processing power.

Another limitation is architectural complexity. The initial design of such an environment can be a somewhat complex process. Ensuring that a multiserver platform performs well requires the organization to pay very close attention to the network architecture, that is, the shared disk architecture, as well as the way the grid is actually configured. It's easy to lose many of the benefits of a parallel-processing environment if the designers make simple mistakes. Getting this right requires a strong relationship among the architects, the business, and the various partners needed to deliver the cloud.

NOTES

1. Without getting into too much detail, a Turing-complete system is one that can, given sufficient time and memory, simulate any other Turing-complete system. In this sense, most spreadsheets technically have the potential to run an entire operating system such as Windows or Linux, even if they don't pragmatically have the horsepower or memory needed to do so.
2. G. Moore, "Cramming More Components onto Integrated Circuits," *Electronics* (April 19, 1965).

CHAPTER **9**

Asset
Management

The goal of a business analytics team is to create value. Getting there involves creating a variety of intermediary assets including processes, reports, and potentially advanced analytics models. Like any other asset, these need attention if they're to be curated and used effectively.

Most organizations take a fairly lackadaisical approach to asset management. Most struggle with:

- Making the transition from often ad-hoc activities into an asset-based approach
- Understanding the value of their assets
- Identifying how to get the most out of their assets
- Linking the effort they expend to the value they create

The solutions described in the next section focus on techniques and approaches to overcome these challenges.

MOVING TO OPERATIONAL ANALYTICS

WHY READ THIS?

When will this help?

Read this if most of your insight is never acted on.

How will it help you?

Using this approach will drive direct value from business analytics.

What are the guiding principles?

- Drive outcomes, not insight
- Start flexible, become structured
- Eliminate bottlenecks
- Always have a plan B
- Function should dictate form
- Watch the dynamic, not just the static

What else should you read?

- Augmenting operational systems
- Coping with information overload
- Scaling past the PC
- Smoothing growth with the cloud
- Reducing time to recommendation
- Enabling real-time scoring
- Blending rules with models

The Background: The Best Answers Are Worthless if They're Not Timely and Actioned

Organizations make countless decisions every day and every single one of these decisions can benefit from business analytics. Unfortunately, few teams actually have the time to support all of these decisions. To do so, they'd not only need to provide insight but also make sure that insight is actually used. When teams rely on *telling* people what to do, it's impossible to close the loop on their recommendations in a scalable way.

The Easiest Way to Action Insight Is through Operations

Analytics is a broad discipline. Sometimes, the best results come from relatively unsophisticated techniques. The simplest data management routines can be tremendously valuable—creating a customer-centric view of all interactions can be as straightforward as a series of SQL scripts. Sometimes, it takes more horsepower, often in the form of predictive modeling and optimization. Improving liquidity while meeting capital adequacy requirements might involve blending portfolio optimization with highly complex simulation-based risk modeling. Regardless of how sophisticated the techniques are, all forms of analytics can generate tremendous value. The key is that they need to be acted on.

When faced with questions, sometimes all that is needed is an answer. An organization might be considering whether to expand its product portfolio. An important first step is working out the market potential for a new product—if the market can't provide enough sales to cover the investment required, it's an easy decision not to go any further. In this situation, insight alone is invaluable. However, the bar rises when it comes to operational activities. Rather than generating one-off insight, the team needs to enable constant, repeatable action, and this transition can be challenging.

Operational Activities Need to Be Robust and Repeatable

Operational analytics usually has a close relationship with microdecisions.[1] Unlike management and support processes, operational processes are aligned to an organization's core business. They often create the organization's primary revenue stream. To improve outcomes in this context, insights need to be as up to date, frequent, and actionable as the processes they inform.

Every time an organization runs a customer-retention campaign, it needs an up-to-date list of people most likely to cancel their services. By having this list, those individuals can be contacted by the call center and hopefully convinced not to cancel. To minimize inventory and stock allocations, inventory-management systems need an up-to-date view of forward demand by product. To have a hope of being accurate, these forecasts need to be based on current sales results.

Even more important, these recommendations need to be actionable. This may seem like a somewhat confusing distinction to a team that doesn't make a distinction between advice and action. Simply put, there are two separate activities that are taking place: One is the generation of insight, the other acting on that insight through an operational process. These involve very different considerations and require different management structures and techniques.

Generating insight requires flexibility. It's hard to know what to look for until one finds it. Operational processes, on the other hand, require repeatability. They need to be fast and reliable. Insight requires creativity and freedom and doesn't necessarily have to provide clear recommendations. It's a blend of intuition, skills, and experience. Operational processes, on the other hand, require strongly defined activities with clear, actionable recommendations. They need to be consistent and automated.

Advice Can't Scale as Much as Actionable Processes

Business analytics drives value by bridging these two activities. To improve microdecisions, insight is synthesized into a strong recommendation that is then operationally executed, driving measurable value. In practice, most teams struggle to bridge this gap efficiently or effectively.

Initially, business analytics teams often give operational staff the insight they need as required, positioning themselves as the "group with the answers." Although insights are still operationally executed in this model, none of it happens at a systems level. Every request is met by a research project, and everything is driven by intuition, communication, and manual action.

This isn't a sustainable or scalable approach. Members of the team may start by being on-call as necessary but over time, this becomes impossible. There's simply more demand than they can meet. To make their lives easier, they standardize their insight-generating processes into some form of technical asset that they can run as necessary.

Rather than providing insight through intuition and interactive applications, they start automating their processes. This may be as simple as a spreadsheet or custom application or as complex as an actual technology asset with associated metadata. What's important is that, by the time the team gets to this point, it has created a strongly defined process that produces repeatable outputs. In effect, it has eliminated the intuition and communication but still retains the manual action. Every time it needs to provide insight, it accesses and manually uses its analytical assets.

This works, albeit usually briefly. Unfortunately, it cements the team as a permanent bottleneck and constrains its ability to deliver economies of scope. Supporting operational activities is a time-consuming task, and doing so makes it difficult to expand into new areas. If decisions are made many times a day and data changes regularly, the team needs to use their assets at least daily. This takes time, drives focus on value-maintaining activities, and distracts from value-creating activities.

This creates tension. On one hand, the team needs to demonstrate tactical value. If the insight they generate isn't acted on, they can't deliver any value. On the other hand, they're often tasked with identifying and driving strategic value in the form of competitive differentiation. This is impossible when all their time is spent supporting tactical activities.

Why Should You Care?

Teams facing these challenges tend to exhibit some common symptoms:

- They become overutilized and spend most of their time answering ad-hoc questions.
- A high proportion of their insights are never acted on unless the team is directly involved in operational process.

Trying to support an operational team with near-real-time analysis is hard work. Operational processes are never ending and without a large team, it's easy for an analytics team to be totally consumed through responding to ad-hoc requests. This heavily limits the scope of the analytics team as well as their ability to turn business analytics into a competitive differentiator. Although tactical activities deliver returns, spending all the team's time on tactical activities prevents the team from developing sources of sustainable competitive advantage.

Another common symptom is an excess of insights. Teams suffering from these forces tend to have more answers than actions. Their ability to support operational processes is constrained by the size of the team. Because of this, they will inevitably generate many insights that they are unable to capitalize on due to time constraints. This is both frustrating and costly—every insight that isn't acted on is wasted effort and carries an opportunity cost.

What Not to Do

One solution is to hire more resources and align the analytics team with the operational team. This overcomes the immediate challenges but limits growth and scope. Analytics becomes a functionally aligned activity rather than an enterprise capability. Future growth is only possible by hiring more resources, an expensive proposition with poor productivity measures.

Another solution is to take the manual processes and automate them by involving IT. Although this is directionally correct, it still runs the risk of inhibiting efficiency and creating process-management challenges. Migrating assets into production requires strong governance; every change needs to be exhaustively tested before being deployed. There are many checks and balances, and this is for good reason: Systems fail if inputs and outputs are not totally consistent, and having operational processes fail can be a costly exercise. Although governance is essential, it needs to be fit for task. It's here that things usually become unstuck.

Software Development Migrations Models Are Not Analytical Migration Models

To mitigate these risks, many IT systems are based on a well-established process of migrating assets between three environments:

1. Development
2. Test
3. Production

Development is where assets are first created. These assets are normally relatively few in number and based on a series of well-defined requirements. At any point in time within this environment, different assets will be in various stages of development; upstream and downstream assets may be running at different versions depending on the development cycle.

Once the asset is finalized and ready for release, it is migrated into the Test environment where it can be exhaustively tested in line with other associated version-locked assets. Importantly, these assets replicate those currently in production. Finally, after passing or failing those tests, the assets are promoted or demoted to production or development, respectively. Production is where actual operational processes are actively running.

This approach is a gold standard in systems management and is often used in data management as well as business intelligence. It provides a strong level of governance and control and works well for situations in which requirements can be well defined up front. Unfortunately, it fails to align with how business analytics works.

Classic Software Migration Models Rarely Work in Business Analytics

Because this is such a well-established process, many IT departments will immediately try to fit all insight generation activities into this model. Unfortunately, applying this as a standard across all business analytics activities creates complexity and limits innovation. Although similar, the activities that occur within a classic development environment are only a subset of the activities that usually take place as part of insight generation.

In their day-to-day business, any given analytics team will often generate:

- Insights without any resulting asset, such as by doing ad-hoc analysis to answer a specific question. This may not even take the form of a final report; it might be an interactive query run while on the phone.

- A small set of assets that will eventually make it into production. These will usually involve both development and testing activities, such as a model that predicts the propensity to purchase a product (along with validating it against a hold-out sample).

- A large number of assets that will never make it into production. These are usually candidate models that, for a variety of reasons, lack sufficient predictive power or robustness to justify their use as either an operational model or a potential challenger model. These assets will often be shelved but may be reexamined at a future point in time.

There are two things here that limit the applicability of traditional asset migration models. The first is the frequent lack of up-front requirements. The second is the need to be able to generate a large number of assets that will never make it into production. Neither of these fit well within the classic development/test/production migration model.

Strong governance in these situations adds needless overhead and limits the agility of the analytics team. Instead of being constrained, the team needs the freedom to discover new insights with an expectation that it will be able to migrate its resulting assets into production at a later stage. Enforcing strong process governance during this creative stage limits an organization's ability to innovate, drive productivity improvements, and be creative.

The How-To Guide: Establish a Dedicated Operational Analytics Framework

This real solution revolves around separating these logical activities into two well-defined environments:

1. A discovery environment
2. An operational environment

Often called a sandpit or a workbench, the discovery environment is lightly governed. It's often managed by the business at a metadata/asset level, if not at an application or hardware level. Although there are similarities between the discovery environment and a development environment, a critical difference is the lack of predefined uses.

Where a development environment usually has well-defined uses, a discovery environment is more akin to a technology playpen for analysts to search for undefined solutions.

It's extremely important to remember that this does not eliminate the need for *all* forms of governance and control. Teams still need data stewards and the like to drive efficiency and reuse. Pure chaos is still chaos! When effectively managed, though, the team maintains its freedom to experiment and innovate. Once finalized, insights are packaged and transformed into assets.

Assets developed to a point where they can be used operationally are then migrated into an operational environment. This environment has some fundamental differences to the discovery environment, usually involving:

- Higher service levels
- Greater reliability levels
- Different technologies that support operational execution (common examples include rules engines, in-database scoring processes, and real-time decisioning systems)

Scalability and job-time completion are critical in this environment. Because these assets are used to augment operational processes, driving better microdecisions can't be made at the cost of timeliness or reliability. Should someone take down the operational environment because of a badly formed query or a late result, the business starts losing real money! This is in stark contrast to a discovery environment in which system downtime is merely frustrating.

By using this approach, the team stops being a bottleneck. They still generate insight quickly. However, that insight takes the form of an asset and is embedded within operational processes. Rather than manually communicating insight, the team takes a systems-based approach to business analytics.

Once an asset has been migrated into the operational environment, there's no reason why the classic test/production asset-migration model can't be used to manage risk. Scoring processes need to be validated against their original models, and data-management routines need to be validated against operational, rather than warehouse, data.

Operational Pricing Optimization

This all may seem somewhat confusing, especially to a team used to operating purely in an analytical sandpit. Because of this, it's helpful to consider a practical example. Most electronics stores face a variety of complex issues. One of the biggest industry drivers is the new-product lifecycle—to sell their products at premium prices, they need to have currently popular items in stock.

Popularity, however, has a shelf life in consumer electronics. On one hand, technology changes. On the other, so does industrial design. It's bad enough that certain offerings may be out of favor compared to a few months ago. To sell them, the store will probably need to discount and take a profitability hit. It's even worse when they still have products on the shelves that are approaching end of life—the biggest discounts in the world are unlikely to help move products if the technology is out of date!

Working out which products tend to sell well in which season is a great example of discovery-based analytics. So is working out typical product life cycles for given classes of goods, Although these are great insights to have and will likely help buyers and planners make better purchasing and planning decisions, they're unlikely to guide day-to-day decisions.

Where analytics *can* help day-to-day decisions is in working out how big a discount the organization should offer to make sure they sell through their product by a given date. In practice, this might involve a blend of price elasticity analysis, sales forecasting, and optimization. The output of this analysis would be a series of pricing recommendations by product/store combinations. This helps redefine prices every day based on current sales data and helps drive margin increases— prices can be set to maximize gross revenue by taking advantage of discriminatory pricing.

The chain may have thousands of products, each of which is offered in different colors and configurations. Because of all these possible combinations, it's quite easy to end up with anywhere from 50,000 to 100,000 unique stock keeping units (SKUs). Ideally, every single one of these would be considered for markdown across every single store in the chain. If the chain has a few hundred stores nationally, the organization could potentially generate close to a million sales forecasts, price elasticity estimates, and optimized prices every single day.

This is obviously a tremendous amount of information to communicate. The best approach is to move to operational analytics. The team builds all the models they need to support their forecasts and optimization processes within the discovery environment. These models are packaged into assets and migrated from the discovery environment into their operational environment. Because of the tight integration that's needed with their planning and pricing systems, this operational environment has significantly higher service level agreements in place.

Every night, the models can be rerun with overnight point of sale data. The ideal price to sell through by a given date would then be calculated and the results delivered directly into the organization's planning systems. These jobs are extremely time sensitive and have to complete successfully within a given window. By the time the stores open in the morning, every department manager has a list of markdowns that apply to their specific market catchment, stock, and sales forecasts.

The team still has freedom to improve the overall process through innovation or creativity. As they refine their forecasting and optimization processes by experimenting and prototyping, they migrate these updated assets from the discovery environment into the test area of the operational environment. Once validated, these changes are promoted into the production area of the operational environment, ensuring business continuity without sacrificing flexibility.

Benefits and Limitations

The immediate benefit of this approach is a substantial increase in productivity as well as direct economic return. Because insights are now generated by automated processes that leverage technology assets, the team eliminates the need for manual analysis in supporting operational activities. Their focus shifts from answering questions to creating deployable assets and developing competitive differentiation.

Because these assets augment operational processes, they help drive return. This approach also allows the team to substantially scale their activities to support many more operational processes. In practice, this can improve the productivity of team members by many orders of magnitude!

A parallel benefit is that this approach maintains the team's ability to innovate. By avoiding all the pitfalls that go along with strong governance during the discovery process, the team preserves its capacity to be creative. This is a critical component in transforming business analytics into a competitive differentiator.

The biggest limitation is usually linked to the handover point between the two environments. By necessity, the operational environment needs to support the assets generated in the discovery environment. Although this approach usually reduces the risk of generating nonexecutable insights, if not effectively managed it can still be possible to create assets that are incompatible with the operational environment. As such, leveraging this pattern does not negate the need for oversight or governance—it simply minimizes it.

MEASURING VALUE

WHY READ THIS?

CASE STUDY

When will this help?
  Read this if you can't explain the value of your work.
How will it help you?
  Using this approach will help quantify the value of business analytics.
What are the guiding principles?
- Drive outcomes, not insight
- Automate everything non-value-added
- Know what you are worth
- Keep things simple
What else should you read?
- Augmenting operational systems
- Moving to operational analytics
- Measuring performance
- Measuring effort
- Understanding the data value chain
- Linking analytics to value

The Background: Without Tangible Returns, It's Impossible to Transform an Organization

Business analytics is a driver for economic value. Unfortunately, that's only true if that value is actually measured. If not, everyone else in the organization will probably claim credit for better results. When teams don't measure the value they create using a standard framework, they inevitably struggle to communicate their worth or attract further investment.

Organizations Have Finite Resources to Invest

Running a successful business is primarily about managing scarcity— resources are limited and regardless of whether you are in the public sector, the private sector, or running your own business, success comes from effective use of resources. Organizations only have so much to invest, and to get maximum return, they need to pick the right areas in which to invest.

For smaller organizations, this is relatively easy; their choices are normally limited by their size. If you're a five-person business, the decision whether to invest in an enterprise grade ERP is pretty easy. However, as organizations become larger and more complex, their options increase substantially, and choosing between options becomes increasingly difficult.

Decisions Needs to Be Made Based on Return

All organizations have a finite budget. Unfortunately, they also usually have unlimited ideas, all of which would require varying levels of investment to commercialize. A bank might focus on driving customer retention through better complaints management. Or it might focus on increasing the number of products per customer through targeted cross-selling. Or it might even focus on driving average credit per customer through better risk management and channel usage.

Every option has the potential to drive better outcomes. Unfortunately, choice can lead to paralysis—deciding where to focus is more challenging that it would initially appear. Because the outcomes are so different (retention, products per customer, and revenue), making direct comparisons would seem to be impossible. Which is better: retaining five customers or lending an additional $50,000?

With the right data, this should be an easy decision. Funding should be directed at the activities that drive the greatest return on investment. This is great in theory but in practice, there's a major flaw. Implicit in this is an assumption that organizations are rational and able to make decisions based on measurable outcomes. Sadly, this is rarely the case when it comes to business analytics. More often than not, the team has a poor grasp on the value it creates. Without this understanding, the team rarely knows where it should focus.

Usually, the team will be able to explain the benefits it has delivered through a variety of statistical measures. This, quite simply, isn't good enough—talking about classification improvements is accurate but useless jargon to someone unskilled in statistics. What most people are interested in are *economic* outcomes, not *mathematical* results. When it comes to justifying its effort, the team struggles to link its insights to outcomes, so it ends up trapped in a cycle in which its effort goes largely unrewarded and its growth remains constrained.

Why Should You Care?

The simple test to see whether an organization suffers from these challenges is to ask what kind of returns a given initiative delivered. Organizations with immature value-measurement capabilities usually hesitate, stutter, and struggle to give any hard measures.

At best they will normally refer to decreases in the time it takes to do business-as-usual activities, productivity gains, or better decision making. It's true that this is better than nothing. In the absence of anything else, it's still a positive outcome! However, it also greatly undermines the ability of the business analytics team to sell the value of their work to the rest of the organization.

Because it can't point to any tangible outcomes, the rest of the organization becomes hesitant to fund further initiatives. This isn't always because of a lack of trust—even trusted teams can be starved of funds. It's simply because there are other initiatives on the table that *do* have measurable outcomes. Funds are limited and a cost-conscious organization channels money to the areas of highest return.

Tactically, this makes sense. Strategically, it greatly limits the ability of an organization to establish a true competitive advantage through business analytics. It creates a vicious cycle in which a lack of funds limits growth. This in turn reduces the odds of future return. More often than not, the team regresses to business as usual, loses motivation, and eventually sees its competencies suffer from turnover.

What Not to Do

The obvious solution is to start measuring the impact and effectiveness of each business analytics initiative. This is actually the right solution, but there's a catch—the measures need to be comparable to other initiatives. When they aren't, the team makes a major misstep that undermines their effort.

Value measurement serves two purposes. It helps:

1. Communicate the value of business analytics to the broader organization
2. Channel investment to where it will make the greatest difference

Having comparable measures is critical. A team *can* define its own measures independently to the rest of the organization. It may even succeed in quantifying its value. However, when those measures aren't comparable against other initiatives, it will normally end up with strong organizational support but no funding.

Most organizations have, at best, a cursory understanding of how business analytics works. This awareness declines as analytical sophistication increases. Although a competent analyst can explain a report in a matter of minutes, it can sometimes take days to explain how true mathematical optimization works in an operational context. Education is important, but it's a time-consuming process and few teams have the time or resources necessary to educate everyone.

Value measurement helps bypass this by focusing attention on what's important: the outcome. Rather than explaining the *how*, it focuses on the *what*. Nothing clarifies attention like being able to demonstrate a doubling of net margin to a retailer or halving services costs with no impact on outcomes to a social services department! Having the right measures in place helps build organizational support.

Having support is a great start. However, it doesn't guarantee funding. Investment decisions are usually made based on a combination of political and financial factors. Support helps with the politics, but it does nothing for the financials. Value measurement also helps in this context by providing a series of comparable measures that benchmark the relative value of different initiatives.

As a practical example, an organization might be trying to decide between two initiatives. One might focus on increasing the rate with which products are cross-sold to existing customers. The other might focus on reducing the rate at which customers are churning. In the absence of value measures, the organization will usually make the decision based on opinion and "strategic priorities." Even worse, it may only get to that point after excessive debate and delay.

Knowing the comparative economic worth of these initiatives changes things dramatically. In the presence of value measures, the organization will usually priorities the initiative with the higher net return. It will usually do so with little disagreement or delay.

When it comes to measuring the value of business analytics, teams tend to priorities what they consider important. Unfortunately, establishing unique measures undermines a major point of value measurement: the ability to compare different initiatives. Therefore, despite apparently doing the right thing, teams make their lives harder.

The How-To Guide: Establish a Standard Value Measurement Framework

The real solution is to establish a standard set of common measures that are automatically calculated for all initiatives, regardless of their objective or functional alignment. By necessity, these represent minimum common criteria for all projects, not an exhaustive list of potential sources of value.

Their worth lies in their *chunkability* and *commonality*, not in their comprehensiveness. Because they represent the smallest set of measures possible, they are easy to communicate and remember. Because they are common among initiatives, they allow decision makers to directly benchmark otherwise incomparable investments. Their focus is on what's been achieved, not on the effort that's needed to deliver the project or the underlying characteristics of the analytics.

Value is a relative concept—to be truly useful, it needs to be compared against other options. To get the most out of these measures, it's important to remember that their value is in being a *relative* measure, not an absolute measure. Even though they carry absolute estimates, those estimates are largely meaningless without something to compare them against. Whether a return of $10 million on the investment is good or not is largely dependent on *how else* that same money could have been used.

Setting up a comprehensive value-measurement framework is a topic in its own right. However, it's useful to be aware of typical measures. The two major classes of value (or business) measures are:

1. Financial outcomes
2. Activity outcomes

Financial Outcomes

Financial outcomes link economic contribution to processes and activities. They give the team the ability to quantify its worth in a highly measurable and business-relevant way. By focusing on economic outcomes, it translates what are often fairly abstract activities into something the financial side of the organization can relate to. Common examples often include:

- Gross revenue generation
- Gross cost avoidance
- Simple return on investment
- Realized rate of return
- Net economic value

Activity Outcomes

Activity outcomes capture the other side of the coin. They track outcomes that may not necessarily be economically quantifiable. They often link to nonfinancial performance indicators and aim to capture operationally driven business outcomes.

Because they're not economic in nature, they rarely help justify funding. However, they do play a key role in building political support. When properly designed and targeted, they align directly against peoples' performance measures. Because of this, they help fulfill the what's-in-it-for-me factor.

Financial measures are usually standard among organizations. There are only so many ways you can calculate net present value. Activity measures, on the other hand, can vary substantially. Because they're aligned to operational activities, they're almost totally dependent on the business problem being solved.

Examples could include:

- The proportion of offers accepted through direct-marketing activities.

- The number of correctly and incorrectly identified cases of fraud.

- The number of times a report is accessed by the organization.

- The final quality of a given good, as measured by deviation from ideal design.

- The level of accuracy of a demand forecast.

Each of these is an activity-based measure of the level of success being achieved by a process. For example, a direct-marketing group may be specifically tasked with improving marketing-communication relevancy. Many countries place limits on how frequently customers can be contacted. Because of this, frequency of contact becomes an important consideration for a marketing group interested in optimizing their contact strategy.

Every unsuccessful contact prevents the organization from making another offer that may be more relevant. Increasing the proportion of offers accepted, therefore, represents a direct demonstration of activity improvement. By applying more accurate predictive models, this acceptance rate might increase. This improves revenue as well as one of the primary metrics of concern for the team. In these situations, both the financial *and* activity measures help the team achieve its key performance indicators.

Benefits and Limitations

The biggest benefit to organizations that establish a single value measurement framework is that they get clarity over which initiatives drive the best business outcomes. This helps focus investment on high-returning areas and, by doing so, builds trust in the use of business analytics. This, in turn, drives future investment. The importance of this can't be understated; without trust, change is impossible.

Another major benefit lies in productivity gains. Because there is a single set of common measures that get applied irrespective of the initiative, delivery teams eliminate the need for speculation and research. Rather than trying to reinvent the wheel for each project, delivery teams leverage a standard list of measures. Efficiency comes having confidence and clarity on what a process *should* look like, streamlining processes to make them as simple as possible, and having a standard value-measurement framework helps drive both.

The biggest limitation is usually complexity. The temptation is always there to create an overly comprehensive value-measurement framework, one that measures everything under the sun. There's nothing wrong with this approach as long as data-capture processes are automated and new initiatives simply leverage existing information-management processes.

Unfortunately, this is rarely the case. More often, processes need to be rebuilt from scratch for each initiative. Although not inevitable, this is usually because the outcomes, input data, and information-capture activities vary by project. When they do, the team needs to invest substantial time in mapping the overly comprehensive value-measurement framework to a variety of new operational platforms. This undermines efficiency and negates many of the advantages of a standard value-measurement framework.

Another significant limitation is that the outputs are only as good as the assumptions and processes used to capture and measure them. Having the wrong measures in place can actually undermine good projects. If the core set of measures revolve around customer retention, it's very easy to end up in a situation where an initiative drives massive margin improvements but no retention improvements. With the wrong measures in place, this project may seem like a failure despite delivering millions in incremental revenue!

Establishing a value-measurement framework is an essential component of a well-functioning team. If they can't sell the value of their work, who will?

MEASURING PERFORMANCE

WHY READ THIS?

When will this help?

Read this if you don't know which of your assets need attention.

How will it help you?

Using this approach will help you understand where you do and don't need to focus your maintenance effort.

What are the guiding principles?

- Automate everything non-value-added
- Eliminate bottlenecks
- Keep things simple

What else should you read?

- Coping with information overload
- Allocating responsibilities
- Scaling past the PC
- Moving to operational analytics
- Measuring value
- Measuring effort

The Background: Without Knowing Where the Problems Are, It's Impossible to Fix Them

A byproduct of business analytics is a large number of intermediary assets. Every single one of these assets degrades with time, and to maintain their value, the team needs to monitor and maintain them. Unfortunately, this isn't an easy process. It's impossible to know where to focus if these assets aren't directly comparable. Given the breadth of activities involved in business analytics, it's rare to have this level of comparability by default.

Assets Degrade with Time

Business analytics generates value by transforming raw data into actionable (and actioned) insight. This transformation process involves generating a variety of assets that go through a fairly standard development process, even if the specific activities can vary.

Teams will start by aggregating, transforming, cleansing, and deriving analytical information from a variety of source systems and data warehouses. The team then uses this information to create one or more analytical assets. These assets can include models, reports, dashboards, or decisioning rules. Once these assets have been created, the team will then deploy those assets into operational processes to help drive better outcomes in a measurable way.

As most things do, these information assets degrade with time. Behaviors and markets change and, as they do, the assumptions behind the assets shift. Over time, the insights the assets provide become less relevant to the organization or they experience decreasing predictive accuracy.

At some stage, this gradual degradation creates unacceptable risks. If the quality of these assets degrades too far, the insights they provide may actually be of a lower quality than alternative processes. Taken to an extreme, it's possible for a predictive model to provide predictions worse than a random guess!

Keeping a close eye on asset quality helps teams manage this risk. If models degrade past an acceptable threshold, the team can redevelop or retire the model, thereby managing the organization's overall exposure. A prime example lies in identifying and managing fraud. Financial transactions can be scored to create a probability-based estimate of whether any given transaction is likely to be fraudulent. High-probability transactions are then flagged and sent across to an investigations team for follow-up.

Unfortunately, this is also one of the most dynamic areas of business analytics. Most teams see behaviors shift rapidly in this field—as soon as criminals know what the organization is looking for, they change their behaviors to avoid those patterns. Because of this, predictive models can degrade surprisingly rapidly.

Monitoring Assets Requires Time

This creates significant risk. Leaving a bad model in production past its useful lifespan can give the organization a false sense of confidence. Everything looks fine right up until they have to declare an extremely costly loss!

The challenge in monitoring asset quality is that it comes at a cost. On one hand, the team needs to deliver new initiatives, each of which establishes a new operational process and creates incremental measurable value for the organization. On the other, it needs to ensure that already deployed operational processes continue delivering value. At a minimum, the team needs to make sure that processes run successfully, that insights are acted on, and that the value they create is measured.

When processes rely on one asset, monitoring the *quality* of this asset is fairly straightforward. The value of the asset is almost directly related to the economic value it creates. Things become more complicated when the process relies on multiple assets. If the process *creates* measurable value and that value is declining over time, the team needs to understand which assets are the cause behind this reduction. Determining this takes time, and that time must be drawn from a finite resource pool.

Things are even worse with assets that focus on loss avoidance like risk or fraud models. Because these assets *prevent* loss, a high-quality asset can seemingly produce exactly the same results as a low-quality asset as long as the events they try to predict don't happen. When criminals are looking elsewhere, both good and bad models may fail to fire.

Unfortunately, when criminals *do* strike, bad models may still fail to fire. This makes it extremely hard for the organization to know whether the lack of detection is a good or a bad outcome. The only answer is to constantly monitor asset quality against known cases.

This puts teams in a difficult situation. They need to spend time monitoring asset quality. Unfortunately, this takes time away from delivering new sources of value to the organization. Consequently, they become stuck in a situation where they must either compromise and reduce their scope of operations or carry excessive risk.

Why Should You Care?

The simple test to see whether an organization is suffering from this challenge is to review how often existing assets are audited. At best, these audits will normally occur annually. At worst, they may never happen!

The main reason this is so insidious is that in the short term, it carries minimal cost and massive benefit. By ignoring asset hygiene and simply focusing on whether processes successfully completed, teams apparently free up substantial amounts of time to focus on other higher-value activities. Initially, this seems to be a successful strategy. Over time, however, their risks mount and the odds of their experiencing a damaging blow to their credibility increases.

The Team That Destroyed Its Value through Neglect

A great example lies in one team I worked with that was responsible for creating analytically based retention models. Over a number of months the team had successfully developed and deployed a relatively sophisticated process to identify customers likely to churn within the upcoming two months. These predictions were fed into the organization's warehouse where they surfaced in the contact center's outbound communications system.

The project had been a massive success for the team. In the first few months of operation, the newly designed process had been significantly better at targeting customers likely to churn. With the support of the direct-marketing team, the team had managed to reduce churn by almost a fifth, a major success in anyone's book!

Unfortunately, members of the team had become so enthused with their success that they had immediately focused on their next initiative. They completely ignored the need to monitor the quality of the assets they had put into production. Instead, they put the bare minimum of checks in place to make sure that the process completed successfully each month.

For a long time, this actually seemed to be a good strategy. The time they saved had generated significant returns. Over the next year and a half they successfully kicked off another five initiatives, each of which was either in-flight or in operation. Unfortunately, things came crashing down late in the second year.

Over a three-month period, the churn predictions suddenly stopped working. In the first month, the organization chalked it up to random chance. In the second month, the organization started to become concerned. The team allayed their concerns by pointing out that all their checks and balances still indicated that the process was running properly. In the third month of bad predictions, the team was being called into the office of the chief marketing officer to explain.

When the team did the quality assessment that they should have done from the start, they realized two things. First, the organization's customer demographics had been shifting over the previous year. Many of the organization's segment characteristics had moved outside the boundaries of the assumption they originally used to develop their models.

Second, and more damningly, they discovered that their models had not been updated for three months. A change in the warehouse's schema had meant that some highly significant fields were no longer being carried across during their data extraction processes. Because the fields were still present in their analytical datamart, the process completed successfully. Unfortunately, because they were no longer being updated, they contained old data. Therefore, the models had been making the same predictions for three months straight.

Over time, the team managed to rebuild their reputation. However, they lost a significant amount of face, cost the organization substantial money, and could have avoided these issues had they followed good asset management practices to begin with.

What Not to Do

The obvious solution is to start benchmarking the quality of the team's assets. This is the right approach, but it comes with a significant drawback—it decreases the ability of the team to diversify its activities across multiple problems. The time the team spends monitoring and auditing its assets is time it takes away from other value-creating (rather than value-maintaining) opportunities.

Because it often appears that there's no other choice, the team ends up trying to maintain a difficult balance of spending *enough* time auditing assets without spending *too much*. In practice, there's no easy answer on how much time (or how frequently assets are reviewed) is right. As with all difficult questions, it depends. Although this is the truth, it's also not exactly the easiest advice to manage by.

The How-To Guide: Establish a Standard Quality-Measurement Framework

Like measuring value, the real solution is to establish a quality-measurement framework that gives standardized, comparable measures. By having a default list of analytical measures that are applied by default every time an asset is pushed into production, the team can ensure constant visibility over asset quality, driving significant economies of scale.

Analytical measures help focus attention on the assets and processes that most need it. More than anything else, they help the team focus its redevelopment, refactoring, and redesign efforts in the right areas.

These measures track asset *quality*. They track inherent characteristics and give the team visibility over how assets change over time. They help the team understand:

- How well their assets are aligned with organizational objectives.
- How effectively assets are performing.
- How much their environment has changed and how strongly these changes will affect their assets.

By having clear visibility over these measures, teams know which assets need immediate attention and which can wait. When these measures aren't tracked, the team can easily waste time examining or refactoring perfectly good assets. This, admittedly, is fairly abstract. It helps to consider a practical example to illustrate why these measures are so important.

Tracking model quality and reliability affects the team's ability to determine when a model's accuracy has degraded past a useful threshold. If a model is allowed to degrade too far, it may actually produce results that are worse than a random guess. Equally though, refreshing or redeveloping models too frequently creates significant opportunity costs. That time could have been spent creating new competencies or developing new assets.

Quality measures vary by application, algorithm, and asset type. However, common quality measures include:

- **Accuracy measures.** The ability of the model to make correct predictions.
- **Improvement measures.** The ability of the model to make better predictions than existing processes.
- **Deviation measures.** The degree to which underlying data is changing over time.

Accuracy Measures

Accuracy measures help teams track, understand, and compare the ability of models to make correct predictions. They are often used to help managers decide which approach to use out of a collection of models or processes.

Models create a prediction based on either a series of business rules or statistical inferences. When these predictions are incorrect, they can be incorrect in two ways—they can either predict that the event *would* occur and it *didn't* (also known as a *false positive* or *Type I error*) or they can predict that the event *wouldn't* occur and it *did* (also known as a *false negative* or *Type II error*). Understanding the likelihood of each of these is essential when their cost to the organization is disproportionate.

One example of how these can affect the value of a model lies in a model built to identify fraud. If the expected value of a fraudulent transaction is extremely high, the organization would normally want to *minimize false negatives as much as possible*. Given the high cost of a missed detection, it may be better for the organization to deal with false positives and spend additional amounts on investigation rather than experience the significant losses associated with a missed detection.

On the other hand, if the expected losses from a missed detection are relatively low and investigation resources are heavily constrained, an organization may decide that efficient identification is the most important outcome. The most valuable model in this context might be one that has a high number of correct predictions *and the smallest number of false positives*. Minimizing false positives is important because each false positive represents an investigation that won't lead to a successful prosecution, limiting the effectiveness of the resource-constrained investigations team.

Improvement Measures

Improvement measures help managers measure the degree to which analytical assets add value beyond alternative (and existing) processes. Because they're a relative measure that can be directly compared against alternative challenger processes, they're often used to set a lower threshold below which models need to be redeveloped or refreshed.

A new predictive model should, in principle, provide better predictions than current processes. This establishes the minimum level of predictive accuracy a model needs to achieve. By analyzing the frequency with which an event occurs in the general population when current processes are applied, a manager can set a floor that represents the organization's level of accuracy should nothing change. For example, if 5 percent of all offers are accepted through direct marketing activity using current processes, the model should at least achieve an acceptance rate higher than 5 percent. If it doesn't, the champion process offers an equivalent or better outcome.

Because this measure represents the model's level of accuracy above existing processes, this improvement is often referred to as *lift*. As models degrade, this lift decreases. Eventually, the model will be only be as good as or worse than the processes it replaced.

Tracking how this lift changes over time is a vital consideration in working out the ideal time to refresh or redevelop a model. If it is redeveloped too frequently, the value created by the refresh may be less than the value created through a new-growth initiative. If it is left too long, the value being lost through inaccurate models may outweigh the value being delivered through growth initiatives.

By tracking these measures, managers can make an objective decision on the optimal point in time to refresh or redevelop models. Additionally, they can establish various processes and business rules to automate notification processes, reducing the time spent by their team analyzing model accuracy.

Deviation Measures

The final types of commonly captured quality measures are deviation measures. These measures help managers understand how rapidly their external environment is changing around them. They are often used as an input into deciding how frequently models need to be redeveloped.

Models are fundamentally constrained by the stability of their inputs: When the current data being used no longer follows the same statistical characteristics of the data originally used to develop the model, the outputs of the model can no longer be trusted. Determining when the data to be scored has deviated beyond an acceptable point is usually a subjective judgment based on experience. However, without tracking the degree to which inputs are deviating from their original values, it's impossible for an analyst to even be aware of how substantially the assumptions underpinning a model have been violated.

By tracking these measures, analysts have the ability to visualize how greatly the underlying data has deviated from the original sample, and, by seeing this, they can make an informed judgment about whether the model's assumptions need to be reevaluated and the model potentially redeveloped.

Consider a model developed to identify the propensity of customers to be interested in "bleeding-edge" technology products. When a model was initially developed, the organization's original customer base may have been younger and extremely technologically savvy.

Since the model was developed, however, the organization may have expanded into new markets, acquiring more conservative customers.

Because the initial model was developed using a different type of customer base than the organization now has, the assumptions and relationships identified by the model may no longer be applicable. By examining a variety of deviation measures, including average customer age, purchasing patterns, and segment distributions over time, analysts may quickly identify that the likely reason for the model's degraded performance is a changed customer base. Because the organization's current customers may be driven by different behavioral patterns, the original set of inputs into the model may no longer be applicable.

Because of this, analysts may decide that, rather than try to refresh the model, they might be better off simply redeveloping it from scratch, potentially saving a week's worth of work and achieving a better outcome. Critically, this decision would have been extremely difficult to make in the absence of objective deviation measures.

Benefits and Limitations

The biggest benefit of establishing a common quality-measurement framework is risk mitigation. By having access to standard and comparable measures, the team can ensure a minimum level of quality across all assets with a minimum of effort. More than anything else, this helps the team avoid additional work that would otherwise be necessary. By doing so, the team drives economies of scale and scope without having to trade off governance or asset hygiene.

The biggest limitation is the up-front effort needed to define these measures and ensure they are consistently applied. This can be substantial enough to almost form an initiative in its own right! For a team already pressed to the breaking point, taking on this work may seem foolhardy. However, it's an essential part of a longer-term strategy.

Although making the trade-off can drive short-term gains, it comes with extremely costly long-term risks. It's not a question of whether things will eventually go wrong; it's a question of when they will.

MEASURING EFFORT

WHY READ THIS?

When will this help?

Read this if you have issues with productivity and don't know how to improve.

How will it help you?

Using this approach will help focus energy around areas with the greatest potential productivity improvements.

What are the guiding principles?

- Automate everything non-value-added
- Eliminate bottlenecks
- Minimize custom development
- Keep things simple

What else should you read?

- Coping with information overload
- Keeping everyone aligned
- Allocating responsibilities
- Scaling past the PC
- Moving to operational analytics
- Measuring value
- Measuring performance

The Background: Without Knowing Where the Bottlenecks Are, It's Impossible to Fix Them

Although everything's constrained, few things are as constrained as a team's time. Driving efficiency through optimizing processes is one of the easiest ways for teams to improve their productivity. Unfortunately, most teams fail to measure the effort they expend to achieve their outcomes. Without knowing this, the best they can do is guess where to optimize, usually incorrectly.

Efficiency Drives Growth

Business analytics involves a lot of moving parts. An average team may deal with five or more different tools, 20–30 different data sources, a handful of different operational systems, and tens to thousands of models and reports. Even worse, many of their discovery activities are relatively undefined, guided by experience rather than strongly defined processes.

Economies of scope come from taking this unique blend of skills and experience and applying them to solve similar problems elsewhere in the business. A team that has a great deal of success in predicting which products each customer is likely to be interested in will probably also have success predicting which transactions are likely to be fraudulent. Although these are fundamentally different problems, they can both be solved using the same skills, technologies, and possibly even data. These common inputs help drive cost efficiencies.

These cost efficiencies in turn drive competitive advantage. However, there's a fairly big assumption behind this approach: It only works if the team has enough free time to solve other problems in the business. Holding everything else constant, there are only two ways they can create this time. One option is to hire more people. The other is to become more efficient.

Hiring additional people often starts off looking like the more attractive option. It's rarely as effective as it initially looks and it comes with its own challenges. Finding the right people doesn't happen overnight, assuming they can be found in the first place. Additional headcount usually needs to be justified by a business case and budgeted, again requiring substantial lead time. Even if the resources are eventually hired, they usually take a variable amount of time to get up to speed with how the team works, adding even more lead time.

The delays associated with hiring new staff usually encourage teams to initially look inward. Rather than grow the team, they'll try to scale by improving efficiency. At the highest level, there are only three ways teams can improve their efficiency. They can:

- Reengineer their processes
- Use new technology
- Improve their skills

By streamlining their processes, they may be able to achieve the same results in less time. Alternatively, they may also be able to drive efficiencies by using different (or higher-powered) tools. Or if there is a lack of knowledge, they may also be able to drive efficiency improvements by developing new skills or increasing the depth of their existing skills.

Improving the Right Areas Can Be Hard

This all makes sense and is fairly straightforward; it's in the execution where things start to become complicated. There's usually a fixed budget of time and money available for process improvement. There are only so many hours in the day, and most organizations are reluctant to invest large amounts of money in productivity-enabling initiatives.

On one side, teams face fairly hard constraints. On the other, though, there's usually a spectacularly large choice of things they *could* optimize. They could spend their budget on new tools. They could spend their budget on learning new modeling techniques. They could also spend their budget on rebuilding their data-extraction routines. All these may help teams become more efficient. Unfortunately, it's exceedingly unlikely that they will all generate the same degree of improvement. Some of these choices will probably work better than others. Without the benefit of hard data, working out which drive the best results can feel like trying to find a needle in a haystack in a dark room.

Every team is unique. Not only are its skills special to the group but their context varies by organization. Some organizations have exceedingly efficient warehousing processes but very little in the way of operational decision-making systems. Others have extremely good operational systems but an almost total dearth of analytical data. Because of this, there's no easy rule to guide teams in their optimization effort. Instead, each team needs to work out what will work best for it.

In the absence of knowing the answers, the team is usually forced to guess what will help them drive the greatest efficiencies. This carries a high degree of risk. If it picks the wrong area to optimize, it will likely end up spending money and creating delays for little benefit. Compounding this is that, in the absence of hard data, a team is often guided by what it is interested in rather than what will necessarily drive the best outcomes. Our perceptions define our reality and it's what we don't know that can often cause us the most pain.

Why Should You Care?

Teams that don't capture hard data on the effort they expend usually hit a very conservative productivity limit. Their attempts to drive greater efficiencies fail as often as they succeed. This isn't because they can't make things run more efficiently. Instead, it's because the things they reengineer don't always deliver the efficiencies they expect.

The Team That Backed the Wrong Horse

A great example of how this plays out lies in a team I knew that was under significant internal pressure. The organization as a whole had been given a 40 percent productivity-improvement target with no additional headcount. Given the business-analytics team's level of productivity, this should have been easily achievable. Unfortunately, the team was not entirely sure where to start. Despite all members of the team being extremely busy, they didn't have a feel about where the team as a whole was spending its time.

After spending a few weeks reviewing their activities, members of the team came to the conclusion that the vast majority of their time was being spent managing information. This in itself wasn't entirely surprising—most teams spend the vast majority of their time trying to source and transform data! Because of this, the team decided that its focus should be on reengineering its data management processes to drive better productivity and, by doing so, keep the jobs of all team members. By its back-of-the-envelope calculations, the team estimated a roughly 40 percent productivity improvement through process reengineering; what was currently taking them roughly five days to do would drop to three days.

A few months later the team had finally finished reengineering its data extraction and transformation routines. This had required additional training, extensive process reengineering, and the use of a few external consultants. Unfortunately, when they reran their benchmarks, they discovered that, rather than a 40 percent productivity improvement, the team had only managed to achieve a 10 percent productivity improvement. Instead of saving two resource days per week, they'd only managed to eliminate four hours of effort!

On investigation, it transpired that their real issue had nothing to do with the efficiency of the team's processes. Instead, it had to do with its platform. Poor architecture had led to the team's analytical platform having an extremely slow connection to its warehouse. The delays that were experienced in job completion times had nothing to do with coding efficiency. Instead, they were due to a lack of network/back-plane bandwidth. As the team had already experienced, the most efficient code in the world would do little to solve its real problem.

Needless to say, this left them extremely exposed. They had wasted substantial time and money for little benefit, purely because they made their optimization decisions on limited information.

What Not to Do

The obvious solution is to start explicitly tracking effort via timesheets and the like. This has the right intent but usually generates the wrong outcome. Timesheets take time to be complete, time that could have been spent driving greater efficiencies or creating new sources of value. If this overhead is too onerous, people will often start taking shortcuts such as using the same time codes constantly irrespective of what they were actually doing. This is worse than having no information at all; it will actively mislead optimization efforts!

The How-To Guide: Establish a Standard Effort Measurement Framework

Like measuring value and asset quality, the real solution is to establish a standard measurement framework that tracks effort in a comparable way. By having access to a common set of measures that are applied by default to every new initiative, the team can substantially increase its visibility over the amount of effort it is expending.

Technical measures aim to quantify resource effort, time, and utilization. They help direct the team's attention to the areas where optimization will make the most difference. Their defining characteristic is their focus on the activity and effort spent by the team, and, when used effectively, they help prioritize internal optimization projects.

These measures primarily focus on effort in the broadest sense. This cuts across:

■ Technology effort
■ Development effort
■ Operational effort

Technology effort measures focus on profiling and understanding system-level bottlenecks in an objective and rigorous manner. They are a critical input into identifying and prioritizing which platform and environment components require upgrades and the order in which they'll provide maximum benefit.

Development effort measures focus on profiling and understanding the time taken to develop new assets. They are a critical input into identifying potential areas of process improvement, often through mentoring, process optimization, developing new assets, or acquiring new tools.

Operational effort measures are focused on profiling and measuring the time spent conducting operational activities. This often includes responding to ad-hoc queries from the business, running scoring processes, or providing operational reports. They are a critical input into prioritizing activities, developing alternative operational processes, or acquiring new tools to facilitate operational delivery.

Technology Effort

Technology effort measures quantify the effort expended by the analytics platform. Critically, this covers all environments including the discovery, operational, and, potentially, also innovation environments. The primary information source is usually processing logs and other platform-related reporting systems.

The most common measures in this category are:

■ Total execution (or real) processing time
■ Data transfer time
■ Data processing time
■ Computation (or CPU) time

Execution time is usually the total amount of time a job needs to complete. It's for this reason that it's also often referred to as real time. In isolation, it rarely indicates anything other than the jobs that take the longest amount of time to finish. Although it helps to priorities optimization effort based on sheer scale, it rarely identifies why processing jobs are taking a long time. For that, the other three measures are essential.

Data-transfer time tracks the time needed to move data from one platform to the next and back again. This includes movement from source systems to the discovery environment, from discovery to operational, and so on. Excessive time spent in these activities often indicates inadequate network infrastructure or inappropriately designed network architectures.

Some common examples include traversing low-bandwidth public networks or inappropriately scoped interconnection bandwidth (e.g., 100 mb ethernet versus fiber channel). Common solutions include rearchitecting network architectures, moving to incremental data updates rather than retransferring entire datasets every time source data is updated, or limiting the amount of data being transferred to only what's necessary.

Data-processing time tracks the amount of time needed to transform and process data within the analytical platform. Excessive time spent in these activities often indicates storage architecture issues or data architecture issues. Some common examples include inappropriately architected storage platforms (e.g., NAS versus SAN, RAID 5 versus RAID 1+0, etc.) and poor data-management processes (such as creating needless copies of data, excessive intermediary data-processing steps, or inefficient data-quality processes). Common solutions include migrating to alternative storage platforms, optimizing data-management processes, or migrating to 64-bit platforms to increase the amount of memory addressable by the platform.

Computation time tracks the total amount of time spent by the platform performing computational activities. Although it may seem that execution time should match computation time, that's rarely the case. Bottlenecks in other areas of the platform may make execution time significantly longer than computation time. For example, data normally needs to be transferred and transformed as part of most analytical processes. When this creates the bottleneck, the CPU sits idle while it waits for the data-management processes to finish. Because of this, a complex data processing job that may take hours to execute may only involve minutes of actual computation time.

Excessive time spent on these activities often indicates inadequately sized platform-processing capability. Some common examples include having too many users accessing the analytics platform or using inappropriate CPU or platform architectures. Common solutions include migrating to parallel processing/grid platforms or migrating to more appropriately architected hardware platforms.

Development Effort

Development-effort measures aim to capture the amount of time spent creating new assets. They represent an internally focused activity measure and provide critical insight into opportunities for process improvement.

When these measures aren't tracked, the team will often struggle to identify and prioritize how processes should be improved. Without having visibility over the effort being expended by the team developing new assets, it's exceedingly difficult to make objective decisions about where to start optimizing or improving efficiencies.

The most common measurement process to capture development effort involves:

- Identifying the major repeatable activities in developing different classes of assets. These might include problem definition, data preparation, documentation, model development, deployment, and so on.
- Establishing lightweight tracking systems to keep track of the elapsed time spent in each of these activities.
- Establishing aggregate reporting systems to aid in analyzing where time is spent.

One of the important considerations in capturing these measures is ensuring they provide the necessary level of insight without creating excessive overhead. The ideal system requires no analyst time to update. The time analysts spend working is automatically tracked and captured. Unfortunately, this ideal is usually unattainable. Instead, analysts often need to actively track their time.

A fairly lightweight but effective approach involves defining standardized workflow processes, implementing supporting systems, and transparently capturing the time spent within specific activities. When used effectively, moving through the various steps within the workflow automatically captures the date and time the step was completed. By aligning activities against high-level measures, managers can leverage the workflow system to create insight on what tasks are taking the longest time.

Operational Effort

Operational-effort measures aim to capture the amount of time spent conducting operational activities. Much like development measures, they are an internal activity measure and often form a key input into identifying opportunities for process optimization and improvement.

The key difference between operational measures and development measures is that development measures can be aligned against specific initiatives, whereas operational measures often have no ending date. Instead, they represent the time the team spends keeping things working. Capturing these measures often involves using the same approach as capturing development effort.

The primary reason for tracking them is to give the team the ability to objectively balance its response to ongoing business issues versus creating value. When appropriately managed, the analytics team helps provide insight to the organization as well as creating new value for the organization.

When these are out of balance, the team sacrifices value creation or value maintenance. If operational activities consume too much time, managers become limited in their ability to create new value through growth initiatives. The value delivered by the analytics team stabilizes and eventually stagnates. Equally though, if too little time is spent on operational activities and the focus is purely on growth initiatives, the organization often fails to maintain the value created by the analytics team.

Benefits and Limitations

The biggest benefit of establishing an effort measurement framework is that it helps a team maximize its return on investment from internal optimization. Rather than focusing on what's obvious, the team focuses on what will drive the greatest benefit. Having hard data helps reduce uncertainty and minimize the team's risk of wasted effort.

Like measuring asset quality, the biggest limitation is also the up-front effort needed to capture and analyze these measures. The team may need to acquire and establish workflow technology to help them track time between milestones. They will often also need to drop down to a highly technical level in order to analyze and transform system logs into something that helps represent the effort needed for job completion. These usually require investment of both time and money.

NOTE

1. Microdecisions are small decisions made countless times on a day-to-day basis, generally of a customer or client-facing nature. Their proponents include James Taylor and Neil Raden. To read more about them, I highly recommend their book, *Smart (Enough) Systems: How to Deliver Competitive Advantage by Automating Hidden Decisions* (Prentice Hall, 2007).

PART
FIVE

Practical Solutions: Data and Decision Making

Data is the fuel that powers the engine of insight. Good data combined with effective decision making leads to good outcomes. Bad decisions based on bad data can drive a business bankrupt.

Together, they make the difference between an organization that makes the right decisions and an organization that makes the wrong decisions. Becoming better at managing data and making decisions drives real value. Given that a typical team can spend over 80 percent of their time managing information, it's not surprising that small improvements create large productivity gains.

The following chapters focus on how best to manage information, link insight to outcomes, and encourage effective decision making. They cover process design, information architectures, and how best to balance the need for static and dynamic decisioning rules.

CHAPTER **10**

Information
Management

O rganizations spend an absurd amount of time trying to manage
their data. Big data only exacerbates this problem; to take
advantage of an asset, it needs to be fit for purpose.

This is especially true in business analytics. The time a typical team
spends managing data usually dwarfs the time it spends actually creating insight. Despite this, few teams have a plan when it comes to
their data. Rather than see data management as a key activity, they
usually see it as a small part of a bigger process. Through a blend of
heroic effort and sheer will, teams limp along constantly wondering
why their lives are so hard.

This is backwards. Data management is the big, bad, and ugly part
of business analytics. A team without a plan is a team doomed to
inefficiency. Most organizations struggle with:

- Designing their information assets to maximize reuse
- Minimizing the time they spend managing data
- Designing flexible processes that can be used across many
  situations
- Deciding what data they capture and process

The solutions described here focus on frameworks and techniques
that help describe and overcome these challenges.

CREATING THE DATA ARCHITECTURE

WHY READ THIS?

When will this help?

Read this if your data is a mess and you don't know what to do about it.

How will it help you?

Using this approach will help you structure your data to encourage reuse.

What are the guiding principles?

- Understand your data
- It's better to have too much data than too little

What else should you read?

- Moving beyond the spreadsheet
- Scaling past the PC
- Understanding the data value chain
- Creating data-management processes
- Capturing the right data

The Background: Without Effective Data Management It Is Impossible for Teams to Scale

Most problems can be solved with the right data. Many problems benefit from common data. Reusing data to solve different problems is a conceptually simple solution that's remarkably hard in practice. When teams fail to define their data structures in an efficient and reusable manner, they drive inefficiency, cost, and wasted time.

Effective Data Management Enables Cost Efficiencies

Data is the cornerstones of business analytics; without them, it's impossible to make better decisions. Without better decisions, it's impossible to drive value. Ironically, data is also most teams' biggest weakness. Most teams find that managing information is their biggest time sink. It's a rough measure, but the general rule of thumb is that data management normally takes anywhere up to 80 percent of a team's time!

Cutting this time down is easy. Teams simply need to make sure they spend as little time as possible repeating effort. Instead, they should try to reuse their assets and processes as much as possible. It's a simple concept, but it's also one that's surprisingly hard to practice. When teams don't actively drive reuse, they end up spending far more time than they should replicating work that has already been completed.

Isolated Activities Lead to Duplicated Effort

One way many analytics teams drive value is by building models that use what's known today to predict what's likely to happen in the future. These models might predict whether someone is likely to find a job, whether they lied on their tax return, or whether they might be interested in buying a new phone. Even though each model predicts a different outcome, the inputs for all models are often very similar.

Two analysts might build models to predict which customers will be interested in two different products. Despite predicting different outcomes, both models will probably benefit from common inputs; few things are as powerful as using customers' known behaviors over time. Given that these models use common data, it makes sense for the analysts to collaborate and share the load of generating these data. In practice though, this rarely happens. Whether it's due to a lack of communication, personality conflicts, or a host of other reasons, analysts will more often than not work independently.

Rather than sharing their workload, they will spend large amounts of time duplicating the same basic data. Ironically, they will then often complain about how much time they have to spend managing their data! Once their project is finished, they will often do the right thing and upload their data into the analytical datamart or shared file system. Unfortunately, they will rarely let anyone else know that they have done so or where they have put their data. Instead, they will chalk it up as a task they'll get to when they have more time.

When this happens, it's normally a sign of a broader cultural and process problem; usually, the other members of their team is doing exactly the same thing. Instead of a real asset, the team ends up with one silo of divorced information per person. Over time, this breeds complexity, wasted disk capacity, and, in the long run, more work. All this occurs simply because the team lacked a common data architecture.

Why Should You Care?

Managing information is never easy. One of the biggest symptoms of teams suffering from this mistake is their abject fear of data—they usually spend so much time creating, re-creating, and searching for data that they end up with little time to actually create anything of direct value!

Another common symptom is a constant lack of storage capacity. Because teams are so horrendously inefficient at managing their data and driving reuse, they rapidly run out of space. This is regardless of how much additional capacity they are allocated; every increase is followed by a rapid expansion of duplicated data!

Teams that make these mistakes suffer a number of headaches. They lose their ability to audit process without massive amounts of effort. Their processes become unmaintainable by anyone other than their designer. Over time, their data complexity becomes a constraint in its own right. Fixing the problem becomes more and more frightening as the number of processes they use increases.

These problems carry financial costs. Teams require more and more staff to do the same amount of work. They limit their ability to scale or become more productive, and they usually require higher-than-average storage investment to accommodate poor design.

What Not to Do

Putting in place a structured datamart is the obvious solution. However, this requires more than just centralizing data. A great example involves a team I knew that unintentionally discovered the limitations of centralization without guidance or structure.

The Massive Mess of Data

With all the best of intentions, the team's most senior analyst had spent a tremendous amount of time establishing a common analytical datamart with structured data. Unfortunately, he happened to be the only person who actually understood it. In principle, the team had invested more than enough effort to create a common analytical datamart. In practice, it had ended up with an inefficient mess of unlinked tables, each of which had some degree of overlap with other related tables. Even worse, there was no easy way to determine which tables contained source data or processed data, making it almost impossible for the broader team to know what was raw data and what was imputed.

Data management had always been a problem for this team. Things eventually came to a head when they hired a new analyst. Despite a strong resume and a great set of skills, this new analyst took almost nine months to get up to speed with their datamart, all of which were spent being totally unproductive. It was at about that point that the team acknowledged they had a real problem and started developing a truly analytical data architecture.

Messy Data Is Cultural, Not Technological

At some stage, the costs of maintaining an existing architecture outweigh the costs of starting from scratch on every new initiative, and at that point, the team usually decides that it needs to clean things up. Therefore, it sets aside a decent block of time to go through and eliminate redundant data. It would seem as though this should solve the problem. Unfortunately, the real disease has its roots in culture and a lack of a formal architecture. By treating the symptom rather than the disease, the team usually makes two mistakes.

First, members of the team continue to work independently—each member rationalizes his or her own data but ignores everyone else's data. Individually, members of the team drive local efficiency gains. Globally though, they just contribute to the problem. Any temporary efficiencies are rapidly eliminated as people fall back into their usual patterns.

Second, team members rarely place an emphasis on standard process. Because they lack guidelines, each team member ends up developing an individual preferred approach to store and structure data. This may be efficient and creative, but across the team, these

238 ► DELIVERING BUSINESS ANALYTICS

different approaches often make it even *harder* to cross-reference and link information. This further limits the team's ability to reuse its data assets.

Finally, the team rarely gets the most out of its technology assets. Optimizing most storage engines requires specialist knowledge. This information is hard to come by and usually requires experience. The niche nature of this knowledge means that it's rare for everyone (if anyone) on the team to be an expert in storage architecture. When left to its own devices, the team ends up with an underutilized storage platform that costs more than it should.

Overall, the final result is an even more fractured and poor performing warehouse that progressively degrades over time. Bad design makes it hard for the team to understand what it has, where its new data should go, and how it could go about optimizing its existing data assets.

The How-To Guide: Design the Analytical Datamart, Don't Create a Shanty

The real solution is to treat the disease, not the symptoms. The better approach is to define a data architecture that covers:

- A conceptual map of the team's data
- The logical structure of the team's data
- The physical design for the team's data
- A data dictionary that provides a roadmap to the team's primary asset

By describing how their data assets should look, the team sets a series of guidelines that dictate how data is managed. It defines how additional data should fit into its model and what relationships exist between these data elements. It dictates how this data should be stored to drive maximum return on the team's technology investment.

Critically, this design is an evolutionary one. Rather than viewing it as an immutable structure, the team treats it as a roadmap, one that guides data management. As requirements and information sources change, each of these architectural elements needs to be maintained and improved.

The Conceptual Data Architecture

The conceptual architecture describes two things. First, it outlines the major entities within the team's data. An organization's customer base might include entities such as customers, transactions, products, relationship managers, and so on. These entities are described through their attributes. For example, every customer has an address, a preferred communication channel, and so on. Every transaction has a date, a time stamp, and a product or service.

Second, a conceptual architecture describes the relationships between these entities. For example, every customer owns one or more transactions. Every transaction includes one or more products or services, and every customer is linked to a dedicated relationship manager.

The conceptual architecture does a few things for the team. It gives the team a map by which it can triangulate where new data should land. The team might source third-party segmentation data that gives it another perspective on likely behavior patterns. By referencing the conceptual architecture, it's fairly obvious that this should be linked against the customer.

It also makes it easy for everyone on the team to quickly see the team's current and future data assets. Through a single diagram or map, analysts can see their assets at a glance. Importantly, this summary-level view cannot contain the detail about where the data is physically stored or what forms the fields take. There are other architectures that play this role. Instead, the conceptual architecture helps them work out whether the type of data they are looking for exists in the first place.

The Logical Data Architecture

Understanding things at a more granular level of detail is the focus of the logical data architecture. The logical data architecture describes the specific data elements held by the team in a platform-agnostic and business-friendly manner.

It plots out the specific tables, fields, and relationships within the team's data assets and is usually fully normalized to minimize redundancy; it represents the highest level of design efficiency possible. It still describes elements in simple language, often referring to "customers," "postal address," and the like.

By defining and enforcing a logical data architecture, teams can minimize data duplication. As teams acquire new data, they map it into the logical architecture based on the relationships described in the conceptual architecture. If they identify duplicate fields, these fields can be dropped prior to creating them in the datamart.

The logical architecture also provides a real data map. It helps teams understand whether the data they're looking for already exists. Once they've identified the entities they're interested in within the conceptual architecture, they can use the logical architecture to find specific measures. If those measures don't exist in the logical architecture, they know that they'll need to source them elsewhere.

The Physical-Data Architecture

The physical-data architecture is the lowest level of detail. It describes how the logical architecture is actually implemented within the datamart. Rather than referring to tables and fields by plain-English names, they are described by the names used within the database. These are often different due to technology constraints or company standards. Storage engines might not allow the use of more than a certain number of characters in a field name. Or database standards might mandate the use of a two-character identifier in the field name to describe the field type.

Unlike the logical architecture, the physical architecture may not be fully normalized. The fully normalized table structure of the logical data architecture is a great way to efficiently describe the team's data assets. Star schemas are a great way of enforcing referential integrity and minimizing data duplication.

However, these structures are rarely optimized for speed. Different storage engines take advantage of different technical approaches to drive storage and access performance. Tables may often be combined for efficacy or technology reasons. For example, in-memory applications often work best when tables are fully de-normalized, eliminating the need to join data.

These design decisions are normally made based on technology characteristics and performance/usage requirements rather than on the data itself. Because of this, the team needs a way to work out where that data is actually stored and how best to store new data. This, fundamentally, is the role of the physical architecture.

Together, these views help the team rationalize and reuse its current and future data. However, this is of marginal value without an easy way to reference all this technical information.

Bringing These Views Together

Making it easy to reference this metadata is the final step. To do so, the team consolidates these architectures along with a deeper explanation of data elements into a data dictionary. Rather than rely on assumptions and guesswork to work out how fields are calculated or what they mean, the dictionary describes how data is sourced and transformed. This is a dynamic document, subject to constant updates. It becomes the team's primary data reference, giving everyone an easily accessible point to determine how best to source, access, find, and extend data.

Benefits and Limitations

Most benefits come from efficiency and driving asset reuse. On one hand, the team can quickly identify whether the data they're looking for already exist within their datamart. On the other, they can also quickly map their new data into a well-defined structure. This reduces effort and drives storage efficiency.

This also helps drive reuse. Rather than constantly re-creating data, the team's usage model shifts toward checking first, developing second. By doing so, the team increases their efficiency and productivity.

The biggest challenges lie in cultural change and up-front effort. This usually represents a significant change in the way people manage their data. Getting people to change the way they work is hard. It helps to emphasize the benefits of having quick access to already-structured data. However, this falls apart if the architectures and data dictionary aren't updated regularly. Driving the right outcomes is a continuous exercise, not a one-off activity.

Equally though, starting out usually requires substantial effort. The legacy of years of inefficiency usually means that getting things right requires a major project. Properly fixing things might require more up-front effort than the team has ever spent managing and defining their data. However, the long-term benefits from reuse greatly outweigh any short-term costs.

UNDERSTANDING THE DATA VALUE CHAIN

WHY READ THIS?

When will this help?

    Read this if you struggle to explain where data came from our how specific measures were calculated.

How will it help you?

    Using this approach will help you establish data lineage through a business analytics value chain.

What are the guiding principles?

- Understand your data
- It's better to have too much data than too little

What else should you read?

- Moving beyond the spreadsheet
- Scaling past the PC
- Creating the data architecture
- Creating data-management processes

The Background: It's Not Enough to Go from Insight to Action—You Need to Know How You Got There

To get from insight to action, every team needs to meet some common transformations. Unfortunately, most teams forget about the importance of tracking how these transformations affect their original data, and, therefore, they lose the ability to defend *why* they're making the recommendations they are.

Data Governance Benefits from Standardized Transformations

Data is oxygen to a business analytics team. Without it, the team can't survive. Given how important data is, it is sometimes surprising how informally teams design their insight and management processes. To an outsider, a business-analytics team can seem almost magical. They conjure data from the depths of the organization and, by applying various arcane instruments, they somehow create insight.

This sounds pretty cool! The sad reality is that many relatively immature business analytics teams actually buy into this myth. They believe that business analytics is indefinable, characterized by art and experience rather than process and governance. They believe that their value comes from creativity, not repeatability.

As anyone who's had to deal with credit management in the financial sector will attest, this is a fairly naive position to take. When every scorecard and every stress test needs to be justified to a poker-faced regulatory committee, claiming art and magic simply doesn't makes the grade. It's only when teams are put under pressure to explain how a particular number was generated and discover that they can't that they realize they have a real problem. Business analytics *can* and *must* have structure surrounding it, even if the specific activities can't always be defined ahead of time.

Without structure, all a team has is chaos. Chaos is extremely hard to explain. Although the results may still be correct, teams will struggle to convince the rest of their organizations that their numbers are accurate. When they can't defend their results, their recommendations end up being left by the wayside.

Why Should You Care?

Teams that lack structured processes can rarely explain how they came up with their results. Like art, the best they can say is, "We know it when we see it." This may make sense to a team but it rarely flies with the rest of the organization. Doing something as simple as calculating an organization's number of customers can quickly become fiendishly complex.

"Customers" seems like a simple measure. It might, however, mean the number of active accounts, the number of people who have recently bought something, or the number of households that have one or more accounts or services. Each is valid, but each will produce a different number. Whether the number is correct depends on context.

Having ill-defined processes increases the odds of ending up with different results for any given measure. Even worse, this lack of definition also makes it hard to reconstruct how specific numbers were generated. This creates tremendous risk for the team—even though their calculations may be correct *given their assumptions*, their assumptions may not match those made by the rest of the organization. When they don't match, the team's credibility ends up being called into question.

The Danger of Parallel Calculations

One team I knew had developed a variety of models that predicted how much customers would be worth in the future based on their likelihood to purchase additional products. To come up with a financial estimate of a customer's value, they had developed three types of models.

The first were propensity models that determined which products a customer was likely to purchase over the next year. The second were activity models that estimated the variable costs associated with provisioning and activating a new customer. The final set were contribution models that estimated the return for each product sold.

In principle, this all looked good. Together, the models provided highly interesting and apparently useful results. Unfortunately, a pristine surface hid a rotten core; things fell apart when the team shared its predictions with the rest of the organization. The marketing department was on-board with the team's project until the finance department torpedoed the entire initiative.

Unbeknownst to the team, finance had already developed a variety of contribution and activity models. Sadly, finance's models produced vastly different results. Reconciling the two numbers wouldn't have been a problem but for one thing: Because the team hadn't created well-defined and standardized processes, it had no way of easily reconstructing its data.

Rather than capturing and storing its data through each step in the estimation process, all the numbers had been created on an ad-hoc basis. Along the way, the team lost all its assumptions and the specifics of how it had transformed its data. The team *had* documented its project but without these repeatable processes, it was impossible to reconcile the numbers against finance's numbers without re-doing the entire project.

If the numbers had been close, the team probably could have argued measurement error. Unfortunately, the numbers were sufficiently different to imply a completely different strategy. Because finance got there first, finance's numbers carried the real weight. Not only did this call the robustness of the analytics team's analysis into doubt but it also destroyed much of the goodwill the team had built with marketing.

What Not to Do

The obvious solution is to audit and refactor current processes. More than anything else, this is a defensive position. The only time a team knows that its numbers are inconsistent is when the numbers are challenged. When numbers don't match expectations, the team spends a significant amount of time redoing its work to justify its recommendations. This hurts the team's credibility as well as its ability to deliver.

The How-To Guide: Track Data Lineage through the Data Value Chain

The better solution is to ensure that whenever the team creates a repeatable solution, they incorporate governance and standardization best practices during design and not as an after-the-fact quick fix. Good processes are *always* transparent, repeatable, and auditable. This can't happen after the fact if the team really wants to drive better outcomes and validate their work: It's a design imperative. For an analytics team, this means having transparency across all its activities, from acquiring data to generating actionable insights.

Without transparent and repeatable processes, teams are lost in the wind. They struggle to explain how they have created their measures and predictions. They struggle to replicate their innovations. Worst of all, they are constantly pushing into being reactive rather than proactive, justifying their work rather than driving transformation. Tracking lineage creates a number of benefits. It helps drive efficiency. It helps replicate best practices as they're discovered. It gives the team the ability to track data lineage by linking source data to transformation and delivery.

This doesn't mean that every process has to be exactly the same; the activities that go along with creating a segmentation model are vastly different to those involved with optimizing marketing campaigns. What makes many teams give up is the fear that processes vary too much to be defined in any meaningful way. Team size, sophistication, and domain focus all play a massive role in working out what process will work best. However, that doesn't mean that they should be unique every time. Most processes *do* follow five common milestones, each of which involves fairly standard stages of data transformation. By tracking lineage across these five milestones, teams ensure that they can always explain their results and predictions.

The Five Milestones of Data Transformation

These five milestones are:

1. Sourcing raw data
2. Cleansing and imputing data
3. Calculating transformations and derivations
4. Calculating value-added data
5. Translating data into a consumable form

These don't *have* to happen within separate processes; they simply describe the full set of steps that always happen in some form. Separation helps, but only when it makes sense to do so. What's important is that the team works out a way of tracking how each of these transformations affects its original data.

Teams start by getting access to raw data. This usually comes from the warehouse, operational systems, or third-party data providers. It represents items of truth, warts and all. It may be incomplete, it may be inaccurate, and it's probably of variable quality, but it represents the best data available.

Unfortunately, this data is rarely ready for analysis. To get any further, the teams need to increase data quality before they can do their analyses. This might involve standardizing inconsistent naming conventions (such as names and addresses) or it might involve inputting missing values to increase the completeness of the data. By the time teams are finished, they have data that's ready for analyses.

They then take these data and create a variety of derived measures. These are calculated measures that represent changes over time or relationships between data elements. Their aim is to make interpretation or statistical modeling easier and more accurate. For example, the companies might think in terms of market-share changes. To help their businesses, the teams might create a model that uses revenue changes to predict market share data. Unfortunately, the raw data they source from third parties might only show sales by company, not by market share. Using this data would force those interpreting the results to think about things in terms sales volumes, not market share.

To make it easier, teams might derive these percentages from absolute sales figures and store them as additional fields. These derived variables aid interpretability and can help drive model accuracy. The same idea applies to creating binary variables from categorical measures, detrending data, or binning interval values. Each represents additional data generated by the team that relies on specific business rules and assumptions.

Once their data is of high quality and they have generated these additional measures, they need to create their models or reports. These, in turn, generate even more data, usually of an analytical nature. Common examples include predictions, statistically based goodness-of-fit measures, and other model diagnostics such as Gini coefficients.

These extra data *also* needs to be stored. They are used to operationalize the results as well as to allow the team to optimize their activities over time. These measures are often fed directly into an analytical-measurement framework, helping teams work out where their attention would be best spent to drive further efficiencies or accuracy gains.

Finally, all these data need to be reduced into something that's easily consumable. At this point, there might be hundreds or thousands of fields. This is far too much for operational decision making, let alone strategic debates! To make the insight palatable, the team needs to summarize this complex data into a form that's easily interpretable, highly relevant, and easily consumable. Dashboards and reports need to present the bare minimum of useful information.

This also applies to operational use: Predictions need to be structured in a way that allows operational systems to leverage them. For example, a model's prediction might be a value between 0 and 1, representing the percentage probability that a customer might accept an offer. The operational system, on the other hand, might need a binary integer flag that simply identifies whether a customer should receive an offer. To get the data into this state, the team needs to convert the percentage value into a binary value, keeping track of the rules that help set where that cut-off point should be.

Measurement Simplifies Management

Isolating, tracking, and measuring how each of these five activities influences its final results make it easier to run the team. Predictions and calculations are inevitably wrong at some stage. By separating these activities, the team can identify *why* things are going wrong when predictions don't match reality. Once identified, the team can fix it. Having clearly linked milestones also makes it easier to trace data lineage. This gives the team the ability to explain and justify its approach to internal and external auditors.

Rather than try to treat processes like a detailed and well-worn recipe, it's better to treat them as a checklist of discrete activities that need to occur in some form. This gives flexibility while still allowing some degree of standardization. It also helps drive efficiency and reliability by making it easier to debug processes. When all these activities are blended into one giant process, it's usually too complex to be easily analyzed. Separating these activities makes it far easier for the team to maintain, optimize, and debug their day-to-day work.

Benefits and Limitations

Adopting this approach actively reduces risk and simplifies analytical data maintenance. By separating major activities, the team can justify and explain with a minimum of effort and rework every piece of information it generates. It can control and isolate the assumptions from the facts contained in the data. This helps build credibility and gives the team the ability to align its measures and calculations against those generated by the broader organization.

It also directly feeds into the team's optimization efforts. Isolating and tracking changes to data makes it far easier to debug analytical data-management processes. When numbers don't match what the team expects, the team can quickly determine whether it's the assumptions it made or whether it's the data that's incorrect.

The only real limitation with this approach is that processes usually need to be re-engineered. This takes time and money. The resulting reduction in maintenance costs helps justify some of this investment. Unfortunately, many costs are potential and driven by excessive risk. That's a problem that's often hard to justify fixing.

CREATING DATA-MANAGEMENT PROCESSES

CASE STUDY

WHY READ THIS?

When will this help?

Read this if your team spends far too much time managing and manipulating data.

How will it help you?

Using this approach will help you encourage process reuse and drive productivity and quality improvements.

(Continued)

What are the guiding principles?

- Automate everything non-value-added
- Understand your data
- It's better to have too much data than too little
- Keep things simple

What else should you read?

- Allocating responsibilities
- Measuring effort
- Creating the data architecture
- Understanding the data value chain
- Reducing time to recommendation

The Background: Monolithic Processes May Be Efficient but They Are Never Reusable

To build an asset, most people will try to find the most efficient route. Unfortunately, efficiency doesn't always imply reuse—usually, it's easier to create a single, highly complex process than it is to create a modular, reusable process. This limits a team's ability to scale and discourages asset and data reuse.

Efficiency and Reusability Don't Always Go Together

Getting from data to outcomes usually takes a lot of data manipulation. This can be hard and complicated. Even the best-intentioned teams find it easy to make mistakes.

To see how easy it is to make a misstep, consider a team that has exhaustively read this book and taken its principles to heart. It has hired the right people, established the right culture, and actively driven change. It understands the importance of driving and measuring direct returns. Its analytical platform is split into discovery and operational environments. It has connected with the right people across the organization, and it has established repeatable workflows to encourage and drive efficiency.

The team understands that competitive advantage stems from driving economies of scope and scale. Therefore, it tries to make its processes as efficient as possible. This is great, but there's a catch: When efficiency comes at the cost of reusability, it hurts rather than helps. Not everything that is efficient is necessarily good.

Monolithic Data Management Processes Discourage Reuse

This may initially seem counterintuitive but it's easy to see why this is the case when one looks at a practical example. To be as efficient as possible, the team refactors its existing sets of code into highly optimized all-in-one processes covering everything from getting the data to deploying the models. It becomes very efficient, the process executes in record time, and by using one tool, the team minimizes transaction costs.[1]

At first, everything seems great. Processes that used to take days now take hours. Unfortunately, these gains are limited to one project and drive few economies of scope. When the team eventually reviews its overall productivity, it usually finds that delivering projects takes the same amount of time as it always did. The team's technical skills are best in class, but its ability to drive economies of scale or scope is sorely lacking.

By creating monolithic processes, the team makes reuse impossible. Other people on the team struggle to take advantage of the subactivities they're interested in. Someone building a cross-sell model might benefit from having up-to-date customer data. Rather than generate that data from scratch, that person might be interested in reusing data from a separate retention model. Unfortunately, because the process is so monolithic, regenerating that data requires rerunning the entire process.

This also creates problems elsewhere. This retention model might have been built to support a monthly process. When data is updated unexpectedly, the results of other assets can change. It's disconcerting for decision makers when their supposedly static results change every five minutes!

This is especially true for operational processes. A retention model will usually be built to support outbound campaign activity. If this happens once a month, churn propensities also need to be regenerated every month. Cross-sell models, on the other hand, may have different requirements. Rather than running monthly, they might run continuously, based on online browsing behaviors. This would require near-real-time scoring to take into account the customer's latest browsing behavior, and that's where things fall apart.

One process runs monthly. The other runs every second. When the faster process requires data from the slower process, everything usually breaks down. Rather than being generated monthly, retention scores are now being generated every second. This places additional load on the analytical platform and, depending on design, might even bring the entire platform down.

To avoid this, every process ends up reimplementing the same datasets. The only difference is the time period they're aligned to. Rather than reducing the time the team needs to achieve actionable insight, those apparently efficient processes force needless work.

Therefore, despite creating spectacularly efficient projects at a local level, the team fails to drive efficiencies at a global level.

Why Should You Care?

Teams facing this problem tend to think about tables rather than processes. Logically, every table is created through a process. Rather than reusing processes, however, the team focuses on the table. If the table can't be updated easily, the team will create a new table with the information it needs.

This adds overhead and effort. The insidious thing about this is that it's not always obvious—an enthusiastic team can still deliver. It just isn't as effective as it *could* be. In time, it cripples a team's ability to scale. One team I worked with was, in almost every way, a model of best practice: It had the right culture, philosophy, and structure. Despite this, it struggled to get past roughly 10 models per analyst. This wasn't bad compared to its peers but was well behind world-class companies.

In many ways, it was very frustrating. The team knew what it *could* be doing, it just couldn't get there. Not until it reviewed its processes in detail did the team realize the real problem: It didn't reuse anything!

Every time the team created a new model, it rebuilt data from scratch. Remember, these were data that could be used by *all* their projects. Even though the team centralized its data in their datamart, it never got around to reusing the data between projects!

The irony was that this was entirely because the team had chosen to create hyperefficient processes. Everything from getting data to training its model happened in one process flow. When the next project came around, it was just too hard to pick this apart and reuse the common bits. Instead, the team would start from scratch and re-create the data it needed. Even though its processes were fast and individually efficient, the team's overall efficiency was surprisingly low.

What Not to Do

If reuse is the problem, the obvious solution is just to make sure everything *can* be reused. Because most teams aren't as sophisticated as the one just described, they usually start by trying to centralize everything. They put their processes and data on a common platform and managers mandate that asset reuse is essential.

The problem is that this mandate doesn't solve the core issue. Reusing something only works when it does what a team needs it to do. When processes are monolithic, most of what the process delivers isn't useful for other uses. If only 15 percent of a process is relevant to a new project, picking it apart might take more work than re-creating it from scratch.

Over five projects, the benefits of this overhead probably outweigh the costs. Taken on its own, though, it's faster for analysts to redo the work. They still deliver, albeit at the cost of global efficiency.

The How-To Guide: Separate Data Management into Four Activities

Productive teams tend to structure their processes around four separate activities:

1. Creating common data
2. Building model-specific tables

3. Training models or generating insight

4. Deploying results

Rather than having an end-to-end process that goes through all these steps, the process should be broken into four separate steps. The team can then reuse each separately as needed. These steps are closely related to the five conceptual activities described earlier, but they give the team of way of instantiating what are otherwise largely conceptual activities.

Separate Logically Different Activities

The first step involves sourcing data *not already in the datamart*. These data might come from source systems, the warehouse, or third-party providers. Key activities are sourcing data, cleansing them, standardizing them, and imputing any missing values.[2] The goal is to deliver this new data to the right place in the analytical datamart based on the logical/physical data architecture. Once the logic has been built, it's packaged and placed in a common area where it can be scheduled and/or used by other people.

The next step involves structuring data to train models or build reports. This involves doing two things. Firstly, data from the first step needs to be joined with data already in the warehouse. Secondly, derived variables not already in the datamart need to be created. These variables will change during the development process; unlike the tables created in Step 1, this table will constantly change structure until the final model is built.

The goal is to end up with a table that can be used to create a model/report as well as score ongoing data. Because it's specific to the model or report, the odds of reuse are low. However, it still needs to be separate to scoring processes for reasons that will be covered shortly.

Step 3 involves generating insight. The analyst uses the modeling table to build a candidate model or report. If successful, it is converted into an operational process in Step 4. If not, the analyst goes back and re-works Step 1 and 2 to build a new candidate asset. When eventually successful, the new variables derived in Step 2 will normally be included in the Step 1 process. This makes them available in the datamart for everyone to use. The goal is to create an asset that drives a better result than current processes.

Steps 2 and 3 are separated to ensure operational flexibility. Model development is rarely time constrained. Data processing delays can be frustrating, but they rarely break anything. Operational scoring is very different—processes need to complete within specific time frames. By separating data extraction from scoring, the team can pipeline individual processes (or run processes in parallel) to make sure the end-to-end process completes at the right time.

The final step involves taking the asset and pushing it into operation. Models are converted into highly efficient formulas that simply score new data. Reports are packaged and pushed into operational environments. The analyst then schedules Steps 1 and 2 to update as frequently as needed and links the output against the converted asset. Then, the whole process is usually migrated to an operational environment and embedded within relevant processes. The goal is to make the end-to-end process as automated as possible.

Reuse What Is Necessary, Not What Is There

Keeping these steps separated helps ensure flexibility, maintainability, and drive efficiency. As data change, the team only needs to profile and rework relatively simple processes. Comparatively, complex end-to-end processes are a devil to debug. They also help drive asset reuse; processes can be called and reused as necessary. Data, by default, land in the datamart in a cleansed form, and derived variables are flagged and separated.

Returning to the case study, realizing this was an AHA! moment. When the team profiled its data use, it realized its problems were driven by a lack of reuse. Developing and deploying a new model took the team roughly two weeks. Of that, a whole week was needed just to get the data in order. When the team split its process into these four steps, initially its development time went up to two-and-a-half weeks! This was disappointing, but expected; doing things properly needed more work than the team was used to.

As planned, though, the team's efficiency grew over time. Within three months, its development time dropped to just under a week. By making a small change and folioing these four separate steps, the team more than doubled its productivity. It went from being able to handle 10 models per analyst to 20 per analyst, a strong improvement.

Benefits and Limitations

There are many benefits in using this approach. On one hand, the team gets clarity. Workflows become standardized and expectations are clear. Over time, the team becomes more productive. The team drives greater asset reuse, and it becomes easier to migrate processes into production.

The biggest limitation is the extra effort that's initially needed. To a team under pressure, this extra workload can seem impossible. In these cases it's important to understand whether the pressure stems from inefficiencies in data management. If so, the only real answer is to cure the disease rather than the symptoms. The team needs to address and solve the core problem: ineffective data management. Until it does so, it will continually be constrained.

CAPTURING THE RIGHT DATA

CASE STUDY

WHY READ THIS?

When will this help?

Read this if you don't know what types of data you should capture.

How will it help you?

Using this approach will help you make sure you have the right data for the problem at hand.

What are the guiding principles?

- Think about competencies, not functions
- Drive outcomes, not insight
- Understand your data
- It's better to have too much data than too little

What else should you read?

- Creating the data architecture
- Understanding the data value chain
- Creating data-management processes

The Background: When There Is More Data Than Time, Everyone Needs to Make Hard Choices

The move to digital infrastructure has transformed the way we manage business. Every transaction and interaction is captured and available for analysis. Unfortunately, there is usually more data than there is time to spend analyzing data; we are profoundly better at capturing information than we are at understanding it. For a team tasked with generating insight from data, this presents an interesting problem. Regardless of how skilled the team is and how effective its technology is, at some stage the team needs to make the hard decision about what data it should try to analyze.

There Is Usually More Data Available Than Is Being Analyzed

Organizations are drowning in data; any organization that isn't should be concerned for its future. It's probably not because the organization is unique. More likely, it's because the organization is not managing its business effectively.

Every transaction and interaction generates data. When customers make purchases, call to complain or compliment, or become loyal customers, they generate data. When the bank rejects a transaction for being potentially fraudulent, the organization generates data. When customers comment online about their experiences, they generate data. Any organization that complains about a lack of data isn't missing data. It is just not capturing the data.

Data is valuable. With the right skills, organizations can uncover patterns and generate insights that might otherwise be impossible to detect. Knowing that certain customers prefer blue widgets to brown widgets drives competitive advantage—organizations armed with this knowledge can rationalize their products and drive sales, generating better results. Business analytics is the enabler that transforms insight into value.

This is a worthy, if somewhat daunting goal—faced with an overwhelming amount of data, it's often hard to know where to start. To see why, consider an organization interested in driving better customer engagement. Because happy customers are less likely to look elsewhere, the organization might measure its success on its ability to drive retention through better engagement.

It's impossible to build a better relationship without knowing what their customers are interested in. The fastest and most efficient way to build this know-how is through business analytics, and business analytics require data. To define a list of potential projects, the team decides to go back to basics—rather than start with the ideal, it starts with what it has. An initial scan across the organization's data repositories might find the following:

- Free text-based customer-contact center interactions
- Customer-based prior purchasing history
- Market preferences, captured through focus groups, containing both structured and free text information
- Online social-media interactions
- Aggregate sales histories by product and geography
- Application forms containing large amounts of free text information
- Price-dependent sales volumes

Any or all of these might prove valuable. The catch is that analyzing all this information requires time and a variety of different competencies.

Different Types of Analysis Require Different Skills

Broadly speaking, getting the most out of data requires at least two different types of skills. One is the ability to analyze numerical and categorical data (structured data). The other is the ability to analyze free text (unstructured and semistructured data). As a general rule, people who can perform one of these skills are rarely skilled in the other;[3] being skilled in parametric analysis is very different from being skilled in ontologies, parts of speech, tokenization, or sentiment analysis.

Because of this skills divide, the team is forced to make a choice. There is clearly more data than it has time to analyze. The team is also seemingly constrained in many ways: It has existing skills, which may or may not align against each of the datasets available. Working out the best approach, given this context, can become a major challenge. It has to start somewhere; the question is just where?

Why Should You Care?

The core problem is one of prioritization. To drive results, the team needs to pick an approach and any or all of the data available to them might give them the insight it needs. The team's main risk is time; as with all projects, it still need to deliver in a reasonable time frame. Unfortunately, there's rarely enough time to try every possibly approach.

Teams that make the wrong choice usually show one of two symptoms. If they pick the wrong data or the wrong approach, the outcomes they deliver may be no better than existing processes. On the other hand, teams that try to use everything usually become paralyzed by indecision and run out of time. It's always possible to build the most comprehensive model in the world. It's just that that rarely happens on the first attempt—sophistication takes time.

The Team That Picked the Easy Option Rather Than the Right One

An analytical marketing team I knew provided a great case study of how painful this indecision can be. It was a newly established team keen to make its mark on their company. As is often the case, its immediate priority was to try to help its direct-marketing counterparts reduce churn rates.

It realized during scoping that it had three major sources of data. The first was a database of contact-center interactions in free text format. The second was a comprehensive record of all customer transactions over the last five years. And the third was a collection of web logs that tracked customers' browsing history.

It made sense that unhappy customers would probably call to complain or try for a discount. This suggested that the team would probably be best off starting with the data from the contact center. A frank assessment showed that the team had little experience in analyzing unstructured data. They did, however, have strong skills in numerical analysis.

Given its skills in numerical modeling, the team decided to start with the transactional data. Had the team been working for a telecommunications company, this would probably have made sense. Customers about to churn often change their usage patterns to avoid what they see as unfair costs. Unfortunately, it wasn't working for a Telco—the company was an insurer. The team's analysis found some degree of relationship between claims and churn, normally due to an unhappy claim experience. The predictive strength of this relationship was, however, relatively weak. When the team compared its models against its existing processes, it found its models were only marginally better. Pragmatically, it was probably more cost effective to keep contacting customers in the month before the customers' policy renewals were due.

In the end, the team had little to show for its three-month project. Rather than question its assumptions, the team instead decided to look for other opportunities to use the transactional data it had spent so much time sourcing and cleansing. A year later, the team had made little progress.

What Not to Do

It's essential that an analytical team define their data architecture. Conceptually, this is simple. Practically, this implicitly involves prioritization; creating structure from chaos takes time and effort. For most teams, there are more data than can be consolidated in a reasonable time frame.

The obvious solution is to align the team's data-acquisition strategy against its strengths. If the team is strong in analyzing structured data, focusing on skills-based prioritization suggests that it should source and use structured data first. The strategy becomes one based on form rather than content.

Sometimes, this works. By happy coincidence, the data the team has fits with the problems they are trying to solve. Usually though, there's some degree of mismatch. The team starts treating everything like a nail simply because all it has is a hammer. When they hit a nail, they succeed. When they find a screw, they struggle.

The How-To Guide: Use What Works, Ignore the Rest

The better approach is to start with the problem and work backward. Rather than choosing data based on its existing skills, the team described in the case study should have chosen its data based on value. The team was aware that the contact-center information was more likely to have leading indicators for churn. Despite this knowledge, the team based its decision on comfort rather than likely value.

To define the approach based on likely value and not the form of the data, teams need to either:

- Qualify out because of a lack of skills.
- Source the right data and develop new skills.

Sometimes, developing new skills simply isn't an option. If the problem requires data that the team would not be able to analyze, given current skills, it sometimes makes sense to not even try; there is rarely a lack of other opportunities. Instead of spending time creating an average outcome, the team is probably better off finding a different problem that aligns with their current skills.

Otherwise, the team should base its approach on what's likely to work, not on what it is comfortable doing. Unstructured and semi-structured data are tremendously valuable; surveys and customer feedback can give insights that are otherwise impossible to identify. This carries through to the team's data strategy; rather than prioritizing data acquisition based on form, the team acquires data based on content and information value.

In practice, data is data. Debating the merits of unstructured *or* structured data is missing the point. The question isn't which is better. The real question is which will produce the best outcome.

Benefits and Limitations

By shifting from a form-based strategy to an outcomes-based strategy, the team increases its odds of success. Using highly relevant and descriptive data usually improves the accuracy of its recommendations. This increases the team's value to the organization, creates value for the organization, and builds trust.

The biggest challenge that goes along with this is that the team usually needs to put a strong emphasis on developing new skills.[4] It may not have the skills needed to analyze social-network data, social-media data, or web logs. That doesn't mean it shouldn't develop those skills; it needs to move outside its comfort zone and accommodate cost and risk. Good outcomes require the team to use data that's fit for purpose and picking data based on what's easy will, more often than not, reduce the value of the team's recommendations. New approaches mean that analytics will usually need training, and this carries cultural change, a notoriously difficult process.

NOTES

1. In fairness, this is a very optimistic point of view. Prior to being refactored and optimized, many monolithic processes end up being gargantuan in nature and can take hours or days to complete.
2. Don't forget that these changes need to be tracked and auditable. Raw and derived data are very different. There's nothing worse than getting into an argument about specific measures and realizing that, rather than arguing based on the facts, you are arguing based on statistically representative but fictional data.
3. There's no good reason for this other than academic specialization; anyone who has the technical ability to pick up one skill has the ability to pick up the other.
4. Skills don't always need to be internally developed. As covered in earlier sections, leveraging consultants is always an option as long as this doesn't lead to an organization sacrificing its intellectual property.

CHAPTER **11**

Decision-Making Structures

I nsight without execution is worthless. It's obvious that action is a critical part of getting value out of business analytics. However, getting an organization to act on insight carries its own set of problems.

Translating qualitative recommendations into operational processes isn't always straightforward. Insight is intangible—it's often hard to measure it after the fact. Scalability is a constant challenge. Making sure decision making keeps pace with increases in data volumes creates its own set of challenges.

Linking insight to outcome is the final piece of the puzzle. Understanding how best to go about operationalizing insight can be challenging—most organizations struggle with:

- Linking insight to outcomes in a highly scalable and measurable way
- Scaling their decision-making processes to deal with big data
- Driving relevancy in their decision making by taking into account current information
- Taking into account both what's known ahead of time as well as what may not be known in advance

The solutions described in the next section focus on frameworks and techniques that help describe and overcome these challenges.

LINKING ANALYTICS TO VALUE

CASE STUDY

WHY READ THIS?

When will this help?

Read this if you struggle to close the link between insight and value.

How will it help you?

Using this approach will help you close the business analytics loop and demonstrate value creation.

What are the guiding principles?

- Drive outcomes, not insight
- Automate everything non-value-added
- Know what you are worth
- Function should dictate form

What else should you read?

- Augmenting operational systems
- Keeping everyone aligned
- Opening the platform
- Scaling past the PC
- Moving to operational analytics
- Creating data-management processes
- Reducing time to recommendation
- Enabling real-time scoring
- Blending rules with models

The Background: Good Insight Doesn't Necessarily Lead to Good Decisions

It's a hard truth but it's an important one: Ideas are cheap. Given enough time and resources, anyone can generate insight. Convincing someone to actually *act* on that insight is the hard bit. Given how hard it is to overcome culture and trust issues, you would think that the technical and data aspects should be easy in comparison. Unfortunately, most teams still struggle to get these working efficiently.

Effective Teams Go from Insight to Action

Ideally, business analytics involve three major activities:

1. Analyzing data to generate insight
2. Generalizing that insight to other contexts
3. Acting on those generalizations

A team might want to know whether certain types of purchases have higher odds of being fraudulent. By engaging with the investigations team, they might develop a hunch that many purchases in quick succession from a number of different retailers are a good indicator of card theft.

To work out whether this is true, the team might pull a few years' worth of data and analyze it. They may apply a logistic regression to measure the relationship between transaction types and known fraud. Among other things, the final models might suggest that the odds of a transaction being fraudulent double if there are three purchases within half an hour that involve either a petrol station or online retailer.

At this point the team has valuable insight, but to make it useful, it needs to make sure the business acts on that insight. The team starts by sharing its findings with the fraud team. This helps build awareness but does little to change the way the business works. Assuming that the fraud team is willing to act on the insight in the first place, simply having this knowledge doesn't actually help it—even though the team now knows that these types of purchases are suspicious, it lacks the skills or time to be able to find them.

To make it easier for the fraud team to find these types of purchases, the analytics team scores current transactions in the hopes of flagging suspicious purchases. It summarize the results into a report and once it has this rich information, the team sends these focused insights to the fraud team for follow-up.

Insights Need to Be Linked to Action

At least in principle, this seems like it should work. The team has found something interesting, it has generalized the information to make it reusable, and it has directly applied the information in a way that should enable action. Unfortunately, there are still issues. Over time, the team discovers that:

- It is constantly short of time
- It cannot explain the team's value

Because the team is engaged with an operational process, there's a constant stream of new data to be scored. By taking on responsibility for generalizing their models to new data, the team ends up spending most of its time running its process and little time developing new processes.

Every day, the team needs to manually score the latest data. The time it spends scoring this data keeps eating into its ability to deliver new projects. On one hand, this limits the team's ability to create new insights and drive new value. On their other, it puts a great deal of stress and pressure on the team—if they don't score and report on the data in enough time, the investigations team cannot act on the data.

This is bad enough. Even worse is that, despite all this work, the team has no way of working out how much value it has added. Although the investigations team gets a report every day, it rarely has enough time to track how many times it does or doesn't act on the insight. The investigations team may insist that it finds the report useful, but when it comes to asking for more budgets, the analytics team cannot directly quantify the benefits it has generated.

Eventually the analytics team ends up time constrained, stressed, and largely unable to explain its worth.

Why Should You Care?

The team's problems come from two main sources. Namely, it:

- Presents soft insights rather than hard recommendations
- Breaks the link between insight and action

Their first problem is that research rarely leads to action when people are short of time. Most front-of-house staff members are under extreme pressure—it's their responsibility to make sure outcomes happen. Because of this, they rarely have the time to review things in detail. They're at their best when they have access to concise information with clear recommendations. The less time they spend interpreting data, the more they have to spend driving outcomes.

Secondly, the team's report isn't linked to tangible outcomes. It's extremely hard for the team to show that any action was specifically due to its insights. That an investigator drove the right outcome might have equally been due to the investigator's experience, gut-feelings, or the conversations the investigator had with other investigators. Even though the insight might be accurate and useful, it's impossible for the team to relate its effort to value.

There are many case studies of teams that fall into this trap. Consistently, teams become overburdened by their reliance on manual processing. One team I knew ended up spending almost 80 percent of their time doing business as usual. That left just under a day a week per member of the team to spend driving new value and taking care of administrative activities. Unsurprisingly, the team struggled to extend its scope of work or justify further investment.

Over time, the team fell apart. Because it could not explain its value, it could never justify hiring new people. Because it was stuck doing time-consuming boring work, most of the team members eventually went to find new jobs. After a year of this, the team was a shadow of its former structure and the organization folded them into another team that was having more success.

What Not to Do

It's tempting to try and solve these problems by forcing the downstream teams to track and report on the value of analytics. This seems to make sense but rarely works in practice.

In principle, it seems fair that the team that's benefiting from the research should track the benefits of that insight. In practice though, it rarely has the time or interest in doing so. With or without better insight, the team still needs to do its job. Although insight will help the team drive a better outcome, tracking the value takes time away from its *driving* an outcome. Therefore, the first thing the team will cut is time spent helping out another team.

Much of this has to do with the team's operational focus. A business-analytics team, by comparison, should adopt a more strategic point of view. Its role is to drive *organizational* value, not just run an operational activity. Delegating this responsibility to another team might seem to free time but usually just means that the results never get tracked.

The How-To Guide: Don't Just Provide Insight—Establish a Strongly Defined Scoring Process Built on Measurement and Recommendations

The real solution is to move to an integrated scoring model. This requires, at a minimum:

- Process automation
- Strong recommendations
- Value measurement

Rather than manually running processes, the team should convert its processes into assets. These assets can then be deployed into a system dedicated to operational execution where they can be scheduled. Up-to-date data are then automatically extracted from the relevant source systems, translated into a scoring input table, and the scoring formulas applied. The results are then automatically delivered to the destination systems where they can be used by the operational team.

Significantly, these insights are far more refined than the general research delivered in the report. Rather than off-loading interpretation onto the front-of-house team, the process makes hard recommendations. Instead of delivering 30 measures that in aggregate describe the main characteristics of a transaction, the process flags whether a transaction *should* be investigated further. There's no harm in providing richer data to help analysis if the front-of-house team is interested in doing further research, but this data shouldn't be the focus.

Finally, effective operational scoring requires the process to close the loop and capture whether the recommendation was acted on. If the recommendation was "further investigation," the scoring should track whether the investigation took place. By doing so, the team first gains the ability to identify whether recommendations were acted on. It is also able to link insight to outcome, giving the team a launching pad to start measuring the value it brings to the table.

Benefits and Limitations

Teams that adopt this approach drive more tangible value. On one hand, their efficiency gains make them more productive. On the other, they're better at tracking the value of business analytics.

There are few caveats that go along with this approach, the biggest of which is investment. This efficiency comes at a price: It requires the right technology platform and the right architecture.

The tools need to support automation, scheduling, and systems-level integration. The processes need to be packaged, managed, and deployed. When they don't and they aren't, it's impossible to drive any real efficiency gains. By necessity, the team is forced to continue to work with manual processes, sacrificing efficiency for cost. In the long run, this is rarely a sustainable strategy. However, those who are not aware of this solution often think it's the only answer.

REDUCING TIME TO RECOMMENDATION

CASE STUDY

WHY READ THIS?

When will this help?
Read this if you struggle to analyze and process big data.
How will it help you?
Using this approach will help you design your insights investments to accommodate for big data.
What are the guiding principles?

(Continued)

- Eliminate bottlenecks
- Design your platform for use, not purity
- Minimize custom development
- Keep things simple

What else should you read?

- Keeping everyone aligned
- Opening the platform
- Smoothing growth with the cloud
- Moving to operational analytics
- Enabling real-time scoring
- Blending rules with models

The Background: Sunk Costs Can Constrain a Team's Ability to Scale

To make insight actionable, teams need to embed their insights within operational processes. This is usually harder than it seems—despite the best of intentions, architecture isn't always dictated by what drives the best outcome. Sometimes, technology becomes an end in its own right. When this happens, business-analytics teams are usually forced into adopting suboptimal approaches, and their capacity to scale becomes constrained by arbitrary technology decisions.

Automated Scoring Drives Scale

Moving to an operational scoring approach makes a lot of sense. It drives efficiency and links insight to outcomes. However, this process doesn't organically appear—the right foundations need to be in place for teams to eliminate their manual processes.

Most teams that have made the leap to client/server processing start out with a discovery environment, often called a sandpit or workbench. Over time, they realize the value of having a common analytical datamart. They put time and effort into standardizing and sharing their data. They extract data from source systems, prepare it, and then create a variety of assets that generate insight.

To sustain the value they've created, they need to regularly use those assets. Therefore, every month they take current data and manually score the data using their assets. This gives everyone relevant and timely insight, predictions, and recommendations.

By doing this, teams drive real value. Unfortunately, at some point they realize that the vast majority of their time is being spent running operational processes. Instead of generating new insights (and value), they're just reusing their existing assets. Rather than creating incremental value, they're simply sustaining value. They eventually realize that this is largely because they spend too much time manually scoring data. Until they break free from manual work, the way they work will always constrain them.

New Approaches Are Often Dictated by Constraints, Not the Problem

Teams start rebuilding their processes and looking for technology-based solutions. They engage IT and start looking into how best to use their existing assets within their organizations' overall technology architecture. It quickly becomes clear that the organizations have sunk significant money into their warehouses and operational support systems. Unfortunately, the teams' assets are all built using different sets of analytical technologies.

Because of sunk costs, teams are often put under pressure to reuse technology instead of acquiring new technology. To scale and automate processing, IT often recommends that teams rebuild their assets inside the warehouses using warehouse-specific functions.

In practical terms, teams may be pressured to rewrite their scoring algorithms into SQL-friendly code. They may be pressured to translate everything they've created into MapReduce or other processing languages. To someone unaware of the more complex forms of analytics, this seems to make sense—data manipulation functions are pretty consistent among systems, and reports rarely require truly complex algorithms.

Rather than put up a fight, teams decide to go along with this approach. When they finalize models, they rewrite their scoring processes into warehouse-specific code. Unfortunately, over time they find that they are consistently slower than their peers in getting models into production. No matter how skilled they get, when they want to move models into production they need to:

- Convert their scoring codes
- Deploy their scoring codes
- Validate that their scoring codes are consistent when run within the warehouses
- Promote their scoring codes into production

Although the second and fourth steps can be managed, the first and third steps take far longer than would be ideal. Therefore, despite minimizing capital costs, teams carry needless operational costs and lose agility.

Why Should You Care?

Teams fighting against these problems usually:

- Take far too long to move assets into production
- Are limited in the techniques they can apply

The biggest barrier to agility is the time it takes to execute. Converting, deploying, validating, and promoting routines takes time. Simple rules like, "Flag all transactions over $10,000," are easy to implement. Things are a bit harder when it's a complex ensemble model with imputations and other transformations.

If it takes an analyst four weeks' worth of full-time work to get an asset into production, the greatest number of assets an analyst can theoretically manage is between 10 and 13. If, on the other hand, the analyst only needs one week of full-time work to get an asset into production, that same analyst can theoretically manage up to a model per week. This can be up to a 500 percent productivity improvement!

Teams in this situation also often find their choice of approach is limited by their operational systems and coding abilities. Some things are just hard to translate from an analytical context into a warehousing context. Neural networks, for example, are infamously hard to build in SQL. Translating the resulting scoring processes into SQL-based code is possible but, depending on the network's complexity, can be time-consuming.

The effort needed to convert complex processes often acts as a barrier. Rather than spend extra time converting tricky scoring processes, analysts will often compromise and base their choice of algorithms on what's easiest to translate. Decision trees may or may not provide the best prediction. When they become the default option simply because they're easy to deploy, something's normally wrong.

What Not to Do

The obvious solution is to try to raise the skill level of analysts and reengineer processes to make them even more efficient. Teams usually get extra training. In some cases, organizations may even create dedicated model-deployment teams that are responsible for migrating assets into production.

To a certain degree, these help. They help the organization avoid further capital costs, albeit at the expense of operational costs and headcount. However, they fail to resolve the real issue. Assets still need to be converted and validated, and, no matter how efficient or knowledgeable teams become, this always results in substantial overhead.

The How-To Guide: Don't Compromise and Don't Convert—Get the Asset Where It Needs to Be in the Form It Needs to Be

The starting point is to accept that no amount of training or process-based reengineering in isolation will ever truly work. As important as these are in this context, they're always trumped by technology and data. Best practice involves using a systems-based approach to moving assets into production.

Effective deployment involves enforcing three principles wherever possible:

1. Assets should be migrated, not converted.
2. Outcomes should dictate the approach, not platforms.
3. The system should be designed to overcome bottlenecks, not just capitalize on existing investment.

Define the Answer Based on the Problem, Not on Existing Constraints

To solve the problem, one needs to remember the context. An analytics team goes through two broad activities when operationally scoring data. First, it extracts current data and converts them into a scoring input table. Once the team has extracted the data, they need to score them. Scoring involves two things: data and logic. Automation requires a system that is specifically designed to facilitate these functions.

Most organizations have warehouses that provide broad access to common data. This is usually a logical place to land and create the input table. Unfortunately, most warehouses have limited native support for advanced analytics algorithms. Their functions tend to be limited compared to purpose-built tools, and when they do provide appropriate functionality, their sophistication tends to be limited.

In other words, although warehouses are strong on the data side, they're not necessarily as strong on the logic side. Although warehouses can usually support basic scoring logic, they often only support a subset of the functions that teams *want* to use. This limits teams' choices to what the warehouses can support.

Even worse, leveraging these functions usually requires some degree of logic conversion. Every manually converted asset adds risk by potentially introducing bugs into the process. Converting logic also introduces inefficiency by requiring additional effort. In these situations it makes sense to trade off accuracy or relevancy for efficiency. To deliver, teams need to compromise, which is a bad outcome by any measure.

Rather than accept this compromise, teams can choose to reengineer their platform to support their assets natively. Taking into account current technology and architectural methodologies, teams have three broad options:

1. Establish dedicated operational analytics environments
2. Leverage in-database scoring
3. Deploy a purpose-built, in-memory business-analytics appliance

The first approach, the dedicated operational analytics environment, involves establishing separate environments that provide the logic piece of the puzzle. Teams can then pump data from the warehouse through these environments and back to the warehouse.

The second approach, leveraging in-database scoring, involves extending the warehouses' logic functionality to include support for the assets that teams are dealing with. Teams then migrate (rather than convert) their assets from their discovery environments directly into the warehouses. Scoring happens without data ever leaving the warehouses.

The final approach, an in-memory business-analytics appliance, involves migrating both data and logic into a separate platform designed specifically to support high-performance analytical applications. Source data and assets are migrated into this environment and only the results are delivered back to the warehouses for general use. In some cases, the high-performance platforms may even take over the role of enterprise decisioning systems.

Each provides different benefits and limitations—the right choice is largely based on context and constraints.

Benefits and Limitations

The advantage of dedicated operational analytics environments is that it provides a full set of analytical functions with high flexibility. Because the environment usually leverage purpose-built tools, they have the broadest native support for analytical functions.

The biggest disadvantage of such environments lie in data transfer—every piece of data that needs to be scored needs to be copied to and from the environment. In many situations, this might not be a problem. Big data changes things. When there are many terabytes or petabytes of data to be scored, it may be uneconomical to move data back and forth. The cost of the network infrastructure may outweigh the benefits of the process.

In these situations, it makes sense to move to an in-database scoring environment. Rather than just translating scoring code into generic SQL, this approach involves providing asset-level compatibility between the warehouse and the discovery environment. Assets aren't converted; they're migrated. Scoring processes are optimized to leverage warehouse-specific functions, and scoring results are consistent between the two environments.

The biggest disadvantage with this approach is compatibility. Not all in-database functions are equivalent. Standards such as PMML (Predictive Markup Modeling Language) seem to offer a common lingua franca among systems. In practice though, not all systems implement the full set of functionality that PMML offers. Equally, PMML doesn't cover the full set of functionality offered by most business-analytical software! Much comes down to the specific implementation with this approach, and every time an asset needs to be converted rather than migrated, organizations become inefficient and carry risk.

A similar constraint exists with conversion to SQL code. It's important to validate whether this conversion is efficient and comprehensive. When the output is a lowest common denominator of generic code, the first thing to go is normally speed. If the point of in-database scoring is speed, it makes little sense to migrate highly inefficient code into the warehouse!

The final option is to refuse to compromise. Rather than having to choose between functionality and scale, the team might decide to have the best of both worlds. To drive the greatest level of scalability possible, they might decide to put the warehouse and analytical platform in the same environment, deploying an in-memory business analytics appliance. Assuming the data and logic are deeply integrated at a technology level, the team gets the benefit of a highly parallelized and extremely scalable system.

The major benefit of this approach is sheer scalability. When designed correctly, these systems link logic to data across every node in the environment. Problems are broken down into parts and parallelized across the grid, allowing linear scalability as more nodes are added. Because the environment includes a storage platform, data updates can be scheduled in advance rather than on demand. This gives teams a path to manage the costs normally associated with investing in high-bandwidth network connectivity.

The biggest limitation of this approach is sheer cost. Organizations need to fund computation *and* storage, which may not be cheap.

However, in situations where the problems are simply so large that the existing warehouses cannot deal with them effectively, organizations might not have any other choice.

ENABLING REAL-TIME SCORING

CASE STUDY

WHY READ THIS?

When will this help?

Read this if your recommendations are suffering because of tardy information.

How will it help you?

Using this approach will help you improve the relevancy and accuracy of your recommendations in situations of high data velocity.

What are the guiding principles?

- Automate everything non-value-added
- Start flexible, become structured
- Keep things simple
- Function should dictate form
- Watch the dynamic, not just the static

What else should you read?

- Augmenting operational systems
- Scaling past the PC
- Moving to operational analytics
- Creating data-management processes
- Reducing time to recommendation
- Blending rules with models

The Background: Up-Front Analysis Isn't Always Possible

Relevancy and recency have a tight relationship—current information helps drive better decisions. Unfortunately, batch-based processes need to be run in advance. When these are run *too far* in advance or when data changes frequently, predictions usually suffer.

Granularity and Recency Drive Relevancy

Business analytics help take an existing process and make it more effective. Being able to predict what people will be interested in helps reduce the odds that they will be shown irrelevant offers—by making right offers more often than they make wrong offers, organizations drive better results. This applies not only to sales-generating activities; the same principle applies elsewhere regardless of whether you are looking at managing fraud, linking people to services, or managing risk.

Operational scoring helps institutionalize this approach. By tracking acceptance/detection rates and further differentiating treatments, teams rapidly identify what works and what doesn't. By using this insight, they start driving continuous improvements.

This virtuous cycle is a never-ending one. The ideal end point is one of mass customization and the market of one—everyone ends up with an entirely unique treatment based on individual personal characteristics. Rather than adopting a one-size-fits-all approach, the offers an individual receives become highly relevant to that person and only that person.

This differentiation comes from two sources. The first is data granularity. By creating smaller and smaller groupings of people with similar behavioral patterns, teams enhance their models' abilities to isolate differences among groups. They then use these differences to drive different treatments.

The second is data recency. When it comes to predicting what type of phone someone might be interested in, knowing what that individual looked at a year ago is of less use than knowing what that individual looked at yesterday. Most of the time, good predictions come from taking advantage of what's happened most recently.

Current Data Is Better Than Old Data

Knowing how to drive differentiation is one thing. Actually doing it is another, and doing this presents two major challenges. Granularity is usually constrained by scale—moving from one model to a hundred requires teams to become a hundred times more productive. As discussed throughout this book, the answer to this problem lies in process reengineering and effective asset management.

The biggest constraint to recency is a little more complex. Operational scoring processes are normally run in batch on a fixed schedule. The processes that use their outputs dictate this schedule. For example, most organizations run their retention campaigns on a rolling monthly schedule. Every month they call customers at a high risk of cancellation and try to make them an offer they can't refuse.

Because this activity happens monthly, it makes sense to create churn predictions just before the calls are made. That way the models can take advantage of customers' most recent behaviors. Every month the organization consolidates their customer data into one big table. Customers' scores are generated ahead of time, and those with the highest risk of cancellation are passed to the contact center for follow-up.

The models might show that the following are strong predictors of churn:

- Browsing plans and pricing on the company's portal 10 days before a customer's contract is due for renewal.

- Asking the contact center about minimum contract lengths within 15 days of the customer's contract end.

Knowing that these are leading indicators is powerful, but there's an issue. Both events require data that falls within the 30-day modeling window. This is a problem because there's likely to be a lag between when the customer's data is scored and when the customer is contacted. To see why, it's helpful to consider a typical chain of events.

Time Waits for No Person

Assuming the models are applied on the first of the month, they will source what is, at that point, the most recent set of data available. However, the contact center will probably take the full month to contact all flagged customers. During this entire period, it will be using the scores generated on the first of the month to prioritize calls.

The predictions for the customers on day one will be as accurate as they can be. By the tenth day, though, the models no longer include accurate browsing patterns. Although the predictions have remained static, customers have continued to live their lives. By the fifteenth day, the models no longer include queries about minimum contract lengths. Therefore, for half of every month, the models can't include two of the biggest leading indicators of churn.

Even though customers may exhibit these behaviors, by the time the contact center gets in touch with them their scores are likely to be out of date. The more engaged a business becomes, the more recent its data becomes. Every social-media engagement or outbound offer creates another data point. Unfortunately, teams will often be unable to take advantage of this rich source of information when they are relying on batch-based scoring processes.

Why Should You Care?

To a certain degree, every organization suffers from this problem. It's usually when their competitors overcome these challenges that the problem becomes obvious. Those that lag in their markets are constantly on the back foot: They understand why things happen but are too slow to do anything about them until after the fact. This creates two specific problems:

1. They sometimes make outright bad decisions.
2. They carry excessive opportunity cost.

Ideally, decisions are made on perfect information. Although this is unrealistic, it's entirely reasonable that decisions should take advantage of all the information that's available. The longer action lags behind analysis, the greater the risk of making a bad decision. Events will happen in that time gap that, if detected, may have suggested fundamentally different actions.

Usually, the cost of this bad decision is relatively small. If the organization is predicting churn, it may simply have a slightly higher level of churn than it otherwise would have. However, this isn't always the case. If the process is trying to detect fraud, a quick series of fraudulent applications could see the organization out millions of dollars.

Because this can happen within a typical 30-day modeling window, the organization might never even have had a chance to detect the event! Even though the data were there, poor process design probably prevented the organization from taking advantage of them. In this case, delayed insight can quickly become an extremely expensive mistake.

This applies in the other direction too. An offer made based on old insight might still be accepted. However, that doesn't mean that the offer was necessarily the best offer that *could* have been made. More recent insight might have led organizations to make different offers that carried a higher margin or revenue. In that case, lack of recent insight leads organizations to forego revenue.

What Not to Do

The obvious approach is to increase scoring frequency. Rather than scoring every month, teams might start scoring data twice a month. As their data becomes more and more recent, they may start scoring every 10 days, every 5 days, and eventually every day.

Superficially, this works. It's also extremely inefficient and requires a tremendous amount of computational horsepower. To be useful, every job needs to score every single customer. This puts significant load on the warehouses and logic tiers of the analytical platforms. For one model, this may not be an issue. When it comes to hundreds or thousands of models, warehouses are likely to grind to a halt.

This problem tends to hit those with the most data the hardest. A company with a million customers and five products may not have any issues with running their scoring processes more frequently. A company with 10 million customers and a thousand products is a different matter. One organization I worked with discovered this the hard way.

The Team That Brought the Warehouse to Its Knees

This organization had developed a handful of cross-sell models and was interested in incorporating channel preferences into their models. Their original models assumed that every customer had a preference for a single channel (such as ATM, branch, or e-mail). The organization quickly realized that not all products were equal when it came to channel preferences. For example, few people in their market preferred to receive mortgage offers while withdrawing money from the ATM.

To fix this, they decided to model channel/product combinations as a multiplicative relationship. Rather than treating channel and product as independent factors, they made channel preference dependent on product. With 40 products and six channels, the organization quickly realized that it would need to develop and deploy 240 models.

This in itself wasn't an issue—the organization was efficient enough that developing these models was a three-month project. The real issue was that with almost 20 million accounts to be scored, every scoring run took the warehouse an hour's processing.

With 10 models, the organization could get results overnight. With 240 models, however, the warehouse was monopolized for 10 days of every month. Given that the warehouse was also supposed to be supporting other business applications, IT understandably pushed back on allowing this level of modeling granularity. Despite having a strong reason to act, political and technical realities prevented the organization from delivering the value it had identified.

The How-To Guide: Go Real-Time or Go Home

The real solution is to try something different. Rather than prescoring tables on a fixed schedule, teams should, instead, score individual records when they are needed. To ensure recency and relevancy, systems designed this way use the most recent data available. Common examples include monitoring in-stream financial transactions for fraud or identifying a "next best activity" during a customer touch point.

Whether this solution is actually needed is generally dependent on:

- The number of models in operation
- The volume of data to be prescored
- The recency of data included in the model

Depending on each of these, at some stage prescoring data becomes uneconomical. Large numbers of models and data lead to heavy load on the warehouse. Although it's always possible to scale the warehouse to deal with ever-increasing processing requirements, it doesn't necessarily make financial sense to do so. In these situations, real-time scoring becomes the *only* solution that works.

Teams that move to this approach need to be aware of a few key differences. One of the differences between batch scoring and real-time scoring is the need to guarantee scoring times. Depending on the context, real-time scoring processes can be hard, firm, or soft.

Hard processes must *always* complete in a given time frame. In-stream transactional-fraud-detection processes fall into this category. If the system is built to analyze every transaction for fraud before money transfers are committed, a modeling failure may cause the transaction to time out. The fastest way to annoy customers is to prevent them from buying something because the system couldn't respond in time.

Firm processes degrade gracefully when deadlines are missed. Rather than breaking the process, things simply move on when scores are unavailable. They require a lower quality of service and require lower investment. A common example is identifying a "next best activity" in a contact center based on the ongoing discussion. If scoring completes successfully in time, the operator will be able to make a relevant offer. If not, the conversation will still continue, albeit with the absence of analytically based insight.

Soft processes are similar to firm processes with the major distinction being that results can still be used after the deadline has passed. A common example is using browsing patterns to make an offer. Even though the offer may not take into account the last 20 seconds' worth of browsing history, it may still be relevant enough to be useful.

Benefits and Limitations

The biggest benefit of this approach lies in its efficiency. Records are only scored when they need to be, significantly reducing processing requirements. This, in turn, limits investment and enables a level of scale that would otherwise be impossible to achieve.

The counterpoint to this is the need for excellent system architecture. Having to guarantee process-completion times requires a great deal more engineering than a traditional batch-scoring process. For most teams, it matters little whether a scoring process takes an hour or an hour and five minutes. Take this same level of variation across to a real-time process, however, and the results may not only be useless but might actually break operational systems.

As such, this scalability comes at a cost. Real-time scoring systems need to offer a much higher level of redundancy and a higher quality of service when compared against batch-scoring systems. Even so, there are many situations in which this is the only solution that makes sense.

BLENDING RULES WITH MODELS

CASE STUDY

WHY READ THIS?

When will this help?

Read this if you spend too much time managing business rules *or* struggle to take business experience into account when building models.

How will it help you?

Using this approach will help you better handle what you know as well as what you don't know.

What are the guiding principles?

- Think about competencies, not functions
- Understand your data
- Watch the dynamic, not just the static

What else should you read?

- Augmenting operational systems
- Scaling past the PC
- Moving to operational analytics
- Creating data-management processes
- Capturing the right data
- Reducing time to recommendation
- Enabling real-time scoring

The Background: Focusing on What We Know Means Missing What We Don't Know

There are things we know and things we don't know. Teams that focus on the first usually miss the second. Rules and known behaviors are great for identifying known patterns. However, of more interest are usually the deviations that signal fundamental changes.

Abnormal Behaviors Are Interesting

Analytics is often focused on isolating the interesting. It's one thing to know that someone regularly spends $50 a month. It's far more interesting to know that their spending dropped to $35 last month. A smart organization starts asking:

- Are they shopping somewhere else?
- Has their situation changed?
- Are they unhappy with our service?

The answers to these questions might drive further revenue or reduce the odds of the customer going somewhere else. This would have been impossible had the organization not been able to distinguish between what is normal and what is abnormal.

These leading patterns appear everywhere. Investigators might notice that money launderers tend to cycle transactions through countries with limited regulation. To do this as efficiently as possible, the launderers may transfer relatively large amounts at once.

By knowing this, the organization can create a rule that flags any transaction over a certain amount to those countries. Whenever the rule fires, the transaction is then halted for further investigation.

Static Rules Create Significant Management Overhead

Rules like these are an efficient way of codifying front-line experience. Unlike more sophisticated forms of analytics, they have the advantage of being easy to understand and interpret. Even better, they also don't require historical data in order to train them—as long as the rule can be defined, it can be deployed. Unfortunately, their strength is also their greatest weakness.

Those same launderers might eventually work out how the organization is identifying them. To avoid detection, they may start splitting their transfers into two transactions, both of which are under the rule's trigger point. For a while, this works and they fly under the radar. Eventually though, investigators uncover their new approach and create a variety of new rules, all aimed at identifying these newly discovered behaviors.

This "arms race" continues indefinitely. Both parties make their behaviors and detection rules progressively more complex. Unfortunately, the launderers always have the advantage—as long as they keep doing things differently, they can constantly stay a step ahead of the investigations team.

Even worse, the team needs to deal with ever-increasing management overhead. Historical rules may no longer be applicable. Unfortunately, the organization has no way of determining which rules should and shouldn't be kept in operation—because they worked once, they may work again. Over time, maintaining and updating this global set of rules becomes a job in its own right.

Why Should You Care?

Organizations struggling with this situation:

- Are constantly on the back foot.
- Have a large collection of rules that rarely fire.
- Are forced to invest in ever-growing rules-management teams.

Because their rules perpetually lag behind the population they're trying to monitor, organizations that rely on static predictions rarely keep up with their market. In some situations, this may not be an issue. Being slightly behind the market in marketing can be like a bad pizza—even when it's bad, it's still better than nothing. In other situations though, lagging behind the market can be costly. Being behind fraudsters is expensive, risky, and rarely acceptable.

Overreliance on static rules also leads to large rule libraries, many of which rarely trigger. Every time a behavior is identified, the team needs to create a new rule. These rules are like wedding gifts—even though they may no longer be relevant or attractive, no one ever wants to get rid of them—just in case.

This cruft creates overhead, and overhead requires management. Over time, maintaining these rule sets becomes a full-time career, justifying an ever-growing team. Whether these rules are actually useful or accurate becomes increasingly irrelevant. Rather than focusing on improving outcomes, the focus shifts to managing the pain.

The Team That Spent More Time Managing Rules Than Adding Value

The scale of this misapplication of resources can be astounding at times. One team I knew ended up growing from 3 people to more than 40, none of whom had a measurable impact on driving quality improvements.

It's easy to ask how this could be possible given how closely organizations track their bottom lines. It was a case of a death of a thousand cuts—at first, the team directly helped reduce fraud. By picking up on insights generated by the investigations team, it successfully deployed operational processes that flagged suspicious transactions. A rapid reduction in fraud justified additional headcount.

Unfortunately, the criminals they were modeling quickly changed their behaviors. The team refined its rules but understandably felt uncomfortable retiring its old rules. Unfortunately, this meant that the team's existing headcount had to focus on maintaining its existing rules. Over time, this cycle kept repeating. Every additional resource started out by developing new rules but ended up spending more and more time maintaining the existing rules.

The team's ability to create value never actually moved beyond its initial returns. Every gain was followed by a subsequent loss as criminals changed their behaviors. Because these losses were so noticeable, the organization kept investing more and more money into the rules team. Although it became a great internal empire, it was also arguably a stunning waste of resources.

What Not to Do

Most organizations try to solve this by restricting these rules to only what is accurate and useful. This seems to make sense. It's also a Sisyphean task.

The value of a rule isn't always directly related to how frequently it triggers. Frequent events may carry a low cost, whereas high-cost events may happen rarely. That a rule hasn't triggered recently doesn't necessarily mean that it's not worth keeping.

Trying to audit these rules creates a large program of work with few benefits. The usual conclusion is that, even though only a small percentage of rules ever trigger, none of the rules should be eliminated. The risk associated with dropping rules is usually seen as being unacceptably high. By doing this work, the team usually throws good money after bad—even though the project's finished, nothing really changes.

The How-To Guide: Take Advantage of the Best, Throw Away the Rest

The true solution stems from remembering that static behaviors are only part of the picture. Modeling the dynamic is equally important, and an effective detection/management strategy requires coverage across both.

Static rules work best with things that are known. This knowledge can come from research, analytics, or field intelligence. Over time though, nothing remains static—given enough time, everything's dynamic. The assumptions we operate under become increasingly irrelevant. Picking up and acting on these shifts is what differentiates a proactive team from a reactive team.

Ideally, the team blends static and dynamic rules, each targeting different behaviors. The team limits static rules to the most parsimonious set possible. Rather than trying to model all possible behaviors, the team instead uses dynamic measures to differentiate standard behaviors from abnormal behaviors. By doing this, the number of static rules in production decreases substantially. This helps organizations reduce overall team sizes without having to sacrifice quality or outcomes.

To see how this works in practice, consider a financial institution interested in proactively identifying credit card fraud. A well-known static trigger might involve flagging any transaction sourced from Eastern Europe involving an online purchase when the individual lives in a Western country.

At a global level, this is usually accurate. At a local level, however, this rule may not always be applicable, especially if the individual is from Eastern Europe. By modeling customers' purchasing patterns and identifying breaks from their typical geographic and vendor preferences, the financial institution can improve accuracy without having to identify the specific pattern ahead of time.

By blending the two approaches, the organization can handle both knowns and unknowns. Static rules cover the knowns, whereas dynamic rules help uncover the unknowns. This moves it ahead of the curve and minimizes the number of resources it needs to allocate to maintenance.

Benefits and Limitations

The biggest benefit from this approach involves moving from constantly fighting fires to getting ahead of the curve. Rather than constantly responding to risks, the organization increases its ability to identify and manage them before they manifest. Even better, the organization can move that much closer to a market of one, driving toward a true one-to-one engagement model. Every person is considered based on his or her personal behavioral patterns, creating person-level predictions and assessments.

The biggest disadvantage is normally political. Pure rules engines can become significant assets in their own right, regardless of how much value they actually create. Reengineering the organization's approach can sometimes involve a significant shift in resources. This can threaten power bases and cause significant discomfort. However, if these resources are being applied to relatively unproductive tasks, it makes little sense to preserve a bad approach just because.

Appendix

The Cheat Sheets

AUGMENTING OPERATIONAL SYSTEMS

Enterprise Resource Planning (ERP) systems are the backbone of most organizations; without them, things would fall apart. They help streamline operational activities and drive efficacy through repeatability. However, the benefits they bring through process efficiency only go so far; once processes are efficient and standard, what then?

Getting ahead of the competition requires more than efficiency. Predicting the future is better than reacting to the past, and greater insight supports better decisions. Unfortunately, most ERP systems are designed around efficiency and repeatability and are relatively lacking on the predictive side. Sometimes, this is because of technical limitations. Sometimes it's due to implementation choices.

The key to continuous return lies in making processes smarter and the easiest way to do this is through leveraging analytics. When existing processes don't offer these functions, it's tempting to hard-code the smarts into the ERP system. More often than not, this is a mistake.

Hard-coding analytics into functional processes creates a number of problems, many of which are only obvious after the fact. The better approach is to generalize analytics functions and make the smarts reusable elsewhere in the organization. By developing parallel analytical processes that augment the ERP system, the organization can leverage these capabilities elsewhere in the business. This helps drive competitive differentiation.

(Continued)

Separating analytics from ERP processes gives the business the ability to drive better results everywhere, not just within a single, functionally aligned ERP process. When correctly applied, this approach encourages competitive advantage and drives economies of scope.

BREAKING BOTTLENECKS

CASE STUDY

There's only so much time in the day. When it comes to finding answers to hard questions, business analytics teams shine. Unfortunately, when everyone needs answers, demand often outstrips the team's ability to deliver. When this happens, the organization ends up waiting for answers and the team loses credibility.

The obvious solution is to hire more resources. Unfortunately, this isn't always an option. The money may not be available, shareholders may not be receptive to increased structural costs, or there may simply be skills shortages. Finding the right people at an acceptable price can be hard.

Regardless of how good the reasons are, a team that can't deliver ends up being seen as a liability. Liabilities are eventually eliminated. Given this threat, another option is to preserve power by hoarding information. By acting as the gatekeeper, they can survive, at least for a while.

Needless to say, neither of these are scalable or effective solutions. They come with direct and indirect costs that create more problems than they solve. The more effective solution is to alter the delivery model. Rather than solve problems by brute force, with more people, the team should lift the organization's capabilities as a whole by moving to a mentoring/self-service operational mode.

Instead of being the insights team, the team should shift its focus to being an enabling team. It balances insight generation with quality control and enablement. By doing so, the team helps the organization as a whole improve and eliminate its role as a bottleneck.

CASE STUDY

OPTIMIZING MONITORING PROCESSES

Assets degrade with time. Models underperform, reports lose relevancy as the contexts they were designed for change, and data-management processes break as the structures they rely on are modified. Staying on top of and fixing this general degradation requires attention and effort. Unfortunately, they're usually the most scarce resource in any business analytics team.

Business analytics teams face constant time pressure. There's always more data that *could* be analyzed and more value that *could* be created given enough time. As the team increases its remit, focusing attention in the right areas becomes harder and harder. Unfortunately, every new asset adds to the general monitoring overhead carried by the team. Every success leads to more work, which maintains rather than adds value.

Because of this, it's easy to see why efficiency becomes such a big deal. To identify value, the team needs to generate new insights. To enable value, it needs to make sure those insights are operationally deployed. To realize value, it needs to make sure that those same insights are acted on. To maintain value, it needs to make sure the assets behind those processes are accurate, current, and valuable. That's a lot of work!

Small efficiency gains can make a big difference. Having a few extra hours a week can mean the difference between more models or stagnation. However, efficiency doesn't happen by magic. To drive it, processes need to change. Given that it's hard to automate intelligence or creativity, streamlining asset review processes are the obvious starting point.

The usual approach is simply to limit the time spent reviewing assets. The team minimizes the amount of time it spends reviewing logs or analyzing value creation for potential errors or issues. Although this is better than either reviewing assets too frequently or not at all, it's still not perfect. If the assets are fine, the team has wasted valuable time. If the assets are degraded, the team has probably been in operational use for longer than would have been ideal. Each outcome is suboptimal.

The better solution is to automate the monitoring processes. Instead of manually reviewing assets on a fixed schedule, the team moves to a management-by-exception model. Rather than manually check to see whether anything's wrong, the system itself takes care of the busywork and team members only get involved when asset performance drops below an acceptable threshold.

ENCOURAGING INNOVATION

CASE STUDY

Innovation is a hard concept to pin down. Sometimes, innovation is evolutionary; improvements come from making existing processes better. Sometimes, innovation is revolutionary; improvements come from discarding existing approaches and blazing a new path. Sometimes, innovation is easy; sometimes, it's hard. The only constant is that it requires a hunger for creative destruction and an environment that allows flexibility and experimentation. This is counter to how most organizations work.

Organizations are generally bad at fostering innovation. This shouldn't be surprising: most organizations are designed around repeatability. Running a business isn't easy, and uncertainty undermines efficiency. There's a reason organizations emphasize consistency and governance.

Organizations interested in innovating face a dilemma. On one hand, innovation requires flexibility. On the other though, efficiency comes from structure. Given this inherent conflict, it's not surprising that organizations usually struggle to drive continuous improvements once they see successes in business analytics. Initial successes are met with inertia and, eventually, stagnation. The answer isn't to try and create one solution for all problems. Rather than trying to make one system that meets all requirements, overcoming the inertia of strongly defined processes involves bypassing them entirely.

The better solution revolves around creating separate but linked business models. By capitalizing on the power offered by different frameworks driven by different requirements, organizations can achieve the best of both worlds. Most teams are targeted on driving efficiency and evolutionary improvements. Other teams are given the flexibility they need to drive disruptive innovation. Everyone, however, is measured on their ability to drive better outcomes.

By establishing an entirely separate but integrated operational model, organizations harness evolutionary and revolutionary innovation. Everyone leverages the same data assets. Everyone integrates into the same operational processes. There are well-defined processes to turn revolutionary innovations into business-as-usual processes. By separating experimentation from continuous improvement, organizations can innovate and test new approaches without impacting business as usual.

COPING WITH INFORMATION OVERLOAD

Making sure everyone moves in a common (and hopefully correct!) direction requires organizations to make decisions. Knowing what has and will happen makes it far easier to decide what to do, but there's a catch: we only have a finite amount of time to consider our options before we need to decide what to do. When our information sources outstrip our ability to consider them all in a reasonable time frame, our decisions suffer.

Some of these decisions are major: restructures, mergers, and acquisitions all fall into this category. Although these can make or break a business, they happen relatively infrequently. More common are the smaller decisions like choosing which customer to contact, which product to offer, or which claims should be paid. Individually, these decisions seem minor in comparison to the major decisions. However, they're made thousands of times a year and, because of their sheer volume, these small decisions can drive enormous outcomes.

Many organizations make their decisions based on experience and intuition. It's true that experience is a powerful force. It's also true that building experience takes time. The real problem is that people with the right experience are few and far between!

Business analytics offers a more scalable solution, one that's especially effective in guiding microdecisions. By applying increasingly sophisticated techniques over time, organizations can drive continuous improvements in predictive accuracy. This ability to scale is one of the things that makes business analytics a competitive differentiator. Unfortunately, this scale creates its own problems: too much insight leads to information overload.

Experience is powerful. So is business analytics. The real answer isn't to rely on one *or* the other. The better approach is to take advantage of process automation and shift focus away from areas of little impact. Blending business analytics with experience-based decision making can help mitigate this conflict. Business analytics helps organizations achieve economies of scale and scope in decision making. Experience helps overcome the limitations of statistically and rules-based decision making. By combining the two, more attention can be paid to areas in which it will have the greatest impact. Doing so improves efficiency and productivity and enables greater returns.

KEEPING EVERYONE ALIGNED

Business analytics is a team sport. Those who are responsible for insight rarely own the outcomes they try to predict. To get from insight to action, each and every team needs to come together as a seamless whole.

This level of coordination rarely just happens. Ensuring a large, extended team stays aligned takes more than a little attention and effort. Making this effort isn't optional; badly managed coordination introduces delays, uncertainty, and risk.

Activity without structure is little more than chaos. Undefined activities are notoriously hard to manage. However, too much structure is needlessly constricting and hampers innovation. Even more than in many other disciplines, it's hard in business analytics to predict what will work.

Success comes from realizing that the answer isn't heroic effort *or* management by meeting. Instead, the team should encourage the use of lightweight process-management techniques. Rather than trying to coordinate through checkpoint meetings, the team should coordinate by using workflow management systems. Doing so improves efficiency, increases agility, and significantly reduces risk.

ALLOCATING RESPONSIBILITIES

Things rarely work perfectly on the first try. We learn by doing, and whether it's gardening, developing an application, or writing a book, the first cut is rarely the last. Things take time to get right.

This is equally true in business. Success comes from understanding what's working and what isn't. Things that do should be replicated and extended. Things that don't should be re-engineered or eliminated. By reusing existing assets and strengthening specialized skills, teams can streamline delivery and improve quality. Being *globally* efficient requires the team to replicate its learnings *everywhere*, not just in all initiatives delivered by the person who discovered the improvement.

Effective teams understand that their real goal is value creation. This is about more than just developing insights; they need to make sure those insights are actioned. Given that it's the value chain that realizes return and not any specific activity within the value chain, it's a small step from here to giving people responsibility for the end-to-end process. Rather than manage at an activity level, people are made responsible for everything from insight to action.

This helps increase the odds of having successful projects. Putting them in charge of the outcome rather than managing individual activities helps create focus. It also helps encourage continuous improvement; owning the entire process makes it easy to identify and deliver incremental process efficiencies. What it doesn't do is encourage *global* improvements. Processes are built based on an individual's preferred approach rather than the team's best approach. Good ideas are rarely replicated elsewhere.

The better approach is to separate outcomes from the work that's needed to get there. Someone always needs to be responsible for the initiative. However, that person doesn't necessarily need to do all the work him- or herself. In fact, people should apply their unique skills across multiple initiatives. Accountabilities and responsibilities should be based on functional activities, not end-to-end process ownership. This helps drive efficiencies across different initiatives and increase *overall* efficiency, not just *local* efficiency.

OPENING THE PLATFORM

CASE STUDY

In an ideal world, demand dictates a team's size. Resources are hired based on workload and every project is met with the management and delivery resources it needs. More often, the opposite is true: resources and workload rarely match due to turnover and changing business needs. People find other jobs, leaving holes in project plans, and management defines high-priority projects that *have* to be delivered on top of business-as-usual activities. The team ends up with more work than it can cover.

Being put under this kind of pressure is never enjoyable. When demand outstrips supply, hiring people may seem like the right thing to do. Ironically, this rarely solves the problem. It takes time to hire new staff, time that the team often doesn't have. Even if the team found additional staff, new staff people may not have the right skills, and it takes time for them to get up to speed.

(Continued)

In these situations, there are only really two options. The team can try and leverage resources from other areas of the organization *or* it can temporarily engage external resources. Neither of these are inherently bad solutions. Usually though, other areas of the organization rarely have spare capacity. For this reason, contractors and consultants fill a valuable role. On one hand, they help smooth out volatile workloads. On the other, they provide easy access to specialist expertise.

For all their advantages, they also carry subtle risks. Firstly, many consultants will, by default, retain the assets they've created and only deliver the outcomes. Once their work is finished, the intellectual property and assets they've created leave with them. When the assets need to be re-calibrated, re-designed, or re-built from scratch, the organization is forced to re-engage the original consultant. Secondly, it discourages organizations from developing their own competencies. In the long run, this hinders an organization's ability to turn business analytics into a competitive advantage rather than a functional benefit.

The better solution is to open the organization's analytical platform and embrace external providers into the fold. Under this model, all resources, internal or external, *have* to use a standard centralized platform and follow common processes. This consistency ensures that, regardless of which resource does what work, anyone will be able to pick up the work of those providers at a future date and understand it.

By adopting this approach, the organization can ensure that intellectual property remains with the organization. As it develops its sophistication over time, the organization is free to convert business analytics from a functional benefit into a strategic advantage.

MOVING BEYOND THE SPREADSHEET

CASE STUDY

Every organization needs insight; action without insight is just chaos fueled by guesswork. Getting high-quality insight, however, can be surprisingly difficult. Counterintuitively, the most obvious approach is usually the wrong one.

In 1983, VisiCalc launched an industry. Numerical analysis, previously the domain of the universities, started to become commonplace. Today, our iPhones have literally thousands of times more processing power than Apollo 11. As processing power has increased, so has the availability of analytical software. Spreadsheets, scripting languages, and statistical tools are becoming a commodity. Even the most basic software offers the ability to do techniques that were once cutting-edge like regressions, curve fitting, and ANOVAs. It's getting to the point where it's hard to click on an icon without bumping into analytics in some form.

Given the prevalence of these tools, it's tempting to just take the path of least resistance. If it's the pre-installed spreadsheet on one's computer, so be it. Sometimes, this makes sense, especially if it's a one-off activity or you are interested in just playing around. When it comes to trying to use business analytics to generate repeatable value though, this creates more problems than it solves. On the positive, it's cheap. On the negative, it limits economies of scale and sometimes reduces output quality.

The better approach is to reconsider what the strategic objectives of the analysis are and choose the tools that support those objectives, rather than just those that are handy. Over time, this helps the organization scale, helps reinforce the perception of business analytics as a specific competency, and helps drive operational value. This movement away from spreadsheets to purpose-built tools represents the first real technological step to capitalizing on business analytics.

SCALING PAST THE PC

CASE STUDY

Getting past spreadsheets is a great start. However, it's only the beginning of the journey. Eventually, there's more than one person in the team and the group dynamic needs to change from a collection of individuals to a team working together.

The easy approach is to stick with the status quo and go with what people know. It's tempting to give people the freedom to choose their own tools and let them install them on their personal computers. Desktop software licenses are normally fairly inexpensive, and as long as things stay on the PC, it's easy to keep IT out of the loop.

(Continued)

The advantage of this approach is that it keeps things relatively simple. It capitalizes on preexisting experience. Unfortunately, it also eliminates many of business analytics' characteristics that foster economies of scale.

The better approach is to move from the desktop to a client/server environment. Analytical data should be centralized and standardized. By encouraging team members to reuse information, the team directly reduces the time it needs to develop insights. Migrating to a server environment also allows the team to start leveraging automation, a major source of efficiency. This drives up productivity and, in turn, drives substantial cost advantages.

CASE STUDY

STAYING MOBILE AND CONNECTED

For many, working in the same place day after day is a luxury they can't afford. In the constant drive to increase agility and reduce operating costs, many organizations take advantage of an increasingly mobile workforce. For many teams, this presents a challenge. For server-based processing to work, one needs reliable access to the server. This is easy to guarantee when everyone's grounded in one spot. When resources become mobile, the situation becomes more complex.

Mobile resources cannot always guarantee acceptable network performance back to their server environment. 4G-based mobile telephony and the like can sometimes provide sufficient bandwidth for analytics-focused road warriors. Unfortunately, this is expensive, and many organizations simply can't afford the ongoing cost of large data transfers to and from the analytical platform.

On one hand, guaranteeing acceptable mobile network performance may be cost-prohibitive. On the other though, moving back to a purely desktop-based processing model requires the team to sacrifice all the efficiencies and reuse that goes along with a server. As with most things, every solution has its exceptions. The traditional client/server model negates the need for local storage or processing beyond what's necessary to run the client software. However, there are situations in which users may need the best of both worlds.

In these situations, those that need it leverage a hybrid of local and remote processing. They maintain a local installation of all necessary software (within reason) but migrate their local assets back to the central repository as they finalize their work. This is a solution based on necessity rather than elegance; ideally, it is avoided as much as possible. Other solutions such as the use of virtual private networks (VPNs) are preferable. However, sometimes this is the only solution that makes sense.

Compared to many of the other solutions described in this book, this one is remarkably straightforward. The most important thing is to simply be aware of it as well as its limitations.

SMOOTHING GROWTH WITH THE CLOUD

CASE STUDY

Centralized processing provides numerous advantages. It encourages the use of standardized processes and allows organizations to manage their insights as assets. Even better, it allows them to integrate these assets into operational systems.

Unfortunately, these benefits come at a cost. Governance requires control and often the organization needs to sacrifice flexibility to achieve this control. As organizations solve more and more problems using the same competencies, they capitalize on economies of scope. The catch is that the demand for processing power or storage can quickly outstrip server capacity.

In principle, this is easily resolved. By upgrading the server, the team can continue uninterrupted. In practice though, this usually results in the team coming to a complete halt; upgrading servers takes significant lead time, in some cases as much as a year in advance! By the time the team finally gets the capacity they need, the market may have moved on.

The answer isn't to move away from a client/server architecture. Instead, it's to transform this hardware-constrained model into one that's extremely flexible: the enterprise cloud. By decentralizing processing and moving from a single-server environment to a grid-based multiserver environment, the platform can be expanded as needed. These upgrades can even occur without affecting existing discovery and operational processes. Even better, it can take advantage of low-cost commodity hardware.

This greatly simplifies the critical path within any upgrade project. Because minimizing downtime is no longer the major driving concern, coordinating

(Continued)

resourcing that is available becomes that much easier. Although it requires more planning and potentially more up-front investment, taking advantage of a cloud-based architecture reduces operational and project risk while also smoothing the volatility that normally goes along with upgrades.

MOVING TO OPERATIONAL ANALYTICS

Creating insight is easy. All it takes is the right skills and having enough time. Getting people to act on that insight, on the other hand, is hard. They need to trust it and they need to have it when they need it, not when it's too late. Even more importantly, they need to see the link between it and their better results. The alternative's a missed opportunity—when organizations don't take advantage of insights, nothing changes. The business achieves the same (or a worse) level of performance as it has historically.

To make a meaningful impact, the right information needs to be available to the right person at the right time. The easiest way to do this is by making insights operational processes in their own right. The problem is that, usually, insight is just something people do through a combination of intuition and experience. It's rarely repeatable or generally accessible.

Transforming intuition into a repeatable process involves two philosophical leaps. First, the team needs to focus on assets rather than on insights. Second, the team needs to understand the difference between discovery analytics and operational analytics. This changes how organizations manage their insights. Rather than just being intangible ideas, they generate technical assets that can be embedded within or integrated into operational systems. They define processes and create platforms to help move these assets from discovery into operation, thereby directly driving better outcomes.

Having standardized processes and platforms to manage this migration drive accuracy and efficiency. To prevent operational disruption, every change needs to be tested and validated prior to deployment. Making this process repeatable and transparent provides obvious efficiencies: the faster an organization can migrate an asset into production, the greater its market agility. The more it scales to deal with microdecisions, the greater the positive benefits the team can drive.

MEASURING VALUE

Given that business analytics aims to drive economic value, it's somewhat ironic that most organizations are as bad as they are at quantifying the value of business analytics. They often focus on productivity gains, better decision making, or improved agility, none of which are very firm measures when it comes to assessing the financial impact of business analytics. Tell a chief financial officer that you've improved productivity and, more often than not, he or she will ask you who they can fire!

Organizations that cannot quantify the value of business analytics rarely develop any true form of competitive advantage. Because they don't know how much their effort is worth, they usually struggle to justify any broad changes to the way the business operates. They also generally find it hard to compare and assess the relative worth of different initiatives. This makes it hard to focus investment to where it will make the most difference. At best, business analytics ends up being a niche exercise, functionally aligned and generally misunderstood.

The better approach is to have a standard set of business measures that are applied to all business analytics initiatives, regardless of where they exist within the organization. This helps guide investment to where it will drive the best outcomes as well as clearly communicate the value of business analytics. This drives further investment, which, in turn, leads to economies of scope, cost efficiencies, and higher-quality outcomes.

MEASURING PERFORMANCE

Business analytics is a complex discipline. Large-scale systems have many moving parts, and keeping the engine running takes effort. At any given moment there's a multitude of things that *could* be going wrong; models may stop performing, reports may lose relevance, or data-processing jobs may fail. For an organization interested in maximizing their competitiveness from business analytics, keeping a firm hand on how their assets are performing isn't optional.

(Continued)

Like many things, this is harder than it first appears. Good hygiene requires the team to constantly track asset quality. Low-quality assets should be flagged, redeveloped, or retired. High-quality assets should be left alone. Unfortunately, tracking asset quality takes time, time that could be spent delivering new value-creating initiatives. One option is to ignore ongoing asset quality and focus purely on value creation. When organizations make this trade-off, they may make short-term gains by having the opportunity to deliver more initiatives.

These gains usually come at the expense of long-term risk. Putting excessive trust in low-quality assets can cost serious credibility if the organization makes bad decisions based on those assets. Spending too much time monitoring asset quality, on the other hand, carries significant opportunity costs. Time spent manually reviewing and auditing asset quality is time that *could* have been spent creating new sources of value for the organization.

The better solution is a third path. By defining a standard analytical measurement framework that becomes a mandatory component of all new initiatives, the team can have all the benefits of rigorous asset management with minimal management overhead. This requires up-front design effort, but it is well worth it. By having standard measures to draw on, the team manages risk, drives efficiencies, and keeps the focus on driving economies of scope.

MEASURING EFFORT

CASE STUDY

Creating value requires effort and time; assets don't build themselves. Part of the trick is making sure insights are useful, accurate, and actionable. The other part is generating them with as little effort as possible without affecting quality. Driving efficiency helps the team achieve economies of scale and scope by giving it the freedom to deliver other value-creating initiatives.

Creating and operationalizing insight can be a highly complex process involving multiple data sources, toolsets, competencies, and teams. It's rare that these all equally impact the time it takes to get to an outcome. More often than not, a small subset of activities consumes the vast majority of time and effort. Counter-intuitively, those activities that are the most complex may not consume the most time. To optimize their effort, teams need to know which activities affect delivery times the most.

Teams often optimize based on their perceived (and not necessarily real) inefficiencies. In the absence of hard data, this amounts to little more than guesswork. It may work or it may not. Optimizing the wrong activities can see teams spend significant time and money for relatively little return.

The better solution is to establish a standard-effort measurement framework that quantifies the effort and time expended in getting to an outcome. By relying on hard data, teams greatly increase the return on investment they get from process and platform re-engineering.

CREATING THE DATA ARCHITECTURE

CASE STUDY

Data is a business analytics team's greatest asset; without data, the team is nothing. Given how critical data are to a team's success, it's somewhat ironic how bad most teams are at managing their most valuable resource.

A hallmark of business analytics is its ability to drive economies of scope. By reusing assets and skills across multiple business problems, teams reduce average production costs. This creates cost advantages, which, in turn, generate competitive advantage. Critically though, this assumes that the team's assets *can* be reused across multiple business problems. If there's a sequence to enabling reuse, data is *always* at the start of the chain.

Analysts aren't usually lazy. Given a problem, most will manage their data as efficiently as they can within their constraints. The key problem is that these local efficiencies rarely translate into reusable assets. Data become tightly wedded to the processes they inform, and each analyst ends up re-creating already finished work. This increases operational costs through needless data storage. Even worse, because analysts don't have well-defined structures from which they can source the analytical data they need, their teams end up spending most of their time doing non-value-added data-management activities.

To increase their efficiency, teams need to manage their data as the valuable assets they are. This requires more than loosely defined, ad-hoc schemas and nonreusable structures. As the team's primary information assets from which all their value stems, efficiency and reuse comes from defining their data's conceptual, logical, and physical characteristics. By using this framework to help guide design, teams drive asset reuse, ensure storage and architectural efficiency, and leverage their technology to the fullest.

UNDERSTANDING THE DATA VALUE CHAIN

Business analytics use and produce large amounts of data. Assets need a broad and deep set of inputs to be accurate and relevant, and these assets, in turn, create large amounts of analytical data in their own right. This sheer volume of information creates a management problem.

Losing track of how information gets modified exposes the team to operational risk, because business analytics revolve around transforming data, it's dangerously easy to end up in a situation in which the team cannot explain how and why a given piece of data has changed. This calls outputs into question and damages credibility. Establishing effective analytical governance requires more than defining processes. The team needs to be able to reconstruct how every piece of processed information was generated. This helps manage operational risk and improve the quality and trustworthiness of analytical outputs.

In generating insight, every action a team takes either sources, transforms, or augments its existing data. Every step requires the team to make assumptions. Keeping track of these assumptions involves understanding the data-value chain. To create robust and defensible results, the team needs to:

- Source raw data.
- Cleanse and impute data.
- Calculate transformations and derivations.
- Calculate value-added data.
- Translate data into a consumable form.

To get from insight to action, every team needs to make sure its processes go through each of these transformations. The rigor a team needs to apply in doing this varies by context. The governance required to support credit scoring is usually very different to that required in marketing. What doesn't change, however, is ensuring that all processes meet and track these requirements in some form.

CASE STUDY

CREATING DATA-MANAGEMENT PROCESSES

As discussed in the previous two sections, getting actionable insight involves a fairly standard value chain. Teams need to get data. They need to make sure that data are clean and complete. They need to alter and extend the data to fit their purpose. Finally, they need to create insight from that data and make sure they are acted on.

Conceptually, this is pretty elementary. In practice, though, teams need to actually make these milestones real in some way. This inevitably involves creating processes that do one or more of each of the activities within this overall value chain. Doing all these steps in the one process can sometimes seem like the smarter choice—the team can reduce the number of tools needed as well as the number of processes it needs to monitor and manage.

These are both true. Unfortunately, these benefits only outweigh the costs when everyone works independently. Reuse is a critical part of driving economies of scale, and adopting this approach creates monolithic processes that discourage asset reuse. One of the best reasons to keep things separate is that it makes everything flexible. Loosely coupled processes flex with changing requirements, even to the point of being able to combine real-time with non-real-time applications.

Efficiency comes from taking the five milestones and implementing them as four activities. These are:

1. Creating common data.
2. Building model-specific tables.
3. Training models or generating insight.
4. Deploying results.

Much as how logical and physical data architectures are related, these are a practical way of making sure everything stays flexible. Although they overlap, one is conceptual, whereas the other is instantiated.

CASE STUDY

CAPTURING THE RIGHT DATA

Every organization has more data than it knows how to use. If it doesn't, it's either not being honest or not tracking its business. Working out how best to use this data is difficult because analyzing data offers opportunities and picking the right ones is harder than it looks.

Faced with a choice, most teams tend to pick the easy option: they analyze what they are comfortable analyzing. This is a mistake; comfort rarely equates to value. Most teams' comfort zones revolve around numerical data. Of highest interest is transactional data, largely because it needs to be well structured and has more numbers than text. Unfortunately, taking this approach ignores the vast reserves of text-based data most organizations have been stockpiling.

This creates an interesting problem. Ironically, most teams have become highly skilled in analyzing what makes up the minority of their available data. This isn't because structured data are easier to analyze; it's because that's where most skills lie.

When determining how best to go about solving a problem, it's tempting to pick data based on comfort levels. The team defines its approach based on using the data they are most comfortable with. This is the reverse of how it should be; the better approach is to work backward from the outcome and use the data that drives the best outcome. Rather than letting skills define scope, outcomes should define the skills. If the question is, "Structured or unstructured data?" the answer should be, "Whatever drives the best return."

CASE STUDY

LINKING ANALYTICS TO VALUE

Driving and quantifying the value of business analytics can be difficult. One of the hardest things for a team to accept is that although their insights might be relevant and powerful, that doesn't necessarily mean they're valuable.

Teams are often time-constrained. For most, it's a big enough struggle to get the right insights to the right people at the right time. Sadly, even when they do, things can still go wrong. Those people may not act on those insights. Having insight is one thing, acting on it another. Even when they do, the value of that insight can be hard to quantify. It's hard to know whether the decision was based on the insight or some other factor.

In a worst-case scenario, the team has a major problem. Because the team presents insights and not recommendations, people don't act on the team's advice. Everyone nods, but no one acts. Because the team's value chain is broken, it cannot directly link insight to action. Even when the organization does the right thing, it's hard to prove it was because of the team's insight rather than experience.

Until the team overcomes this issue, it constantly struggles to demonstrate the value of business analytics. Success comes from establishing scoring processes that are integrated with the front-of-house decisioning system. By automating scoring processes and delivering recommended actions to those with the power to act on them, the team gains the ability to scale, to start measuring the value of business analytics, and to drive better outcomes.

REDUCING TIME TO RECOMMENDATION

CASE STUDY

Operational scoring drives efficiency and helps teams link insights to value. However, a good or bad design can make or break a process, especially when one starts dealing with big data. When processes and systems are architected correctly, teams can scale their scoring to levels that might otherwise seem impossible.

Scoring processes only involve two steps. First, the team needs to prepare the data to be scored. Then, it takes new data and scores them. Despite being conceptually simple, network, data, and technology architecture play a big role in dictating how operational scoring process should be designed. Picking the right approach needs to take into account an organization's objectives and technology landscape.

In the absence of awareness and forethought, many teams end up simply taking their existing approach and extending it. This doesn't always work and can, in some situations, actively hurt the teams' delivery capabilities.

Taking into account current technologies and methodologies, there are three general solutions:

(Continued)

1. Establish a dedicated operational analytics environment.
2. Leverage in-database scoring.
3. Deploy a purpose-built, in-memory business-analytics appliance.

These aren't hard divisions; the lines between them can become somewhat grey at times. However, they form a useful model to consider how best to design an operational scoring platform. Working out which approach is best requires a good understanding of the constraints inherent in each.

ENABLING REAL-TIME SCORING

CASE STUDY

Relevant treatments drive better outcomes. The tricky thing is that relevancy is often dictated by timeliness. When customers are in the market for phones, they may only be open to influence for a week or two. Their interests will probably be colored by what they have most recently seen through their research.

We often only have one chance to make an offer. Making the right offer leads to a conversion, whereas making the wrong offer may lead to a cancellation. The best way to increase the odds of making the right offer is to use as much relevant information as possible. Factors such as browsing history, recent interactions, and direct feedback can all be used to fine-tune an offer.

As long as things stay constant, batch-based routines usually give good-enough recommendations, even though they may use old data. Unfortunately, batch-based routines provide inaccurate recommendations when things change rapidly. The answer doesn't lie in more frequent scoring processes, either; trying to score every customer every time new information is captured is hardly a scalable approach. Much as trying to make a square peg fit into a round hole is destined for disappointment, trying to force traditional scoring models into a real-time context is an exercise in futility.

When information is dynamic and recency is more influential than history, the limitations of batch-based scoring become overwhelming. Rather than scoring tables ahead of time, the organization needs to score transactions in real time.

BLENDING RULES WITH MODELS

CASE STUDY

There are many ways to predict what will happen. Some patterns apply everywhere and rarely change. Regardless of where one looks, the same behaviors consistently emerge. Sometimes, however, patterns are individual and change rapidly. Items of interest emerge, not through consistent behaviors but, rather, through deviations from normal patterns of behavior.

Ideally, working out what to do involves leveraging both types of patterns. Unfortunately, many organizations end up believing that it's a case of either/ or rather than and. When they fall into this trap, they sacrifice efficiency *and* accuracy.

The better solution is to adopt a hybrid approach, one that capitalizes on the best aspects of each technique. By doing so, organizations deal effectively with the static *and* the dynamic and do so in a highly efficient manner.

Glossary

Advanced Analytics
A subset of analytical techniques that, among other things, often uses statistical methods to identify and quantify the influence and significance of relationships between items of interest, groups similar items together, creates predictions, and identifies mathematical optimal or near-optimal answers to business problems.

Aggregation
A process by which variables are summed based on a classification or temporal hierarchy. Common examples include totaling all sales for a given time period or geographic region.

Agile Development
A software-development methodology that emphasizes iterative and incremental development driven by cross-functional collaboration and co-location.

Algorithm
A finite series of well-defined steps that achieve a desired outcome. These steps may be deterministic or include random or probabilistic elements.

Analytics
A data-driven process that creates insight. These processes incorporate a wide variety of techniques and may include manual analysis, reporting, predictive models, time-series models, or optimization models.

Analytics Platform
A technology platform that provides standardized tools, an ability to collaborate, and the ability to migrate insight into operational processes.

Assets
Items of economic value created by a team through the application of competencies and tools. Within a business-analytics context they are normally intangible in nature and often include models, processes, and electronic documentation.

Big Data
A colloquial term referring to exceedingly large datasets that are otherwise unwieldy to deal with in a reasonable amount of time in the absence of specialized tools. They are different from normal data in terms of volume, velocity, and variety and typically require unique approaches for capture, processing, analysis, search, and visualization.

Big Data Analytics
The process by which highly scalable techniques are applied to big data to drive value out of data volume, velocity, and variety.

Bounded Rationality
The theory that personal rationality is bounded by our ability to process information, our cognitive limitations, and the finite time we have to make a decision. Although our decisions are still rational, they are rational within these constraints and, therefore, may not always appear to be rational or optimal.

Business Analytics
The process of leveraging all forms of analytics to achieve business outcomes by requiring business relevancy, actionable insight, performance management, and value measurement. These business outcomes are typically tangible and/or intangible values of interest to the organization.

Business Intelligence
A broad classification of information-systems-based technologies that support the identification and presentation of insight. Common historical usage referred primarily to reporting-focused systems, but usage of the term has been broadened by some to include all forms of insight generation (including exploratory data analysis and predictive analytics).

Champion/Challenger Process
A process that benchmarks alternative processes against the currently selected process. If an alternative challenger process outperforms the current champion process, the champion process is usually replaced with the challenger process.

Churn
A term that refers to a customers going to a different provider. Depending on the context, it may refer to a total migration away from the organization in question to a reduction in consumption.

Community Detection

The process by which a full graph of personal connections is decomposed into communities and subcommunities. These can be defined by a variety of factors including strength of relationship, frequency of contact, or type of contact.

Competencies

Reusable and generalizable skills held by a business analytics team. One common example is the ability to build predictive models.

Competitive Advantage

A strategic advantage held by one organization that cannot be matched by its competitors. This advantage may or may not be sustainable and, if it is not, may eventually be replicated by its competitors.

Conceptual-Data Architecture

The conceptual architecture outlines the major entities within the team's data and describes the relationships between these entities.

Contagious Churn/Viral Churn

A situation in which individuals cancel their services because other people in their network have canceled their service. Common reasons include being made aware of better options and pull-through by leveraging positive network externalities.

Continuous Improvement

A management methodology through which organizations drive continuous incremental improvements to outcomes and processes. It has strong relationships to evolutionary innovation.

Cross-Sectional Modeling

A variety of methods that focus on analyzing time captured across entities at a specific point in time. Common applications include identifying differences among groups, relationships among outcomes and causal factors, and creating predictions.

Cross-Sell

A process by which new, not overlapping products are sold to existing customers.

Cruft

Software or processes of low quality that creates "technical debt" and makes future modification costly and difficult.

Data Cleansing
The process of detecting, removing, or correcting incorrect data.

Data Dictionary
A reference by which a team can understand what data assets they have, how those assets were created, what they mean, and where to find them.

Data-Management Process
A series of well-defined steps that take source data, conduct a series of operations on them, and deliver those operations to a predefined location.

Datamart
A shared repository of data, often used to support functional areas within the business. It is sometimes used as the direct access layer to the data warehouse.

Data Quality
A broad term that refers to the accuracy and precision of data being examined. Data that exhibits high quality correctly quantifies the real-world items they represent.

Data Warehouse
A shared repository of data, often used to support the centralized consolidation of information for decision support.

Decision Tree
An algorithm that focuses on maximizing group separation by iteratively splitting variables.

Derived Variable
A variable not included in the original data but based on the underlying characteristics of the source data. Common examples include calculating a three-month moving average and calculating recency, frequency, and monetary statistics.

Discounted Value
The value of an item after taking into account the cost of time.

Discovery Environment
A logically defined and usually separate area within an analytics platform that provides users with the ability to create assets and generate insight.

Economies of Scale
The process by which the average cost per output falls as production increases.

Economies of Scope
The process by which the average cost of production falls as the scope of activities increase.

Enabling Initiative
A business analytics initiative focused on creating processes or assets needed for either a planned growth initiative or to deliver evolutionary efficiency improvements.

Enterprise Platform
A centralized analytics environment based on a defined set of tools that supports the entire organization.

Enterprise Resource Planning
A variety of software-based systems that aim to standardize processes and information management within organizations, typically focusing on operational processes including finance and accounting, supply chain and logistics, inventory management, and resource management.

Ethernet
A high-speed networking standard used for local area networks, typically capable of speeds up to one gigabit per second.

Evolution
Within the context of business analytics, the incremental improvement extension of existing processes or capabilities, often involving adaptation of modification.

Fiber Channel
A high-speed networking standard often used for storage networks, running on both twisted-pair copper and fiber optic.

Firm Process
A process that degrades gracefully when deadlines are missed, with the caveat that results returned outside this time frame are discarded as being useless. A common example is identifying a next-best activity in a call center.

Gains Chart
A visual representation of lift.

Grouping Model
A type of model specifically focuses on grouping similar individuals or entities together based on multidimensional information. A common example is a customer segmentation model.

Growth Initiative
A business-analytics initiative focused on creating value. It tends to have fairly well-defined deliverables, fixed time frames with expected end dates, and involves the creation of new assets and processes.

Hard Process
A process that must *always* complete in a given time frame. If the process does not complete, the entire transaction fails. Common examples include most real-time applications such as operational transactional processing and real-time billing.

Hax and Wilde's Delta Model
A way of looking at competitive advantage that looks for ways of maximizing the customer-value proposition to achieve maximal customer bonding. It describes three broad strategies: best product, total customer solutions, and system lock-in.

Hedonic Pricing Analysis
An econometric technique that aims to identify and quantify the underlying factors that drive demand in a heterogeneous market. A common example is within real estate, where prices, location, distance from main roads, the number of bedrooms, and the overall square footage all contribute to the final price the market will bear.

Heuristics
An experience-based technique for solving problems that emphasizes personal knowledge and quick decision making.

Hot Desking
A reservationless shared desk that is used by multiple people within any given time period.

Hoteling
A reservation-based shared desk that can be used by multiple people within any given time period but is usually booked out for given periods of time.

Ideation
The process of generating and communicating ideas. It includes the innovation process and should eventually lead to commercialization.

Impute
The process of estimating likely values for missing data, taking into account the statistical characteristics of broader population, often simultaneously trying to minimize the bias introduced through estimation.

In-database Processing

A technique involving migrating logic processing away from a generalized computing tier and into the database. A common example in analytics is transforming analytical-processing steps into native database execution logic and deploying this logic into the database.

Independent Variables

A term referring to the inputs used within a model. They are typically unrelated to each other but should exhibit some form of causal relationship toward the outcome being examined.

Infonomics

A relatively new field that focuses on how to quantify, manage, and leverage information as a business asset.

Information Theory

A branch of research pioneered by Claude E. Shannon that focused on the quantification of information.

Innovation

Within the context of business analytics, the process of delivering a different approach. Sometimes, this different approach may be evolutionary. At other times, it may involve high amounts of disruption.

Intangible Value

The immeasurable worth of an asset of outcome to an organization. Common examples include job satisfaction and the ability to make better decisions.

Join

See Merge.

Kryder's Law

The trend for magnetic disk storage to double annually, leading to significant ongoing increases in storage capacity. It was defined by Mark Kryder while he was at Seagate.

Lift

A common statistical measure that represents the degree of improvement one or more alternative classification processes offer over an existing process.

Linear Programming

A technique within operations research that maximizes or minimizes an objective function by varying inputs given constraints. It relies on the assumption of a linear relationship between inputs and outputs.

Logical-data Architecture
The logical-data architecture describes the specific data elements held by the team in a platform-agnostic and business-friendly manner. It plots out the specific tables, fields, and relationships within the team's data assets and is usually fully normalized to minimize redundancy and represents the highest level of design efficiency possible. It still describes elements in simple language, often referring to customers, postal address, and the like.

Market Failure
An economic condition in which the allocation of goods by the market creates an inefficient outcome. In the absence of intervention, the free market will achieve a suboptimal result. Common examples include the creation of negative market externalities such as pollution or the abuse of shared public grounds, commonly known as the *tragedy of the commons*.

Merge
A process by which two or more tables are combined into one, matching them using one or more common fields. A common example involves combining customer data with purchasing data to create a single table that incorporates all available information.

Microdecision
A small decision made many times by many workers at the front line of the organization. They usually have a significant impact on organizational performance due to their sheer volume.

Microsegmentation Modeling
A segmentation approach that creates very high numbers of segments, often in the thousands.

Model
An abstracted view of reality. Within analytics, it often refers to a mathematically or logically defined function that helps simplify multidimensional information into a small set of useful measures.

Model Deployment
The process by which models are migrated from a discovery environment into an operational environment and used to provide ongoing scoring processes.

Model Development
The process by which models are created.

Monte Carlo Sampling

A process by which samples are repeatedly drawn with replacement from an existing population. Typically, Monte Carlo sampling is used as an input-generation process to run a variety of simulations and capture the resulting outputs.

Moore's Law

The trend for the number of transistors on an integrated circuit to double roughly every two years, leading to significant ongoing increases in computing power. It was defined by Gordon E. Moore, cofounder of Intel.

Multivariate Analysis

A form of statistical analysis that includes more than one variable at a time.

Net Present Value

A more advanced financial measure that calculates net return, taking into account the time value of money.

Network Attached Storage

A storage device on a network deployed in such a way that it appears as a discrete file server available to multiple clients on a network.

Neural Network

An algorithm that conceptually mimics the learning patterns of biological neural networks by adaptively adjusting a series of classification functions in a nonlinear nature to maximize predictive accuracy, given a series of inputs.

Nonparametric Statistics

A branch of statistics that makes no assumptions on the underlying distributions of the data being examined. In general, the tests are far more generalizable but sacrifice precision and power.

Operational Activity

An ongoing process focused on preserving existing value. It tends to be more process driven; has no fixed end date; and leverages existing assets, capabilities, and processes.

Operational Analytics

The process by which strong recommendations based on analytics are aligned and integrated with operational processes to drive better microdecisions.

Operational Environment
A logically defined and usually separate area within an analytics platform that provides users with the ability to deploy assets into processes and workflows to support operational activities.

Operations Research
A subset of analytical techniques that apply mathematical optimization techniques to identify optimal or near-optimal answers to business problems. It is often used to support inventory optimization and supply-chain optimization, and to optimize the allocation of scarce resources.

Opportunity Cost
The cost of the next-best choice to someone who has picked from a series of mutually exclusive options. It represents the option forgone.

Optimization Model
A type of model that aims to maximize or minimize a target outcome by identifying the best inputs or settings to use given a series of constraints. Common examples include optimizing production or delivery schedules to minimize total cost or routing time.

Organizational Planning
The highest level of strategic planning, typically focusing on identifying the markets in which the organization will or will not compete, targeting acquisitions, or creating key competencies and cultures.

Parametric Statistics
A branch of statistics that assumes the data being examined comes from a variety of known probability distributions. In general, the tests sacrifice generalizability for speed of computation and precision, providing the requisite assumptions are met.

Payback
A simple time-based measure that quantifies the period of time needed to recoup the cost of investment.

Performance Management
The application of technology, process, and psychology to manage behavior and results and facilitate the delivery of strategic and tactical objectives.

Petabyte
An SI-defined measure of data storage equal to 1,000 terabytes. For comparison, a single commercial single-sided dual-layer DVD can store up to 8.54 gigabytes.

Physical-Data Architecture

The physical-data architecture is the lowest level of detail in data architecture. It describes how the logical architecture is actually implemented within the datamart and describes elements by their technical (rather than business) names.

Porter's Five Forces

A framework to consider industry structure as defined by Michael Porter. It aims to identify attractive industries based on the threat of new entrants, the threat of substitutable products, the bargaining power of consumers, the bargaining power of suppliers, and the degree of competitive rivalry within the industry in question.

Predictive Modeling

A process by which the underlying relationships behind an outcome are identified, quantified, and used to create predictions for new information. These are often statistically based. A common example is using information about customers who have canceled their phone service to statistically identify and quantify the major leading indicators that suggest someone will cancel. These indicators are then translated into a scoring process and used to score existing customers, helping to identify those who are at a high probability of cancellation. Once identified, they can then be contacted before they cancel, potentially making a unique retention offer to discourage them from going to a competitor.

Pricing Analytics

The application of analytics to specifically support calculating optimal prices and understanding the relationship between prices and demand through price-elasticity models.

Propensity Model

A type of model that specifically focuses on creating predictions around the likelihood of an individual performing a particular action. Common examples include the propensity of them to default on a loan or to purchase a given product.

Quality

A comparative concept that described the relative ability of two or more competing processes to drive outcomes. A higher-quality process drives a better outcome when considering a full variety of direct and indirect sources of value. Quality is subjective, and depending on organizational and personal objectives, the perception of which process is higher quality may vary.

RAID 0+1

A storage technique that involves stripping information across multiple physical disks without parity and then mirroring the array onto another array, delivering speed and redundancy at the cost of available storage. RAID stands for Redundant Array of Inexpensive Disks.

RAID 5

A storage technique that involves stripping information across multiple physical disks while preserving redundancy through parity bits. RAID stands for Redundant Array of Inexpensive Disks.

Recursive

See Recursive.

Refactor

A process by which existing code or processes are reengineered or re-structured to improve nonfunctional aspects without impacting outcomes. It is usually done to make existing assets more manageable, efficient, and maintainable.

Relational Model

A type of model that aims to identify relationships of interest and quantify the strength of relationship between individuals or entities. Common examples include market-basket analysis and social-network analysis.

Reporting

A process by which insight is presented in a visually appealing and informative manner.

Research Initiative

A business analytics initiative focused on delivering insight. Although they are often an enabler to value creation, they usually do not create any direct value in and of themselves.

Return On Investment

A simple financial measure that subtracts the investment expended from the total returns generated, giving a simple net financial return.

Roadmap

Within the context of business analytics, a defined set of staged initiatives that deliver tactical returns while moving the team toward strategic outcomes.

Satisfice
The process by which people make decisions that try to meet an acceptability threshold rather than an optimal outcome. It is a portmanteau of the words *satisfy* and *suffice*.

Scoring Process
A process by which a predefined model is applied against new data, creating a new variable for each record that contains the result of the model. A common example is calculating the propensity of every customer to churn within a given time period.

Scoring Table
A table containing new data that is to be fed through a model converted to a scoring process, the output of which is usually a series of numerically based recommendations.

Segmentation
A process by which entities within a population are grouped into segments that have common characteristics. This grouping process may be manually, algorithmically, or statistically based and will often take into account anywhere from a handful to hundreds of common attributes across all the entities.

Segmentation Strategy
A strategy that identifies subgroups within the market and treats these groups differently. This targeted treatment can then drive offer relevancy and increase offer attractiveness.

Semistructured Data
Data that, although unstructured, still has some degree of structure. A good example is e-mail: Even though it is predominantly text, it has logical blocks with different purposes.

Sensitivity Analysis
A form of simulation modeling that focuses specifically on identifying the upper and lower bounds of model outputs given a series of inputs with specific variance.

Simulation
A process by which processes or models are run repeatedly using a variety of inputs. The outputs are normally captured and analyzed to conduct sensitivity analysis, provide insight around likely potential outcomes, and identify bottlenecks and constraints within existing processes or models.

Simulation Modeling

An analytical technique that often involves running models repeatedly using a variety of inputs to determine the upper and lower bounds of possible outcomes. This simulation process is also sometimes used to identify the likely distribution of outputs given a series of assumptions around how the inputs are distributed.

Single View of Customer (SVoC)

A consolidated view of all customer information within an organization.

Soft Process

A process that degrades gracefully when deadlines are missed where the results returned outside this time frame are still useful. A common example is using browsing patterns to make an offer; even if the person has a more recent browsing history, the offer may still be relevant.

Spreadmarts

A colloquial term for the painful situation in which spreadsheets are turned into datamarts in their own right. They tend to create significant management complexity and discourage data reuse.

Social Network Analysis

The application of analytics to analyze relationships among individuals, often to help with contagious churn or viral marketing.

Storage Attached Network

A storage device on a network deployed in such a way that they appear to be locally attached to the operating system.

Stress Testing

A form of simulation modeling that focuses specifically on identifying the response of a model under specific, often highly negative scenarios. Common examples include testing the profitability of a bank given catastrophic levels of mortgage defaults or modeling extreme macroeconomic conditions.

Strongly Defined Process

A series of steps that is clearly defined, is repeatable, can be automated, and leads to the creation of value.

Supply-chain Optimization

A process, often leveraging operations research, that aims to improve the efficiency of a given supply chain. Common targets include minimizing delivery time, reducing total cost of delivery, minimizing inventory held on hand, and minimizing the total number of distribution centers needed.

SWOT Analysis
An input into a strategic-planning process defined by Michael Porter. It focuses on identifying an organization's strengths, weaknesses, opportunities, and threats.

Tactical Revolution
The process by which deliberate incremental improvements can be leveraged to create sufficient free time to allow the delivery of growth initiatives.

Tangible Value
The quantifiable and measurable worth of an asset or outcome to an organization. Common examples include financial improvements and saleable market value.

Terabyte
An SI-defined measure of data store equal to 1,000 gigabytes. For comparison, a single commercial, single-sided, dual-layer DVD can store up to 8.54 gigabytes.

Time-series Analysis
A variety of methods that focus on analyzing time-stamped information, often with an emphasis on identifying relationships between events and outcomes as well as creating predictions.

Tools
The basic building block through which most assets are created. They can be internally developed or purchased off the shelf, but without an appropriate set of purpose-built tools, a business analytics team is unable to create any new assets.

Total Cost of Ownership
A simple financial measure of the total costs of an initiative, covering services, software, hardware, support agreements, internal transfer pricing, training, and all other associated costs.

Training Table
A table containing data that is be used to develop a model.

Transaction Costs
The inherent cost associated with conducting a transaction in some form. Common examples include search and information costs, bargaining costs, and policing and enforcement costs. When the business negotiates with IT to modify IT's approach to business analytics, the organization as a whole usually incurs all three of these costs.

Transformation
A mathematically defined way of taking data and altering it based on a generalized mapping function, often with the goal of creating a different way of looking at the data in an easily reversible way. Common examples include taking the natural logarithm or exponentiation.

Trending
A process by which underlying trends are identified within time-related data. These trends may be manually, algorithmically, or statistically identified and may be extrapolated into the future to aid planning.

Type I Error
A term that refers to incorrectly rejecting a null hypothesis. It is also sometimes termed a *false positive*. It is used when an outcome is incorrectly identified as having happened, such as when a customer is incorrectly identified as having committed fraud.

Type II Error
A term that refers to failing to reject a null hypothesis when it is false. It is also sometimes termed a *false negative* and used when an outcome is incorrectly identified as not having happened, such as when a customer has committed fraud but has not been accurately identified.

Univariate Analysis
A form of statistical analysis that focuses on one variable at a time.

Unstructured Data
Data that does not fit into a structured data model or does not fit well into relational tables. Common examples include binary information such as video or audio and free-text information.

Up-Sell
A process by which customers are upgraded to more expensive products, replacing their existing products.

Value
The intrinsic and extrinsic worth of an asset or outcome to an individual or organization.

Viral Marketing
The application of direct marketing with the goal of leveraging an individual's personal networks to promote a message, increase mindshare, or drive pull-through sales through positive network externalities.

VRIN Resources

Resources that lead to competitive advantage as suggested by the resource-based view of the firm. They are characterized by being valuable, rare, inimitable, and nonsubstitutable.

Weakly Defined Process

A series of steps that leads to the creation of value, is based on guidelines, and relies on the skill and ingenuity of the analyst to complete successfully.

Further Reading

In researching this book I came across many sources that I found valuable. Although specific references have been acknowledged in the text, I felt that it might be useful for other researchers to have a guide to what I found interesting, insightful, or simply useful.

Although not everyone involved in business analytics *needs* to read these references, everyone will benefit from reading them. To save time and provide context to many of the concepts discussed in this book, the list has been ordered in a suggested reading path.

Stubbs, E. *The Value of Business Analytics: Identifying the Path to Profitability.* Hoboken, NJ: John Wiley & Sons, 2011.

Davenport, T. H., and J. G. Harris. *Competing on Analytics: The New Science of Winning.* Cambridge, MA: Harvard Business School Press, 2007.

Christensen, C. M., J. Dyer, and H. Gregersen. *The Innovator's DNA: Mastering the Five Skills of Disruptive Innovators.* Cambridge, MA: Harvard Business Review Press, 2011.

Govindarajan, V. *The Other Side of Innovation: Solving the Execution Challenge.* Cambridge, MA: Harvard Business Review Press, 2010.

Davenport, T. H., J. G. Harris, and R. Morison. *Analytics at Work: Smarter Decisions, Better Results.* Cambridge, MA: Harvard Business Review Press, 2010.

Pirsig, R. M. *Zen and the Art of Motorcycle Maintenance: An Inquiry into Values.* New York: William Morrow Paperbacks, 1974.

Brooks F. *The Mythical Man-Month.* Needham, MA: Addison-Wesley, 1975.

Drucker, P. *Innovation and Entrepreneurship.* New York: Taylor & Francis, 1985.

Hubbard, D. W. *How to Measure Anything: Finding the Value of Intangibles in Business.* Hoboken, NJ: John Wiley & Sons, 2010.

Taylor, J., and N. Raden. *Smart Enough Systems: How to Deliver Competitive Advantage by Automating Hidden Decisions.* Upper Saddle River, NJ: Prentice Hall, 2007.

Franks, B. *Taming the Big Data Tidal Wave: Finding Opportunities in Huge Data Streams with Advanced Analytics*. Hoboken, NJ: John Wiley & Sons, 2012.

Crosby, P. B. *Quality Is Free*. New York: McGraw-Hill, 1979.

Deming, W. E., and M. Walton. *The Deming Management Method*. New York: Perigee Books, 1988.

May, T. *The New Know: Innovation Powered by Analytics*. Hoboken, NJ: John Wiley & Sons, 2009.

Glass, R. *Facts and Fallacies of Software Engineering*. Needham, MA: Addison-Wesley Professional, 2002.

Juran, J. M. *Quality Control Handbook*. 1st ed. New York: McGraw-Hill, 1951.

Frisch, R. *Theory of Production*. Dordrecht, The Netherlands: D. Reidel, 1965.

Panzar, J. C., and R. D. Willig. "Economies of Scale in Multi-Output Production." *Quarterly Journal of Economics* 91, no. 33 (1977): 481–493.

Sittig, J. "Defining Quality Costs." Proceedings 7th EOQC Conference, Copenhagen, Denmark, 1963, 9–17.

Turner, T. E. "An Economic Look at Quality." *Quality Progress* 2, no. 4 (1969): 16–20.

Sackman, H., W. J. Erickson, and E. E. Grant. "Exploratory Experimental Studies Comparing Online and Offline Programming Performance." *Communications of the ACM* 11, no. 1 (1968): 3–11.

Beck, Kent et al. "Manifest for Agile Software Development." Agile Alliance (2001).

About the Author

Evan Stubbs lives in Sydney, Australia, one of the few places in the world where a 30-hour flight itinerary fails to raise even a single eyebrow. His childhood was mainly spent (often unsuccessfully) avoiding brain-controlling parasites, civil war, and biblical floods. He now spends most of his spare time filling in bandicoot holes in his back yard, avoiding murderous redbacks, writing, and otherwise keeping life (somewhat less) interesting.

He's also the Chief Analytics Officer for SAS Australia/New Zealand and sits on the board of the Institute of Analytics Professionals of Australia. He's a prolific speaker and evangelist for the power of analytics, having written *The Value of Business Analytics*, a book that explains why some teams succeed, whereas others fail. Over the years he's developed human-machine interfaces for concept cars, models that predict criminal behavior, and helped organizations establish analytical centers of excellence.

Index